495
m

WARSHIPS
OF THE WORLD
SUBMARINES &
FAST ATTACK CRAFT

SAR 33-class

WARSHIPS
OF THE WORLD
SUBMARINES &
FAST ATTACK CRAFT

Bernard Ireland

Charles Scribner's Sons
NEW YORK

Printed in Great Britain
Library of Congress Catalog Card Number 79-93214
ISBN: 0-684-16061-7

Contents

Pegasus: note negligible wake when foilborne.

Preface

When, on 21 October 1967, the Israeli destroyer *Eilat* sank off Alexandria after suffering two massive explosions, a new era had dawned for the small warship, for those that had sunk her had not even left harbour. The SSM had arrived.

It was revolutionary because warships had not changed greatly since World War II, advancing in efficiency mainly by dint of becoming even larger, more complex and more expensive. Minor navies relied for their ships on the acquisition of second-hand tonnage from 'first-division' fleets. Western navies had concentrated on the development of AS techniques and SAM systems for, with overwhelming power in their numerous carriers, the major threats were posed by the submarines and aircraft with stand-off missiles which the Soviet Union was building in large numbers. The latter, however, was early in the field with the large, shipborne SSM with a range in the hundreds of miles and designed to counter a carrier group without the hazardous necessity of approaching it.

What could be done for the complex, over-the-horizon weapon could be done the easier for a shorter-ranged system and the SS-N-2 (Styx) followed quickly. Rather a crude missile, relying on radio control and IR homing it, nevertheless, had two things in its favour — it was compact enough to fit into a small hull and, equally important, the West had no antidote available. The crash programme of Komars soon had the Styx at sea in large numbers, forcing the West to develop both countermeasures and its own SSMs; it was fortunate at this time that no East/West maritime war occurred to spotlight the latter's deficiencies.

The commercial implications of these systems that had been thrust upon them were not lost on the West and a rash of SSM-armed FPBs was soon available for purchase. For the first time, smaller fleets could afford new ships with powerful weaponry and the rate of market expansion was matched by a Soviet readiness to transfer Styx-armed craft to any state, however unstable, that could offer any political gain. Fortunately, there is an inbuilt weakness in this arrangement for maintenance of this high technology equipment is usually beyond the resources of the recipients and 'after-sales service' has not proved a Russian strong point.

Successive classes of FACs have followed the normal cycle of warship development, increasing in size until they have merged with the corvette at the top end. The corvette has a future. Slower and more weatherly than the average FAC it can carry a helicopter and both AA and AS weaponry, areas in which most FACs are deficient. Her extra capacity can be used for the equipment necessary for the coordination of a group of FACs or for incorporating the range required for duties such as offshore patrol, vital to those states with developed offshore exploitation. Though there exist enthusiastic lobbies for exotica such as hydrofoils and surface effect craft, it is unlikely that these will have any significant blue water impact for the foreseeable future. Even the airship is to be re-evaluated by the Royal Navy during 1979 but its 72-hour endurance is likely to be largely offset by its poor payload.

The gas turbine, which is gaining universal acceptance in larger warships, has still to oust the robust and cheaper diesel from the smaller craft. Market penetration is likely to be from the top end downward.

Submarines are at a late stage of development and innovation is not so marked. At the high end, the SSBN is still being built by the USA, USSR and France but, in the Trident-armed Ohios, the Americans have produced a monster that is causing them second thoughts. Like the aircraft carrier, its cost and size have escalated to the point where fewer can be built; its bulk renders its concealment on patrol the more difficult. In the quest for higher speed, the Los Angeles class attack submarines have also grown unacceptably. With the successful introduction of cruise missiles such as the Tomahawk it is possible that we may see a new type of intermediate submarine combining both strategic and tactical offensive power within more modest dimensions. While the nuclear submarine has no peer in its designed environment, it is becoming increasingly clear that the 'conventional' still has a great future, particularly for use in shallow or constricted waters. Silent and extremely cost effective, they have entered a new phase in their development.

The space available for data is all too limited in a book of this size; only essential figures are quoted to avoid it growing to an unacceptable length. Dimensions and displacements have usually been rounded to the nearest realistic unit and, where two figures are quoted for submarines, the first applies to the surfaced condition. My thanks, as ever, are due to the seemingly ever-increasing numbers of people who have helped along the way with illustrations or information; they are acknowledged as far as possible but those unnamed, particularly my wife, are not forgotten.

Bernard Ireland
Fareham, 1979

Abbreviations

AAM	Air-to-Air Missile		GM	Guided Missile
AA (W)	Anti-aircraft (Warfare)		GP	General Purpose
AC	Aircraft		GRP	Glass Reinforced Plastic
AD	Aircraft Direction		GT	Gas Turbine
AEW	Airborne Early Warning		HA	High Angle
APD	See LPR		HSA	Hollandse Signaal Apparaten
ASROC	Anti-submarine Rocket		IR	Infra-red
AS (W)	Anti-submarine (Warfare)		kt	Knot, ie one nautical mile per hour
BPDMS	Basic Point-Defence Missile System		LAMPS	Light Airborne Multi-Purpose System
CIC	Combat Information Centre		L (oa)	Length (overall)
CIWS	Close-in Weapons System		LPR	
CODAG	Combined Diesel and Gas (Turbine)		(ex-APD)	Amphibious Transport (small)
CODOG	Combined Diesel or Gas (Turbines)		MAD	Magnetic Anomaly Detector
COGOG	Combined Gas or Gas (Turbines)		MCMV	Mine Countermeasures Vessel
COSAG	Combined Steam and Gas (Turbines)		mm	millimetre
COSOG	Combined Steam or Gas (Turbines)		MTU	Motoren und Turbinen Union
CP	Controllable Pitch		NTDS	Naval Tactical Data System
CPIC	Coastal Patrol and Interdiction Craft		PCE	Patrol Craft, Escort
DC	Depth Charge		PF	Patrol Frigate
DC (T)	Depth Charge (Thrower)		PUFFS	Passive Underwater Fire-Control
DDG	Guided Missile Destroyer			Feasability
DDH	Helicopter Destroyer		qv	Quod Vide (which see)
DLG	Guided Missile Frigate		rpm	Rounds per minute
DP	Dual Purpose		SAM	Surface-to-Air Missile
ECM	Electronic Countermeasures		shp	Shaft Horse Power
ECCM	Electronic Counter Countermeasures		SLBM	Submarine-launched Ballistic Missile
ESM	Electronic Support Measures		SSM	Surface-to-Surface Missile
FAC	Fast Attack Craft		STAAG	Stabilised Anti-Aircraft Gun
FFG	Fast Frigate		STIR	Separate Track and Illumination Radar
FPB	Fast Patrol Boat		TT	Torpedo Tube
FRAM	Fleet Rehabilitation and Modernisation		VDS	Variable Depth Sonar
			V/STOL	Vertical/Short Take-off and Land
			WT	Watertight
			3-D	Three-Dimensional

Pegasus firing Harpoon SSM.

Albania

Little is known about the efficiency of the Albanian Navy, which consists of a collection of small warships transferred either from the Soviet or, latterly, the Chinese fleets. The main components of the force are believed at present to consist of the following units details of which classes may be found under their countries of origin:

Four Kronstadt patrol craft transferred from the USSR in 1958.

Four/six Shanghai II class FAC (gun) transferred from China 1974/5.
Four Hoku class FAC (missile). These are Chinese-built Komar class boats transferred in 1977.
Six P4 class FAC (torpedo). These are Chinese-built and were transferred in 1965.
Over 30 Hu Chwan class torpedo-armed hydrofoils transferred from China in 1968-74.
Two Whiskey class submarines transferred from the USSR in 1960.

Algeria

The major offensive craft operated by Algeria are all currently of Soviet origin (details may be found under countries of origin) and comprise:

Three Osa I class FAC (missile) transferred in 1967.
Three Osa II class FAC (missile) transferred in 1977.
Six Komar class FAC (missile) transferred in 1966.

Six SO-I class patrol craft transferred in 1965-7.
Up to 10 P6 class FAC (torpedo) transferred in 1963-8.

King Corvette

Argentina

	Laid Down	Launched	Completed
P20 *Murature*	1939	1943	1945
P21 *King*	1938	1943	1946

Displacement: 1,000 standard
1,050 full load
Length (oa): 253ft
Beam: 29ft
Draught: 7.5ft
Machinery: Two diesels, two shafts
2,500shp for 16kts

These two little ships are remarkably similar to the PF/River class frigates operated by the Argentine navy subsequent to World War II. Although laid down prior to the war, they were long a-building and it is more than probable that the Rivers were an

influence on their final form. An innovation for the time was the inclusion of a pair of Werkspoor diesels in place of the more customary steam propulsion.

As built, each was equipped with four 105mm guns (a peculiarly German calibre) but have since shed X mounting. They are simple little ships, now used largely for training purposes and typical of the size of ship built at this time by the naval yard at Santiago. This pair was followed in 1956/7 by an 'improved' version, the Azopardos, turbine propelled and of a size and performance with the Rivers, but, rather strangely, the latter couple were discarded in 1973 and have been survived by the Kings.

Lürssen-type 45m FAC (missile)

Argentina

Units: Two under construction (1978)
Displacement: 235 standard
265 full load
Length (oa): 147ft
Beam: 23ft
Draught: 7ft
Machinery: Four diesels on four shafts
14,400shp for 38kts
Armament: Five launchers for Gabriel SSM (1×3 and 2×1)
One 57mm gun
One 40mm gun
Two 21-inch TTs

It is a feature of the basic Lürssen steel FAC hull that it can apparently be scaled up or down without much loss of efficiency. Thus, the Typ 148 of the

Bundesmarine has, since its appearance in 1972, spawned numerous very similar designs in foreign fleets. Argentina, long a country that imported warships, has developed an advanced shipbuilding capability and has passed through a phase where the leadship of a projected class would be built abroad and the remainder built as replicas in home yards, to a point where the design is bought-in for smaller ships and all are home-built.

Such is the pair of Gabriel-armed FACs now building to complement the two gun-armed Intrepidas. Typically Lürssen in appearance, they will pack a very powerful armament in to what is the shortest version yet of the basic hull. To compensate, the full 23ft beam of the longer (158ft) boats has been retained.

With the bridge structure, as usual, arranged in

one compact mass, a large clear space abaft has been kept for the five Gabriel canisters. These fit neatly into an arrangement that features two single launchers firing forward at a fixed angle to the centreline and a triple mounting further aft that can be trained in azimuth. The SSMs, together with the 57mm automatic gun forward, are controlled through the HSA fire control under its familar mast-head dome.

In addition to the DP weapons, a hand operated 40mm gun is sited right aft. Two long 21-inch TTs capable of firing wire-guided weapons can be sited aft, their bases doubling as minelaying racks, but it is doubtful if these can be fitted in addition to the other weaponry and the after gun, at least, would need to be landed to compensate for the added topweight.

Cruising on only two engines the type would probably have a considerable range, necessary for small craft on such a long coastline as Argentina's.

Lürssen-type 45m FAC (gun)

Argentina

		Laid Down	Launched	Completed
ELPR1	*Intrepida*	1973	1973	1974
ELPR2	*Indomita*	973	1974	1974

Displacement: 240 standard
270 full load
Length (oa): 149ft
Beam: 24ft
Draught: 7.5ft
Machinery: Four diesels on four shafts
12,000shp for 35.5kts
Armament: One 76mm DP gun
Two 40mm guns (2 × 1)
Two 21-inch TTs

This pair are lower-powered and slightly larger versions of the missile-armed boats now building. They carry the larger 76mm OTO-Melara forward and a pair of 40mm weapons aft, singled to give b   weight distribution together with the ability of engaging more than one target simultaneously. Whether the excellent HSA fire control can handle this number of aerial targets at the same time is open to conjecture but surface targets are no problem. Pre-fragmented and proximity fused ammunition confer great potential to even a small automatic gun and incoming SSMs would well be engaged if the system is not already saturated. A separate fire control is fitted for the guidance of the long torpedoes fired from the tubes carried aft, German fashion.

Typ 209 Patrol Submarine

Argentina

		Launched	Completed
S31	*Salta*	1972	1974
S32	*San Luis*	1973	1974

These are two standard German Typ 209s (qv). No dates are quoted for laying down as they were shipped from Germany in four prefabricated sections for assembly by the Argentinian navy yard. Two more are planned, possibly to be constructed completely in Argentina.

Ex-US Patrol Submarine

Argentina

		Laid Down	Launched	Completed
S21	*Santa Fe* (ex-USS *Catfish*, SS339)	1944	1944	1945
S22	*Santiago del Estero* (ex-USS *Chivo*, SS341)	1944	1945	1945

These are two standard US Balao class submarines modernised under the Guppy programmes (qv). They were purchased by Argentina in 1971 to replace two unmodernised units previously operated.

Brooke Marine-type 42m Patrol Craft

Australia

Displacement: 220
Length (oa): 138ft
Beam: 23.5ft
Draught: 6ft
Machinery: Two diesels on two shafts
Speed 30kts
Armament: Not yet announced

It is planned to build about 15 of these craft as larger successors to the Attack class. Where the latter are comparatively slow and lightly armed, however, the 42m craft will be capable of better than 30kts and of a size potentially large enough to mount an SSM such as Harpoon, although it is not yet announced officially what the final armament will be. Early drawings indicate a flush-hulled design with a knuckle forward and a monoblock superstructure, without a funnel casing.

Only the lead ship will be built in the UK by Brooke Marine. After delivery in mid-1979, she will be

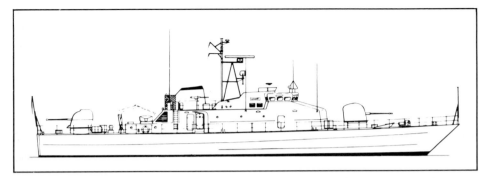

evaluated and the remainder constructed in Australia. The UK-built unit will be named *Freemantle*, and the remainder *Bendigo, Bunbury,* *Cessnock, Dubbo, Gawler, Geelong, Geraldton, Gladstone, Ipswich, Launceston, Townsville, Warrnambool, Whyalla* and *Wollongong.*

Oberon Patrol Submarine   Australia

		Laid Down	Launched	Completed
57	*Oxley*	1964	1965	1967
59	*Otway*	1965	1966	1968
60	*Onslow*	1967	1968	1969
61	*Orion*	1972	1974	1977
62	*Otama*	1973	1975	1978
70	*Ovens*	1966	1967	1969

These are six standard UK-built Oberon class submarines (qv) and the wide disparity in building times is of note. They differ from the RN boats in having some electronics of German and US origin, the latter believed to be in conjunction with the planned purchase of the long range American Mk 48 wire-guided torpedo and encapsulated anti-surface ship Harpoon missile.

Oberon Patrol Submarine   Brazil

		Laid Down	Launched	Completed
S20	*Humaita*	1970	1971	1973
S21	*Tonelero*	1971	1972	1977
S22	*Riachuelo*	1973	1975	1977

These are standard UK-built Oberon class submarines (qv) but with simpler electronics.

Tonelero was rebuilt whilst under construction due to fire damage.

Ex-US Patrol Submarine   Brazil

		Laid Down	Launched	Completed
S10	*Guanabara* (ex-USS *Dogfish*, SS350)	1944	1945	1946
S11	*Rio Grande do Sul* (ex-USS *Grampus*, SS523)	1944	1944	1946
S12	*Bahia* (ex-USS *Sea Leopard*, SS483)	1944	1945	1945
S13	*Rio de Janeiro* (ex-USS *Odax*, SS484)	1944	1945	1945
S14	*Ceara* (ex-USS *Amberjack*, SS522)	1944	1944	1946
S15	*Goiaz* (ex-USS *Trumpetfish*, SS425)	1943	1945	1946
S16	*Amazonas* (ex-USS *Greenfish*, SS351)	1944	1945	1946

S10 and S16 are ex-Balao class boats and remainder are Tench class; all have been modernised under various Guppy programmes (qv) and look similar. Transferred 1972/3.

Vosper (Singapore) 37m FAC (missile) — Brunei

Waspada

A series of three 37m boats has recently been constructed by Vosper Private Limited, VT's Singapore affiliate, for the Royal Brunei Malay Regiment, which operates that state's coastal fleet. In 1977, they disposed of the Brave class boat *Pahlawan* which, with her small SS.12M missiles, constituted the major unit. At the time of writing, information is sparse on the replacement boats but the photograph shows them to be of handsome appearance with the high profile of a craft dedicated primarily to patrol duties. Gun armament is light, consisting of a twin 30mm Oerlikon-Buhrle, 75cal weapons capable of the very high rate of fire of 650rpm/barrel.

The most interesting addition is the brace of MM38 Exocet SSMs aft, imparting greatly increased firepower and continuing the present trend of putting SSMs aboard craft aimed at patrol rather than outright offence (eg rearmed Omani craft). A lightweight Sperry Sea Archer fire control pedestal is sited atop the bridge, part of a system that can operate with radar sensing or with unobtrusive laser, TV or infra-red illumination.

A capacious deckhouse is fitted as an after extension of the superstructure, probably for transport of military personnel over short distance. The very 'open' appearance of the craft *Waspada* shows that she is not designed for use in a major conflict involving nuclear effects. Though *Pahlawan* was gas turbine propelled the new boats are almost certainly diesel powered. A second boat of the class has been named *Seteria*.

Bulgaria

As a member of the eastern bloc, Bulgaria operates a small naval force of Russian-built units to police its short coastline on the Black Sea, very much a Soviet pond. Besides two elderly Riga class frigates (see *Warships of the World: Escort Vessels*) the following craft are operated:

Three Poti class AS corvettes, transferred in 1976.
Up to three Stenka class FAC (AS), transferred in 1978.

Three/four Osa I class FAC (missile), transferred in 1971.
Six SO-I class patrol craft, transferred in 1963.
Six Shershen class FAC (torpedo) transferred in 1971.
Possibly still a few P4 class FAC (torpedo) remaining.
Two Romeo class submarines transferred in 1973.

Details of all these classes can be found under the USSR section.

Algerine Corvette — Burma

Yan Myo Aung (ex-HMS *Mariner*; ex-HMCS *Kincardine*)

	Laid Down	Launched	Completed
	1943	1944	1945

A Canadian-built example of the British Algerine class ocean minesweeper (qv) acting as a corvette. Minesweeping capacity has been retained and a mine-laying facility added. Except for the addition of a commercial type navigation radar on a lattice structure on the bridge, her appearance is little changed from that at transfer from the UK in 1958.

An ex-US PCE-type patrol craft is also operated.

She is the *Yan Taing Augn* (ex-USS *Farmington*, PCE894) transferred in 1965. An ex-US Admirable class MSF is used also as a patrol craft. She is the *Yan Gyi Aung* (ex-USS *Creddock*, MSF356) transferred in 1967.

Cameroun

A pair of Shanghai class FAC (gun) have been reported transferred from China in 1976. The only other craft of note is the French-built 48m *L'Audacieux*, completed in 1976. Although fitted with two quadruple launchers for the short-ranged SS.12M SSM, her speed is under 19kts.

Oberon Patrol Submarine   Canada

		Laid Down	Launched	Completed
72	Ojibwa (ex-HMS *Onyx*)	1962	1964	1965
73	Onondaga	1964	1965	1967
74	Okanagan	1965	1966	1968

Three standard Oberon class submarines (qv) built in the UK naval dockyard at Chatham. Electronics to British standards except for communications compatible with US.

Lürssen-type 36m FAC (torpedo)   Chile

		Completed
80	Guacolda	1965
81	Fresia	1965
82	Quidora	1966
83	Tegualda	1966

Displacement: 134 tons full load
Length (oa): 118ft
Beam: 18.5ft
Draught: 7ft
Machinery: Two diesels on two shafts 4,800shp for 32kts
Armament: Two 40mm guns (2 × 1) Two 21-inch TTs

The southern portion of the immensely long Chilean coast is fjorded and similar to the Norwegian seaboard in its suitability for FAC operation. Weather conditions are severe and distances long so that small craft need to be highly seaworthy and long-legged. This particular 36m type was designed by Lürssen but built by Empresa Nacional Bazan in Spain. It is very similar to a series of three built in Germany for Ecuador as the triple-screw Manta class (qv) in 1971. Bazan has recently built another five (following a Lürssen-constructed lead ship) for the Spanish Navy as the Barcelo class (qv) but, although of the same basic hull and twin screw layout, these carry normally a patrol-boat armament.

In appearance, the craft have a pleasing profile with a compact superstructure set off by a low frame bearing the multi-purpose radar antenna. Both TTs fire forward, with scallops in the gunwhale in front. It is probable that the light scale of the armament reflects the need for a good reserve of stability and allowance of space for large bunker capacity which gives a useful 1,500-mile range at 15kts.

Oberon Patrol Submarine   Chile

		Laid Down	Launched	Completed
22	O'Brien	1971	1972	1976
23	Hyatt (ex-*Condell*)	1972	1973	1976

Two standard UK-built Oberon class submarines (qv).

Ex-US Patrol Submarine   Chile

		Laid Down	Launched	Completed
21	Simpson (ex-USS *Spot*, SS413)	1943	1944	1944

The survivor of a pair of US Balao class submarines (qv) modernised under the Guppy programmes. Transferred along with 20/*Thomson* (ex-USS *Springer*, SS414) in 1961/62. Both refitted in USA 1966-68, but *Thomson* was discarded in 1973. Life expectancy of *Simpson* now short.

Kronstadt Patrol Craft

Up to 20 standard USSR-designed Kronstadts (qv) are in service. Dating from about 1953-57, some were built in the Soviet Union and some in the PRC.

Hai Dau FAC (missile)

Displacement: 250-300 tons
Length: c155ft
Beam: c23ft
Draught: 7ft
Machinery: CODAG Triple shafts
Armament: Six SSM launchers
Four 57mm guns (2 × 2)

There still exists doubt that this design is an operational FAC. If it is, its size is comparable with a Combattante II and geared for surface interdiction. The type is credited normally with launchers for SS-N-2 (Styx) missiles but this would seem unlikely in as much as the canisters are considerably shorter and are carried on very high bases, suggesting a

smaller missile of lower mass than the Styx. A compact bridge structure is topped-off with a GRP dome housing a common fire control for both SSMs and the twin 57mm gun mounting at either end. Those familiar with prewar World War II British destroyers will be amused by the apparent reintroduction of the 'Charlie Noble' galley pipe adjacent to the fire control.

By far the most dominant feature of this enigmatic craft is the high tower aft; raked and faired, it supports various antenna and apparently acts as an air intake, the primary reason for supposing GT propulsion. If so, it is likely that this unit would power a centreline shaft with cruising diesels on wing shafts — but nothing is certain.

Osa FAC (missile)

Up to 80 of the standard USSR Osa I class FACs (qv) are in service. The first 10 of so were transferred from the Soviet Union in 1965-8 and the remainder have since been built in Chinese yards. An improved type, known as the *Hola*, has been reported bearing

no gun armament but up to six SSMs. The lack of gun would seem unlikely but the increase in the number of missiles would agree with the entry into service of a smaller missile than the SS-N-2, as suggested by the *Hai Dau*.

Komar FAC (missile)

A few Komars (qv) were delivered from the Soviet Union about the same time as the above-mentioned Osas and the Chinese have again gone into production with copies, known as the Hoku class. Where in the USSR the Komar was superseded by the Osa, the Chinese appear to have produced both types in parallel and it is believed that up to 50 or 60 Hokus exist. The logistics problem of supplying missiles for all these boats following the severing of

relations with the Soviet Union seems to have been solved satisfactorily by a home-based industry, which must be gaining enough experience to produce its own designs.

The Hokus appear to vary from the Russian-built Komars in having steel hulls and launcher/canisters mounted farther inboard to obviate the sponsons previously necessary. A pole mast is also reported.

Shanghai and Hainan FAC (gun)

Following the introduction by the Soviet Union of the SO-I class of AS patrol craft in about 1957, the Chinese commenced construction of a smaller, but very similar type, designated the Shanghai (later Shanghai I). Where the SO-I carried only 25mm guns and a powerful AS outfit of four five-barrelled MBUs in addition to twin TTs and DCTs, the Shanghai I carried a far heavier gun armament, TTs and DCTs but lacked the projectors. Later units lacked the TTs so it is probable that they were over-ambitious on a small (115ft) hull. Some 25 of this original type are believed still extant but it gave way during the 1960s to an enlarged version, termed the Shanghai II. In this the steel hull has been lengthened to 128ft,

apparently without any corresponding increase in beam. Beyond a token DC rack aft, no AS potential is included in the Type II and the automatic gun armament has been increased very significantly, making them quite potent patrol boats. They appear successful as about 300 seem to be in service, with units transferred also to the navies of Albania, Congo, Guinea, North Korea, Pakistan, Romania, Sierra Leone, Sri Lanka and Tanzania. Although production of the Shanghai II still continues, a larger version, still remarkably similar to but larger than the original SO-I, has been introduced, termed the Hainan. This type has adopted the old-pattern MBU, similar to those on the SO-I, together with its disposition. Its size permits a single 75mm gun to be mounted at either end in additon to four 25mm weapons amidships. Production commenced in the mid-1960s and over 20 are believed to exist, one of which has been transferred to Pakistan.

Hu Chwan Fast Attack Semi-Hydrofoil (torpedo)
People's Republic of China

Possibly inspired by the Russian P8 version of the P6 FAC, where the forward end is lifted at speed on to semi-submerged foils, the Hu Chwan class has been built in large numbers, over 100 serving in the Chinese fleet with a further 30 or so transferred to Albania, four to Pakistan and a small number to Romania, which now builds craft to the same design. Where the P6/P8 was of composite wood-on-metal construction, the Hu Chwan has adopted an all-metal hull, better to withstand the pounding stresses. There are two pairs of foils, a small one right forward and a larger one about on third aft; it is not known what degree of adjustment — if any — they possess but they serve to lift the bows clear of the water whilst the stern rides on the flat sections aft.

The armament is a pair of sided, large-calibre, anti-ship TTs and two pairs of 50cal (12.7mm) MGs in tubs. The bridge is open and surmounted by the rather dated Skin Head radar on a small tripod although, as the type seems to have been built in series for at least the last two decades, many variants must exist.

Also serving in the Chinese fleet are about 100 P6 and P4 FAC (torpedo) (qv) some Russian and some home-built. The conventional P6s have a better radius of action than the Hu Chwans, which are geared to short passages at high speed.

Submarines

The Chinese submarine force is extensive, although composed mainly of recently-built craft to somewhat dated designs. Its composition is believed to be:

About 50 Romeo class patrol submarines (qv). The early boats were Russian-built but have since been added to by Chinese series production. A Mk II version is reported, slightly longer and carrying a more powerful armament.
About 20 Whiskey class patrol submarines (qv). These date from about 1957 to end of Sino-Soviet relations in China. It was the 'drying-up' of components for Russian-designed ships that triggered the development of an indigenous warship-building industry.

People's Republic of China

A Golf class boat (qv) has apparently been built but would appear superfluous until home-produced ballistic missiles, comparable with the unavailable SS-N-5s, can be produced.

In addition, a Chinese-designed patrol submarine (code-named 'Ming') exists, of about a size with the Romeos and presumably, intended as a replacement. A nuclear fleet submarine (code-named 'Han') has also been reported. If the craft exists it means that the Chinese navy is adopting a more offensive nature.

Asheville Patrol Gunboat
Colombia

		Launched	Completed
—	(ex-USS *Canon*, PG90)	1967	1968
—	(ex-USS *Gallup*, PG85)	1965	1966

The two non-missile type Asheville class patrol gunboats (qv) were reported transferred in 1978. No new names yet known.

Typ 209 Patrol Submarine

Colombia

		Launched	Completed
28	Pijao	1974	1975
29	Tayrona	1974	1975

Two standard German-built Typ 209s (qv).

Shanghai II FAC (gun)

Congo

Three Type II Shanghais (qv) are reported transferred from the PRC in 1974-5.

Cuba

The naval forces of Cuba have been strongly reinforced by the Soviet Union following the latter's unsuccessful confrontation with the USA over the siting of ballistic missiles on the island.

At present, the strength is believed to comprise:

Six Osa I class FAC (missile) transferred in 1972-4.
Five Osa II class FAC (missile) transferred in 1976 and 1978.

Up to 20 Komar class FAC (missile) transferred in 1962-6.
Twelve SO-I class patrol boats transferred in 1964-7.
Six Kronstadt class patrol boats transferred in 1962.
Up to 12 P6 class FAC (torpedo) transferred in 1962.
Up to 12 P4 class FAC (torpedo) transferred in 1962-4.

Albatros Corvette

Denmark

		Laid Down	Launched	Completed
F344	Bellona	1954	1955	1957
F346	Flora	1953	1955	1956
F347	Triton	1953	1954	1955

Bellona

Three sisters to the Italian Albatros class (qv) differing in appearance by virtue of prominent shields on the 76mm guns and the large Plessey AWS-1 search radar antenna atop the bridge structure. Four of the type were built for Denmark in Italian yards and funded by the US but *Diana* (F345) was discarded in 1974.

Willemoes FAC (missile)   Denmark

Nordby: note two single Harpoon launchers.

		Completed
P540	*Bille*	1976
P541	*Bredal*	1977
P542	*Hammer*	1977
P543	*Huitfelde*	1977
P544	*Krieger*	1977
P545	*Nordby*	1977
P546	*Rodsteen*	1978
P547	*Sehested*	1978
P548	*Suenson*	1978
P549	*Willemoes*	1976

Displacement: 260 full load
Length (oa): 151ft
Beam: 24ft
Draught: 8ft
Machinery: Three RR Proteus gas turbines of 12,000shp
Two cruising diesels of 800hp CODOG arrangement.
Three shafts 40/12kts
Armament: Four Harpoon SSMs *or* Two/Four 21-inch TTs
One 76mm DP gun

A close similarity exists between this class and the Swedish Spicas (qv) as each stems from the common ancestry of Lürssen in West Germany. The Danish boats, also of steel, have a larger superstructure and also set well aft to balance the mass of the gun and to give it a maximised firing arc. Where the Swedes opted for the home-built 57mm Bofors, however, the Danes have increased the calibre with a 76mm OTO-Melara.

Although designed from the outset as missile boats they have an interchangeable weapon fit with the early units carrying four fixed TTs, two aft and two amidships and P544-548 surrendering the after TTs in favour of four Harpoon SSMs in two, paired, lightweight mountings. (The Danish Navy has standardised on the Harpoon and has fitted it also in the Skram and Juel class frigates — see *Warships of the World: Escort Vessels*). On either side of the bridge are rails for projecting illuminant or ECM rockets.

In common with both the Swedish Jägaren and Norwegian Hauk class FACs, the Willemoes are fitted with the 9LV 200 Mk 2 weapon control system by PEAB, the Swedish subsidiary of Philips. Both missiles and gun can be controlled via the prominent director. The ballistics of the former can be computed by the system, which features frequency agility to resist jamming and pulse doppler tracking of aerial targets to cut out clutter, with all information clearly displayed to the operator.

An interesting departure from the other classes is the fitting of low-power diesels on the wing shaft, in a CODOG configuration, giving the boats an enhanced cruising capacity. Alternatively, all three shafts can be driven by Proteus gas turbines, already well-proven in the Søløven class (qv). They drive cp propellers whose pitch can be varied so as to run the GTs at constant optimum speed or reversed to give astern power without requiring any change of direction in the rotation of the prime movers.

Søløven FAC (torpedo)   Denmark

Søulven

		Completed
P510	*Søløven*	1965
P511	*Søridderen*	1965
P512	*Søbjornen*	1965
P513	*Søhesten*	1966
P514	*Søhunden*	1966
P515	*Søulven*	1967

Displacement: 95 standard
115 full load
Length (oa): 99ft
Beam: 25.5ft
Draught: 7ft
Machinery: Three Proteus gas turbines 12,750shp
Two cruising diesels. Three shafts
53/10kts
Armament: Two 40mm guns (2 × 1)
Four 21-inch TTs (4 × 1)

In 1959, Vosper launched in the UK a pair of the fastest torpedo craft to date, the Brave class for the Royal Navy. They were the first to use the marinised version of the Proteus gas turbine, with one unit on each of three shafts. No cruising machinery was fitted and the fixed pitch propellers required reversing gearboxes. Their conventional, high speed planing hulls were extremely beamy and constructed of laminated wood on light alloy framing, with a welded light alloy superstructure. The West German navy ordered one of the type for evaluation, together with a two-engine version known by Vosper as the Ferocity class (both of these now serve in the Greek navy (qv); each was completed in 1962).

Soon afterward, the Danish navy ordered the lead pair (P510/511) from Vosper, together with licence for the construction of a further four in the Royal Dockyard at Copenhagen. They compared interestingly with the Falken class boats then recently completed by the Dockyard to a basic Lürssen design, which were built also by the latter yard as the Silbermöwe class and which, too, ended their days in the Greek navy. These classes were diesel driven and very seaworthy but little advanced from the World War II S-boats. The Søløvens represented a one third increase in speed but this trend in turn has been eclipsed by a return to larger, round-bilge hulls driven at more moderate speeds.

It was the intention to use the British boats as interchangeable MGB/MTBs and, in the former guise, they would have exchanged a pair of tubes for a new and fully stabilised 3.3-inch gun developed from an Army weapon. In the event this proved too cumbersome and nothing larger than 40mm guns were ever fitted. The Danish boats were an improvement in the incorporation of a pair of low-power diesels on the wing shafts for cruising purposes.

Seven further boats were built by Vosper for Libya and Malaysia as the Susa and Perkasa classes (qv) and these are a further variant in that they have a primary armament of the small French-built SS.12M anti-ship missiles. The latter group has since been discarded.

Narvhalen Patrol Submarine

Denmark

		Laid Down	Launched	Completed
S320	*Narvhalen*	1965	1968	1970
S321	*Nordkaperen*	1966	1969	1970

These are hybrid Danish-built boats similar in characteristics to the Norwegian Ula class (qv). In appearance however, they are configured like the German Typ 205 (qv) of which the Ula type (known as the Typ 207) was a deeper-diving derivative. At

present, the German and Norwegian design departments are working on a new 750-ton design to be known as the Typ 210. It is reported that Denmark may build up to six of them under licence.

Nordkaperen

Delfinen Patrol Submarine   Denmark

Springeren

		Laid Down	Launched	Completed
S326	*Delfinen*	1954	1956	1958
S327	*Spaekhuggeren*	1954	1957	1959
S328	*Tumleren*	1956	1958	1960
S329	*Springeren*	1961	1963	1964

Displacement: 580 surfaced
650 submerged
Length (oa): 177ft
Beam: 15.5ft
Draught: 13ft
Machinery: Two diesels 1,200bhp
Two motors 1,200hp
Two shafts 14/13kts
Armament: Four 21-inch TTs

These elegant little boats were the first built by Denmark post-World War II. They were contemporary with the French Arethuse class (qv) and similar in size, outfit and function, ie inshore patrol. It is probable that their diving capabilities are less than the French boats in view of the shallow approaches to Danish waters and their performance is also less by virtue of having twin-screw propulsion where the Arethuse design opted for single. There are four TTs, all forward, backed by the usual active and passive sonar outfits.

Three of the class were built in sequence with a fourth, *Springeren*, added later and taking her name from an ex-British U class boat latterly returned to the UK. There would seem to be a good chance of the Delfinens being phased out as the new Typ 210s are constructed.

PCE-type Patrol Craft   Ecuador

		Completed
P22	*Esmeraldas* (ex-USS *Eunice*, PCE846)	1944
P23	*Manabi* (ex-USS *Pascagoula*, PCE874)	1943

These are of the US-built 180ft steel-hulled PCE (qv) and were transferred in 1960. They have short funnels but are otherwise very similar to the Dutch Wolf class (qv for picture).

Lürssen-type 45m FAC (missile)   Ecuador

Quito

		Completed
LM31	*Quito*	1976
LM32	*Guayaquil*	1977
LM33	*Cuenca*	1977

Displacement: 260 tons full load
Length (oa): 147.5ft
Beam: 23ft
Draught: 8ft
Machinery: Four diesels on four shafts
14,000shp for 40kts
Armament: Four MM38 Exocet SSMs
One 76mm gun
Two 35mm guns (1×2)

This trio of boats comprise an improved version of the West German Typ 148 (qv) to which they are very similar. Although their hulls — again steel-built — are slightly shorter they have an up-rated MTU diesel installation for a higher speed. The general layout is similar but they carry an enhanced point defence armament in the twin 35mm mounting aft, in place of the earlier design's single 40mm. The Oerlikon 35mm GDM-A has a rate of fire of 550rpm/barrel and can be integrated with the ship's weapon control system for fast automatic response against, say SSMs and using proximity-fused fragmentation ammunition.

It is probable that the class includes also some form of tactical command system for integrated operations with the less complex Manta class torpedo-armed FACs (qv). Whether this approaches the capacity of the German AGIS is not known. The Quitos were built by Lürssen in West Germany, but the closely related gun-armed FACs of the Malaysian and Thai navies (qv) were built under licence in the Far East. Others serve under the Argentinian flag.

Lürssen-type 36m FAC (torpedo)   Ecuador

Manta

		Completed
LT41	*Manta*	1971
LT42	*Tulcan*	1971
LT43	*Nuevo Rocafuerte*	1971

Displacement: 135 tons full load
Length (oa): 119.5ft
Beam: 19ft
Draught: 6ft
Machinery: Three diesels on three shafts
9,000bhp for 36kts
Armament: One 40mm gun
Two 21-inch TTs

In 1965, the Spanish yard of Bazan built four Lürssen-designed torpedo-armed FACs for Chile. These were a sturdy 36m design (qv) and were virtually repeated in the boats for Ecuador, but built in West Germany. These differ from the Chilean craft in having a third, centreline shaft and diesel added and in carrying only half the armament. Another closely similar class is the Spanish Barcelo (qv) designed for use either as lightly gun-armed patrol vessels or as torpedo craft.

Typ 209 Patrol Submarine   Ecuador

		Launched	Completed
S11	*Shyri*	1976	1978
S12	*Huancavila*	1977	1978

These are two standard German-built Typ 209 (qv) a best-selling export submarine, particularly to South America.

Egypt

The Egyptian navy reflects in its composition the alliances of various eras. In the period following World War II, British influence was strong and the larger units are mainly ex-Royal Navy ships of World War II vintage. From about 1956 the country became more firmly committed to the Soviet Union and most of the smaller combatants are of this origin but relations cooled and, from the mid-1970s, when

October class No 207 FAC (missile) arriving in the UK for refit.

Whiskey class patrol submarine.

Romeo class patrol submarine.

Russia made no more spare parts available, Egypt again became Western orientated. Minor Egyptian units include the following:

Six Osa I class FAC (missile) transferred in 1966. Reported to carry SA-N-7 missiles but have been partially refitted with British equipment, particularly electronics.
Three Komar class FAC (missile), transferred about 1964. Still carry SA-N-2 missiles and probably in questionable state of efficiency.
Six October class FAC (missile). These are Egyptian copies of the Komar design and only recently completed. As machinery, electronics and armament are no longer available from Russian sources, the hulls are being fitted out by Vosper Thornycroft in the UK.
Up to six Shershen class FAC (gun/torpedo), transferred since 1967. Some possibly have been modified to carry SA-N-7 missiles.
About 20 P6 class FAC (torpedo) transferred in batches, 1956-72. Some carry multi-barrelled unguided rocket launchers.

A few surviving P4 class FAC (torpedo).
About 10 SO-I class patrol craft, transferred from about 1962. Some have been torpedo armed and some may carry SA-N-7 missiles.

In view of the lack of rounds for the SA-N-7 launchers, removal or replacement may be expected.
Vosper Thornycroft has received an order for six new 52m FAC (missile) but further details are, at present, not available. Two BH7 hovercraft are also reported on order from the UK. In addition, the Egyptian navy operates submarines, as follows: Six Whiskey class patrol submarines, transferred between 1957-62; six Romeo class patrol submarines, transferred in 1966-9. Details of these and other ex-Russian vessels can be found under that heading. That the above submarines have only a limited life left to them is indicated by the recent purchase of the British *Cachalot* of the Porpoise class (qv) and the rumoured order for a pair of French-built Agostas (qv) a type probably better suited to Egyptian needs.

Ethiopia

Formerly operating only a small ex-US netlayer and a selection of gun-armed patrol craft, again mostly of US origin, the Ethiopian navy has taken a decisive turn with the new national regime. Reports state that it has obtained fighting craft from the USSR,

including one Osa II FAC (missile) (qv) and two MOL variants of the basic Stenka (qv). It is hard to see the function of the single Osa II except prestige and the chance to train crews for further transfers.

Turunmaa Corvette

Finland

		Laid Down	Launched	Completed
—	*Karjala*	1967	1967	1968
—	*Turunmaa*	1967	1967	1968

Displacement: 650 standard
770 full load
Length (oa): 243ft
Beam: 25.5ft
Draught: 8ft
Machinery: One Olympus gas turbine 22,000hp
Three MTU diesels 3,300bhp total CODOG
arrangement. Three shafts 35/17kts
Armament: One 120mm gun
Two 40mm guns (2×1)
Two 30mm guns (1×2)
Two AS torpedo launchers

Though 10 years old, the basic Turunmaa corvette is very modern in concept, being dated only in the armament fit. No exact parallel exists, and the type

rates somewhere between the new Italian-built Libyan corvettes (qv) and the larger French A69 (qv).
Capable of long endurance patrols the craft had also to be able to boost rapidly to maximum speed for interdiction. For this, a triple shaft hull was adopted, with diesels on the wing shafts, working through cp propellers and a third diesel interchangeable with a de-rated Olympus gas turbine on the centreline shaft, driving a fixed pitch propeller whose efficiency is enhanced by a duct. A powerful gun armament is fitted, with an automatic Bofors-pattern 120mm weapon forward, an unusually large calibre firing 80 75lb projectiles per minute out to about eight miles. The remaining armament reflects the aircraft threat in the Baltic and consists of two single 40mm and a twin 30mm mounting, all by Bofors.

Fire control is the HSA combined search/track unit in the GRP dome atop the bridge.

The flush-decked hull and continuous deckhouse/bridge structure are fully enclosed and very clean, offering maximum protection from both the elements and fallout. In the sides of the deckhouse amidships are hinged doors which enclose launchers for AS torpedoes, associated with a hull-mounted sonar. DCs are also carried.

That the Turunmaa design still has much to offer is evidenced by three further variants recently armoured by the builders, Wartsila. These are:

An updated basic version with the 120mm gun supplemented by four forward-mounted MM38

Exocet SSM launchers and the secondary armaments' 40mm guns replaced by a single Bofors 57mm weapon.

An AA escort with two single 57mm guns, the twin 30mm retained and French Crotale SAM launcher. Search radars are enhanced and a forward-firing Bofors AS launcher added.

An AS version with a 76mm gun forward and a more powerful twin Oerlikon 35mm OTO mounting amidships. The after end has a pad for a helicopter (for which there is no hangar) and AS torpedoes are launched either by the helicopter or Mk 32 TTs. This version seems to stretch the design too far for use in northern waters but the first two are extremely effective on the tonnage.

Osa II FAC (missile)   Finland

Tuima

Four were transferred by purchase from the Soviet Union in 1975. They were named *Tuima, Tuisku, Tuula* and *Tyrsky* and are similar in appearance to the

standard Osa II (qv) but have fewer mast-mounted antenna. It is reported that five more are being sought.

Nuoli FAC (gun)   Finland

Displacement: 40 standard
65 full load
Length (oa): 73ft
Beam: 21.5ft
Draught: 5ft
Machinery: Three diesels on three shafts
2,700bhp for 40kts
Armament: One 40mm gun
One 20mm gun

Named *Nuoli 1-13* this class was built in Finland and are of a size that is rapidly disappearing, comparable types being the Russian P4 or, more closely, the Norwegian Nasty/Tjeld. Comparison immediately discloses the light scale of the Finnish boats' armament; even allowing for the fact that they have the extra deadweight of a third engine, it would seem reasonable to suppose that a pair of TTs could be shipped if required.

They appear to be built of light alloy and the superstructure of the last four built is marginally lower. The class has Soviet-built machinery and dates from 1961-6. Two further boats, the *Vasama 1* and *Vasama 2*, of the British-built Dark class have now been deleted. That their wooden hulls survived Baltic ice for 20 years was rather surprising.

Ruissalo AS Patrol Craft   Finland

Ruissalo

		Completed
3	*Ruissalo*	1959
4	*Raisio*	1959
5	*Roitta*	1959

Displacement: 110 standard
130 full load
Length (oa): 111ft
Beam: 20ft
Draught: 6ft
Machinery: Two diesels on two shafts
2,500bhp for 16kts
Armament: One 40mm gun
One 20mm gun
One Squid triple-barrelled AS mortar

Bearing a passing resemblance to a British inshore minesweeper this class of vessel has a function more akin to another RN class, the Ford-type SDB (qv), ie that of inshore defence against submarines. For this purpose it mounts a similar weapon in the Squid mortar, together with an armament of light automatic guns. The hull is built of metal but is similar in both size and speed. Another pair of craft, *Rihtniemi* (1) and *Rymattlya* (2) preceded the above three units into service. They are slightly smaller and are fitted for general-purpose patrol duties although they can carry DCs. All are capable of either mine-laying or minesweeping.

Trident FAC (missile)   France

		Completed
P670	*Trident*	1976
P671	*Glaive*	1977
P672	*Epée*	1976
P673	*Pertuisane*	1977

Displacement: 115 standard
130 full load
Length (oa): 121.5ft
Beam: 18ft
Draught: 5ft

Trident

Machinery: Two diesels on two shafts
4,000bhp for 26kts
Armament: Six SS.12M SSMs
One 40mm gun
One MG

Although a major designer and builder of FACs for export, France has little peacetime use for them other than in the training of her fleet in anti-FAC techniques and such patrol duties as fishery protection or safeguarding offshore facilities. The four Tridents are the survivors of a planned 30-boat series, geared largely for colonial deployments for which their modest speed and armament would have been adequate. With diminishing foreign interests came the cancellation of the remainder of the class and they are best viewed as patrol, rather than attack craft.

Of composite construction, the clean-lined hull supports a large superstructure with the mast amidships in the position where the antenna experience minimum acceleration forces. A simple twin diesel-twin shaft arrangement has been incorporated, driving through cp propellers and economical in both fuel and space; the craft can realise a range of 1,500 miles at 15kts.

Only a 40mm gun and light automatic weapons are normally carried but accommodation can be made for six Nord Aviation SS.12 SSM mountings on the after superstructure. These short range weapons carry a 65lb warhead to only three miles, and with the Trident's low speed, it is difficult to imagine against what they are supposed to be used. A class of larger FAC is reported planned.

Combattante I FAC (missile) France

	Completed
P730 *La Combattante*	1964

Displacement: 180 standard
200 full load
Length (oa): 148ft
Beam: 24ft
Draught: 6.5ft
Machinery: Two diesels on two shafts
3,200bhp for 23kts
Armament: Four SS.11 SSMs
Two 40mm guns (2 × 1)

La Combattante is the sole example of the type, perpetuating the name of a famous frigate of World War II. Upon the development of a successful derivative, the design became known as the Combattante I but, beyond sharing their name, it has little in common with the later boats. Although classed as an FAC (missile), the title seems dubious as the twin diesel power is sufficient only for some 23kts and the missiles are small, wire-guided SS.11s in a bulky quadruple mount abaft the superstructure. Their warheads weigh under 20lb and their range is less than two miles. Two 40mm guns can be carried, although the after one is sometimes landed. The hull is of wood and GRP laminated construction and, together with the large superstructure, can provide accommodation for an 80-man detachment, complete with equipment, for short passages.

Combattante II FAC (missile) France

Displacement: 235 standard
255 full load
Length (oa): 154ft
Beam: 23ft
Draught: 8ft
Machinery: Four diesels on four shafts
12,000bhp for 36kts
Armament: See individual entries

When the Russians put their new SS-N-2 (Styx) missile into the small Komar hull about 1960, they produced a cheap warship of great potency. Western navies, still geared to the aircraft carrier strike concept, had been early in SAM development but had neglected the SSM. Thus, when the World War II-built carriers reached the end of their useful lives and proved too expensive to replace, the development of a western SSM was an urgent requirement. Quick off the mark, the French had produced the Exocet (Flying-fish) by 1968, a surface skimmer difficult for a potential target to detect or counter. It was built as a fire-and-forget weapon as little room is available on a small warship for elaborate guidance systems. All that is required is for the parent craft to locate the target and compute the intercept bearing and range; this will put the missile sufficiently close to the target for its own detectors to locate and lock on for the approach phase. The MM38 Exocet is self-contained in a canister/launcher, can be maintained aboard and can take a 375lb warhead to further than 22 miles. Its total dominance of the market has since been challenged, notably by the Harpoon and Otomat.

A suitable vehicle for the Exocet was developed from the basic La Combattante design (qv) but larger and faster with a round-bilged hull for seakindliness built from steel with a light alloy or steel superstructure. 36kts was realised with a four diesel-four shaft arrangement. The superstructure consists of a bridge block, placed well forward to allow space

behind for the SSMs, which need to be placed to fire at an angle to the centreline, so that the rocket efflux will blast clear on the opposite side. Guidance systems permit a maximum target offset of about 30 degrees. A rapid-firing gun armament is fitted, varying according to customer preference — some prefer a mix of 76 or 57mm with 40mm weapons, some a homogeneous 35mm fit. Heavier guns give 'more bang for the buck' against surface targets; smaller ones, when well directed, a good chance of disintegrating an incoming SSM by saturation. TTs can be fitted. Comprehensive fire control surveillance radars are supplied mainly from Thompson CSF or HSA, together with such data links as are necessary for flotila operations. It is common to use commercial wavelengths for electronics to prevent an ESM-equipped target becoming suspicious.

No Combattante IIs have been built for the French navy but may be found in those of Greece, Iran, Libya and Malaysia. It is closely related to the West German Typ 148s, most of which were also built by the CMN yard at Cherbourg.

Combattante III FAC (missile) France

Displacement: 385 standard
425 full load
Length (oa): 184ft
Beam: 26ft
Draught: 7ft
Machinery: Four diesels on four shafts
18,000bhp for 35kts
Armament: Four MM38 Exocet SSMs
Two 76mm guns (2 x 1)
Four 30mm guns (2 x 2)
Two 21-inch TTs

This 'stretched' version of the Combattante II design, has so far, been built only for Greece with a further three, 'Type III B' ordered by Nigeria. With a length of 184ft it is comparable with the Israeli Reshef (qv) or West German Typ 143 (qv) classes and nudges at the top end of the size range for the FAC — beyond this lie larger displacement vessels such as the Russian Nanuchkas (qv) or the Italian-built Libyan corvettes (qv).

The extra displacement allows of a very

comprehensive armament fit with the Greeks opting for a well-proven OTO-Melara 76mm gun fore and aft and a twin, fully automatic 30mm mounting on either side of the afterbridge. This mounting is the Emerlec gun, used also in the American-built CPIC (qv) and based on the 600rpm Hispano cannon. (A possibly better alternative would have been the Oerlikon/BMARC gun, lighter and with a higher rate of fire.) This gun armament, together with four MM38 Exocet SSMs and two TTs mounted to fire wire-guided torpedoes over the transom, German style, give the design good anti-ship capability, with a high survivability. Fire control arrangements are similar to those on the Greek Combattante IIs and a French SATIN automated combat system has been added for the full coordination of operations with the Mk II boats.

Engine power has been increased by 50% to achieve a speed close to that of the smaller boats, to which they are similar in appearance but with a longer bridge structure and a diminutive house aft, supporting a braced mainmast.

Le Fougueux Patrol Craft France

		Completed
P635	L'Ardent	1959
P640	Le Fringant	1960
P644	L'Adroit	1958

Displacement: 325 standard
400 full load
Length (oa): 174ft
Beam: 24ft
Draught: 10ft
Machinery: Four diesels on two shafts
3,250bhp for 19kts
Armament: Two 40mm guns (2 x 1)

Hedgehog AS mortar or 120mm mortar
Disposals: P630 L'Intrepide; P637 L'Etourdi; P638 L'Effronte; P639 Le Frondeur; P641 Le Fougueux; P642 L'Opiniatre; P643 L'Agile; P645 L'Alerte; P646 L'Attentif; P647 L'Enjoue; P648 Lettardi

Between 1941 and 1944 the US Navy commissioned a large number of 173ft submarine chasers (PC), whose function was largely as coastal convoy escorts. They were simple, twin diesel-twin screw ships, built of steel and carrying a basic armament of a 3-inch gun, automatic weapons and plenty of depth charges. Many were transferred abroad after

World War II, some 36 going to France of which some were then taken over by the embryonic naval forces of the states of the former French Indo-China. Those retained by the French Navy were known as the Carabinier class and were rated Escorteurs. They proved to have limitations however, not the least being their short life expectancy and were derated to Patrouilleurs. Being useful craft, nevertheless, an improved class of 17 were built in France in the late-1950s, funded partly by the US Offshore programme and rated Escorteurs Cotiers. Of these, 11 were retained under the tricolor and three transferred to Portugal, and one each to West Germany and Ethiopia.

This improved class, the Le Fougueux group, carried only two 40mm guns, the forward one initially being mounted over the bridge for almost all-round fire. More deadweight was allocated to AS weapons, with an ahead-firing Hedgehog sited forward, sometimes replaced by a single-barrelled 120mm mortar, doubling as both AS and short-range bombardment weapon. Their coastal escort functions now being usurped by the new A69 corvettes, the little PCs are disappearing fast and the three survivors have only a short time to run.

Le Foudroyant SSBN

France

		Laid Down	Launched	Completed
S610	Le Foudroyant	1969	1971	1974
S611	Le Redoutable	1964	1967	1971
S612	Le Terrible	1967	1969	1973
S613	L'Indomptable	1971	1974	1976
S614	Le Tonnant	1974	1977	1980
S615	L'Inflexible	—	—	—

Displacement: 7,500 surfaced
9,000 submerged
Length (oa): 420ft
Beam: 35ft
Draught: 33ft
Machinery: One PWC reactor driving two turbo-alternator sets to power single drive motor Single screw, 15,000shp for 20/50kts 'Get you home' diesel, 2,750bhp
Armament: Sixteen ICBM launch tubes
Four 550mm TTs

When France left the NATO alliance it meant that she had to be self-reliant in the matter of nuclear deterrance and it is a matter of great national pride that she has developed an effective force controlled entirely by her own government and independent of any other powers acquiesence in its use. Although, understandably, the French missiles' performance trails that of the Americans, it, too, is being continuously up-dated.

The first of the French SSBNs, La Redoutable, became fully operational in 1971, deploying 16 M1 missiles, whose size and 1,300-mile range were roughly equivalent to the American A2 Polaris which, by then, had seen 10 years' service. By 1974, the third of class, Le Foudroyant, carried the 1,600-mile M2 which was then developed in power to the M20 for the L'Indomptable of 1976. The latest system, the M4, has been perfected at Muraroa to the point where it is being retro-fitted to the Le Terrible during her current long refit. Reportedly carrying seven MIRV warheads out to 3,000 miles, the M4 equates roughly to the American C-3 Poseidon.

As may be expected when designed around a similar weapon fit, the French SSBNs are very close in dimensions to the American Lafayettes and the British Resolutions. In appearance they, too, have the US-type fin-mounted dividing planes; the casing aft has a less pronounced hump but shows a discontinuity of line forward of the fin. In common

Le Redoutable

with normal practice, only a small defensive armament of four TTs is fitted although these will acquire an increased potency if the Subroc missile is purchased from the US.

The reactor is water-cooled but not under the normal high pressure, a great advantage if it means that the usual noisy pumps can be eliminated. Steam produced via the heat exchanger drives two turbo-alternator sets which generate the power for the single electric propulsion motor. The single shaft can also be rotated by a small auxiliary diesel, giving a 5,000-mile emergency range.

Following general practice, two complete crews are provided to get maximum utilisation from this highly expensive force. L'Inflexible, the sixth unit of the class, has been ordered and will carry the M4.

Gymnote Experimental Ballistic Missile Submarine France

		Laid Down	Launched	Completed
S655	*Gymnote*	1963	1964	1966

Displacement: 3,000 surfaced
3,250 submerged
Length (oa): 275.5ft
Beam: 34.5ft
Draught: 25ft
Machinery: Four diesel-electric generators driving
two propulsion motors on two shafts
2,600bhp for 11/10kts
Armament: Two ICBM launch tubes

When in 1955 the US Navy commissioned its first nuclear submarine, *Nautilus*, other major fleets were also pursuing their own lines of research, the French project being known as Q244. Work proceeded rapidly enough for the first metal to be cut in 1957, before either the British or the Russians. It was intended that she displace about 4,000 tons on the surface and she was laid down in 1958, only to be cancelled the following year. Whether this was through financial stringency or technical shortcomings it is not clear, but the hull lay incomplete for some years.

France, meantime, had left NATO and had to develop her own seaborne ICBM (known as the MSBS). The availability of the hull was fortunate in that it could be rebuilt for a test vehicle and work re-commenced in 1963 to fit a pair of vertical launch tubes into her. Although the diameter of the pressure hull is virtually identical with that of the later, purpose-built SSBNs, the tubes appear to project further and are shrouded in a conspicuously high casing abaft the fin. As the *Gymnote*, she has also been used to check out other submarine systems for the French navy.

A conventional machinery fit was eventually shipped, the four-alternator arrangement suggesting expediency and far too low-powered to give the craft any serious offensive capacity. With a bow-dome of distinctive shape and the double step in the after casing her surfaced profile is unmistakeable. Recently, she has been fitted out for the proving of the M4 missile at Muraroa, late in 1978.

Agosta Patrol Submarine   France

		Launched	Completed
S620	*Agosta*	1974	1977
S621	*Beveziers*	1975	1977
S622	*La Praya*	1976	1978
S623	*Ouessant*	1976	1978

Displacement: 1,450 surfaced
1,725 submerged
Length (oa): 222ft
Beam: 22ft
Draught: 18ft

Machinery: Two diesel-alternators driving one main
or one cruising motor Single shaft
4,600hp for 12/20kts
Armament: Four 550mm TTs

Contrasting with the short, fat submarines now in vogue for middle-distance operations, the Agostas are designed for distant water use and are at the upper end of the size range produced in the west. As with the preceding Daphné class (qv) great efforts have been made to reduce radiated underwater

Agosta

noise, not only in the insulation of machinery but to the extent of making external fittings retractable for the maintenance of clean flow over the hull. The hull shape is typical of modern practice, with the extreme high speed Albacore shape being much modified for better capacity; diving planes are mounted forward, abaft the rounded bow casing that houses the passive sonar arrays and the cruciform control surfaces aft allow of a large, slow-turning propeller for optimum, silent performance.

The main machinery is conventional in having a pair of diesel-alternator sets providing power for both charging batteries and driving the main motor. What is unusual is the addition of a 23kW (about 30hp) electric motor for quiet low speed cruising on station.

Only four TTs are fitted, all forward, for which some 20 reloads are carried. It is assumed that on distant operations, targets present themselves at a rate that could not require a reloading exercise during an attack, bearing in mind that, with modern wire-guided torpedoes, it is no longer necesary to fire large spreads to guarantee a hit. Torpedoes can be launched down to maximum submerged depth of about 1,000ft by use of 'swim-out' techniques, unobtrusive and useful against other submarines.

Mines probably cannot therefore be carried as they cannot be conventionally ejected. The sonar fit is comprehensive and includes long and short (intercept) range sets as well as passive arrays with sufficient spread along the hull to act as a ranging device.

Spain, having built Daphnés under licence, is now constructing Agostas. South Africa ordered two from France but the delivery was blocked for political reasons; the fact that Egypt is reported to be interested in a couple may not be disconnected with this.

A prototype nuclear fleet submarine of about 2,400 tons (surface) is finally under construction after a gestation going back to the 1950s (see under Gymnote). For delivery in 1981/2 she will be only about 237ft in length and torpedo armed. The latter are 21-inch weapons (533mm) in contrast with the 550mm calibre usually favoured by the French and suggests an interest in compatibility with other western navies. If so, this would point possibly to acquisition of an encapsulated Harpoon and/or Subroc. The advanced cruise missiles of the Tomahawk type are also geared to the same tube. Known as the Type SNA72, the second boat is also on order and at least three more are planned.

Daphné Patrol Submarine   France

		Laid Down	Launched	Completed
S641	*Daphné*	1958	1959	1964
S642	*Diane*	1958	1960	1964
S643	*Doris*	1958	1960	1964
S645	*Flore*	1958	1960	1964
S646	*Galatée*	1958	1961	1964
S648	*Junon*	1961	1964	1966
S649	*Venus*	1961	1964	1966
S650	*Psyche*	1965	1967	1969
S651	*Sirène*	1965	1967	1970

Displacement: 870 standard
1,045 submerged
Length (oa): 189.5ft
Beam: 22ft
Draught: 15ft
Machinery: Two diesel-alternators powering two propulsion motors Two shafts
1,300bhp/13.5kts surfaced
1,600bhp/16kts submerged
Armament: Twelve 550mm TTs

Supposedly a development of the Arethuse type (qv) to which it bears a passing resemblance, the Daphné is very different in concept. Rather larger, the design's most obvious difference lies in a reversion to twin screw propulsion, compared with the smaller boat's single propeller; in view of the submerged silence claimed for the class, this is of interest. A change of thought is apparent also in armament, as no less than eight TTs are mounted forward and four

aft. For these, a range of torpedoes is carried and selected according to likely target ie high or low speed, surfaced or submerged etc. Whether this vast battery of weaponry can really be justified and whether the boat's fire control facilities are up to its full utilisation can only be surmised. All have recently been updated electronically, however, and carry a very comprehensive range of sonars. Externally, the majority have a bow dome faired into the line of the stem, but some still have a 'blister' type dome slightly farther aft.

As with other French boats, the outer hull is kept very clear of protrusions that could cavitate and cause noise. A pair of WT aerials is strung aft from the top of the fin but these presumably can be dismantled to avoid any strumming effects when submerged. They are deep diving boats, very successful and a good export line. They can be found also under the flags of Libya, Pakistan, Portugal, South Africa and Spain.

Daphné

Arethuse Patrol Submarine   France

Arethuse

		Laid Down	Launched	Completed
S635	*Arethuse*	1955	1957	1958
S636	*Argonaute*	1955	1957	1959
S639	*Amazone*	1955	1958	1959
S640	*Ariane*	1955	1958	1960

Displacement: 545 surfaced
670 submerged
Length (oa): 163ft
Beam: 19ft
Draught: 13ft
Machinery: Two diesel-alternators powering one
propulsion motor Single shaft
1,050bhp/12.5kts surfaced
1,300bhp/16kts submerged
Armament: Four 550mm TTs

Smallest of the French submarines in service, the
Arethuse class boats were designed for operations in
shallow and restricted waters, particularly against
other submarines. Now over 20 years in service, their
concept varies from modern equivalents eg the West
German Typ 206. One example of this is the ratio
between surfaced and submerged displacement.
Obviously, the smaller the difference between them,
the less ballast the boat requires to submerge,
cutting diving time. This advantage has the penalty
of low reserve buoyancy, rendering the boat liable to
foundering from only a small involuntary flooding. In
conventional submarines it is currently common to

have 15-20% difference in the tonnages for larger
boats and 25-30% for smaller examples (the
Typ 206 has about 50%) to give extra disposable
buoyancy to offset the increased likelihood of being
sunk inshore but where the submarine would bottom
before reaching collapse depth. As the Arethuse
class has only a 19% margin, they can obviously dive
rapidly but follow the older line of thought.

Another common feature in modern boats is a
heavy battery of TTs forward to respond to the busy
situations encountered at choke points. The
Arethuse packs only four tubes and but one reload
for each, which must reduce its capacity for
operations on a busy station.

They are reputed to be well-designed although the
single-screw propulsion (they were among the first
to follow the Albacore experiments but enclosed the
single screw within an aperture forward of the single
rudder) was not repeated in the Daphné class boats
that followed. As with all French conventionals,
diving planes are mounted forward rather than on
the fin and there exists a strong resemblance
between classes, with the smaller boats having a
proportionately higher fin.

Narval Patrol Submarine   France

		Laid Down	Launched	Completed
S631	*Narval*	1951	1954	1957
S632	*Marsouin*	1951	1955	1957
S633	*Dauphin*	1952	1955	1958
S634	*Requin*	1952	1955	1958
S637	*Espadon*	1955	1958	1960
S638	*Morse*	1956	1958	1960

Displacement: 1,635 surfaced
1,910 submerged
Length(oa): 254.5ft
Beam: 25.5ft
Draught: 17.5ft

Machinery: Three diesel-alternators powering two
propulsion motors Two shafts
2,400bhp for 15/18kts
Armament: Six 550mm TTs

Narval

In 1945 in company with the remainder of the Allied navies, the French gained access to German World War II developments and ran several types of ex-U-boat alongside their ex-British and older home-built boats. One of these was a Typ XXI and ran until the 1960s as the *Roland Morillot*. The excellence of her design influenced new French construction as surely as it had American, British and Russian, and the six Narvals, built under the 1949 programme, were very similar in tonnage and dimensions to the XXI, extremely strongly built and of long endurance.

One factor limiting endurance is a large crew and the 63 required by a Narval compares unfavourably with the 50 or so in an Agosta. Automation has accounted largely for this; reducing crews reduces the size of the boat as accommodation, stores and services can also be scaled down and, most important, it reduces the wage bill, probably the most expensive factor in cost over the boat's life.

As built, the design's six bow tubes were complemented by a further pair mounted externally in the casing but these were removed in the class's rebuild in 1965-70. At the same time, the electronics were completely renewed and the machinery replaced, particularly with an eye to noise reduction. Originally, the shaft could be driven either by diesel or electric motor, but when the old Schneider two-strokes were replaced by three medium-speed Pielsticks, the latter were coupled to alternators which power either the main propulsion motors or a small, 40hp, cruising motor on each of the two shafts. Externally, the main alteration was in the squaring-off of the fin profile. In spite of their age, they are still considered good performers and are the largest of the French 'conventionals'.

Gabon

	Completed
P10 *President el Hadj Omar Bongo*	1977

Displacement: 160 full load
Length (oa): 138ft
Beam: 25.5ft
Draught: 6.5ft
Machinery: Three diesels on three shafts 10,500shp for 40kts
Armament: Four SS.12M SSMs
One 40mm gun
One 20mm gun

Originally named *N'golo*, this craft has been constructed by the Esterel yard in Nice, a firm associated more with the production of luxury private yachts. She is beautifully constructed of wood, treated with epoxy resin below the waterline against the attentions of marine boring creatures, and is very much a prestige flagship, carrying a prestige name.

Likely to spend the greater part of her career in official duties, her armament is very light in scale but does include two paired SS.12M mountings forward of the bridge. Unlike the arrangement on the French *La Combattante* (qv) these have no directors and, wire-guided, rely on optical control out to their full range of 5,500m. Only basic navigation radar and communications are fitted.

The Gabonese Navy also operates a half-dozen patrol craft with light automatic armament, three of which are comparable in size with the *Bongo* and have been delivered recently from Italy.

Hai Corvette

East Germany

Units: Names uncertain but reported to include the following: *Bad Doberan; Butzow; Gadebusch; Grevesmühlen; Lubz; Ludwigslust; Parchim; Perleberg; Ribnitz-Damgarten; Sternberg; Teterow* and *Wismar*. Pennant numbers 411-414, 431-434; 451-454
Displacement: 300 standard
370 full load
Length(oa): 187ft
Beam: 23ft
Draught: 10ft
Machinery: Gas turbine 10,000shp
Two diesels 4,800bhp
CODOG configuration 25kts max
Armament: Four 30mm guns (2×2)
Four MBU-1800 AS rocket launchers

These interesting little ships were designed for inshore AS duties and, as such, in the same category as the French Le Fougueux (qv) and West German Thetis (qv) types each of which is also built around an ahead-throwing mortar, mounted forward. The East German design is slightly more modern than the Thetis but incorporates a CODOG machinery layout, a rather doubtful improvement in as much as the gas

turbine output is only 10,000shp giving — if published sources can be believed — only a small speed advantage. Marginally greater acceleration would be possible over the all-diesel but hardly enough to justify the extra complication, unless the actual maximum speed is nearer 30kts, as would seem quite possible.

Russian-fashion, the battery of four five-barrelled AS rocket launchers is all forward, superfired by a twin 30mm automatic mounting of the familiar 'helmet' type, a second one of which is sited aft. Both are laid by the Drum Tilt antenna mounted conspicuously in what would seem to be a hot-spot immediately abaft the funnel. Very similar in layout to the Thetis type, they are rather smaller and, in place of the former's AS TTs carry depth charges in racks, discharging over the broad transom. It would appear also to give them a small mine-laying capability.

Construction appears to be of steel and of very shallow draught. The reported names are those of small towns and hamlets in the coastal strip of Mecklenburg, they contrast strangely with the class name of Hai (Shark).

SO-1 Patrol Craft

East Germany

Four SO-I type boats (qv) probably built in East Germany to complement the Hai class corvettes for inshore AS work. They would appear to be similar to Soviet-built units and are apparently numbered

621-624 inclusive, and named *Wolf, Panther, Tiger* and *Luchs* (Lynx) although not necessarily in that order.

Osa I/II FAC (missile)

East Germany

Twelve Osa I class boats (qv) were reported transferred from the Soviet Union in the early 1970s, reinforced about 1976 by a further three Osa IIs (qv). They are standard production units but rather unusually, are named. These are unconfirmed and thought to include: *Alain Kobis; Arvid Harnack; August Luttgens; Fritz Gast; Heinrich Dorrenbach; Josef Schares; Karl Meseberg; Max Reichpietsch;*

Otto Tost; Paul Eisenschneider; Paul Schulz; Paul Wieczorek; Richard Sorge; Rudolf Egelhofer; Walter Kranmer. Pennant numbers are reported to be 711-714, 731-734 and 751-754 but whether this implies an organisation into three half-flotillas is not known.

Shershen FAC (torpedo)

East Germany

Between 15 and 18 standard Shershens (qv) were transferred from the Soviet Union between 1968 and 1976. Following East German practice, these too have been named. Unconfirmed names include: *Adam Kuckhof; Anton Safkow; Arthur Becker;*

Bernhard Bastlein; Bruno Kuhn; Edgar Andre; Ernst Grube; Ernst Schneller; Fiete Schulz; Fritz Behn; Fritz Heckert; Hans Kopl; Heinz Kapelle; Rudolf Breitscheid; Willi Bausch. Pennant numbers include 811-815, 831-835, 851-855.

Iltis FAC (torpedo)

East Germany

Displacement: 25 standard
30 full load
Length (oa): 56ft
Beam: 11ft
Draught: 3ft
Machinery: Probably two diesels and two shafts 3,000bhp for 40kts
Armament: Two/three 21-inch TTs

The East German coast is not very long, extremely shallow offshore and within easy reach of west-controlled waters. This combination allows for the use of very small, high speed craft of limited range and seaworthiness for a variety of tasks. Such a type is the Iltis (Polecat) class, easily the smallest warship to be considered in this volume but none the less deadly for that. Its aramament is purely offensive and it has no guns to defend itself. Having a very low profile, it can lie undetected close inshore with

engines shut down or idling, loose its torpedoes over the transom and guide them to its target without betraying its presence. The explosion of the torpedo would probably be the target's first indication and also the signal to the Iltis to crash into gear and escape retribution in the resulting confusion, relying on its small size, manoeuvrability and acceleration to get away.

Several versions of the basic Iltis class exist, some are of composite, others of metal construction; a few have raised foredecks for greater seaworthiness and some have three TTs. Hull numbers are of three digits, commencing with '9' and between 30 and 40 of the class are believed to exist. A few of a slightly larger variant, known as the Libelle (Dragonfly) class have been built. Layout is basically similar but incorporates a twin 25mm gun mounting in addition to the TTs. All Soviet-built P6 type have been deleted.

Thetis Corvette

West Germany

		Launched	Completed
P6052	*Thetis*	1960	1961
P6053	*Hermes*	1960	1961
P6054	*Najade*	1960	1962
P6055	*Triton*	1961	1962
P6056	*Theseus*	1962	1963

Displacement: 565 standard
650 full load
Length (oa): 229ft
Beam: 27ft
Draught: 9ft
Machinery: Two diesels on two shafts
6,800bhp for 24kts

Armament: Two 40mm guns (1×2)
One 4-barrelled AS mortar
Four AS TTs

In the event of a European war, the approaches to the Western Baltic and the Danish belts would be fiercely contested. Reinforcements and supplies would have to cross these waters to Norway and eastern bloc warships would need access to the open sea from their Baltic bases. Small submarines would have an important part to play in establishing an enemy control and the Thetis class corvettes were designed to combat them.

They were funded originally as torpedo recovery

vessels but they would seem a little large and fast for this task (the current TRVs are 40-tonners!) and it would appear that the description was no more than a strategem to procure funds at a difficult period.

The hull is typically German in origin, flush-decked with an elegant sheerline and pronounced knuckle forward, designed for dry operation in short, inshore seas. Twin diesels exhaust through a funnel, the presence of which makes the craft look larger than they, in fact, are. Layout is geared to the AS armament with the foredeck devoted to a four-barrelled Bofors launcher, in an optimally effective position. This weapon can project a 375mm rocket every second out to over one mile.

Four, single, trainable AS TTs are mounted adjacent to the gap in the superstructure, with reloads probably carried in the casing abaft the funnel. Attack data is acquired from a hull-mounted sonar (VDS has never been fitted as unsuitable for shallow water use) and *Najade*, at least, has the bridge structure extended forward to house a computer for threat assessment. The torpedoes are wire-guided and have an HSA fire control.

In self-defence, the design is deficient, having only twin 40mm in a Breda L70 mounting aft. They are due to have this replaced by a more effective 76mm OTO-Melara, but even this will have blind areas forward. With no point defence system, these ships would themselves need to be escorted to survive a shooting war in the narrows.

Hans Burckner is a stretched 265ft version of the class and carries the number A1449, denoting her present auxiliary status. She carries a small VDS and, allowing for like deficiencies, could act as a coordinator for the class's group AS activities.

Typ 143 FAC (missile) West Germany

		Completed
P6111	*S61*	1976
P6112	*S62*	1976
P6113	*S63*	1976
P6114	*S64*	1976
P6115	*S65*	1976
P6116	*S66*	1976
P6117	*S67*	1976
P6118	*S68*	1977
P6119	*S69*	1977
P6120	*S70*	1977

Displacement: 300 standard
380 full load
Length (oa): 200ft
Beam: 24.5ft
Draught: 8.5ft
Machinery: Four diesels on four shafts
16,000bhp for 38kts
Armament: Four MM38 Exocet SSMs
Two 76mm guns (2 × 1)
Two 21-inch TTs (2 × 1)

Though classed as replacements for the last of the Jaguars to be transferred out of the Bundesmarine, the Typ 143s are far removed from them in concept and represent the next step even from the Typ 148s (qv). Where the latter are French-designed boats with steel hulls, the 143s are from the Lürssen stable and are wood-planked on alloy frames and steel longitudinals. This makes not only for a more habitable hull but also lowers the boat's magnetic signature. As with the 148s, they have four Exocet canister launchers angled out over either beam from a site abaft of amidships, but the extra length has allowed the substitution aft of a second 76mm gun for the earlier design's 40mm.

The superstructure has grown considerably in length and bears a tall tripod mainmast whose very size suggests that it may be removed in time. Also conspicuous is the dome of the WM27 fire control which is linked to the AGIS data processing system, which, in turn, assesses the most complex of action situations and retransmits data to other, more simply equipped boats. By this means, a single 143 can direct operations of a group of 148s. On either quarter is a tube for the discharge of the long-range wire-guided Seal torpedo, whose run is also guided by the WM27.

Four 16-cylinder MTU diesels power the four fixed pitch propellers and it is interesting that the Germans, having evaluated the merits of the high speed, flat-vee, gas turbine boat through a pair built in the UK (see Aiolos and Astrapi classes under Greece) have stuck to the diesel-driven displacement boat. These have obviously proved more seakindly, have a good range (2,500miles at 16kts) and yet still be capable of 38kts at rated 16,000bhp output. For periods not exceeding two hours the engines can, in fact, be overrun to 4,500bhp.

As the German appear finally to have forsaken the troubled NATO hydrofoil project (see Pegasus PHM class under US) the proposed Typ 162 does not look like materialising and a class of improved 143s is reported under design.

S62

P6112

Typ 148 FAC (missile) West Germany

S52

		Completed
P6141	*S41*	1972
P6142	*S42*	1973
P6143	*S43*	1973
P6144	*S44*	1973
P6145	*S45*	1973
P6146	*S46*	1973
S6147	*S47*	1973
S6148	*S48*	1974
S6149	*S49*	1974
P6150	*S50*	1974
P6151	*S51*	1974
P6152	*S52*	1974
P6153	*S53*	1974
P6154	*S54*	1974
P6155	*S55*	1975
P6156	*S56*	1975
P6157	*S57*	1975
P6158	*S58*	1975
P6159	*S59*	1975
P6160	*S60*	1975

Displacement: 235 standard
265 full load
Length (oa): 154ft
Beam: 23ft
Draught: 6ft
Machinery: Four diesels on four shafts
14,400bhp for 35.5kts

Armament: Four MM38 Exocet SSMs
One 76mm gun
One 40mm gun
Two 21-inch TTs (2 × 1)

Built as unit-for-unit replacements for the first 20 Jaguars disposed of, the 148s represent a blend of proven designs. They are of the French Combattante II type (qv) variant A4L and all were fitted out by the CMN yard at Cherbourg, which also built the hulls, excepting the even-numbered units from *S46* to *S60*, which were sub-contracted to the Lürssen yard.

Armament, besides the four Exocet SSMs, consists of a 76mm OTO-Melara forward and a 40mm Bofors gun aft, which can be removed to release space and deadweight for the carrying of eight mines. These boats are geared to North Sea and Baltic operations and a minelaying capability is important. TTs are not fitted.

They are equipped with a Thomson CSF Vega weapon control system, in which surveillance is the province of the Triton radar whose antenna tops the mast and target tracking is carried out by the Pollux set, whose dish is atop the bridge, coupled to optical sights for emergency or 'quiet' use. The guns follow the latter and, as the 76mm is fully stabilised, data on the ship's movement as well as speed and heading, are fed into the firing computer.

Zobel/Typ 142 FAC (torpedo) West Germany

		Completed
P6092	*Zobel*	1961
P6093	*Wiesel*	1962
P6094	*Dachs*	1962
P6095	*Hermelin*	1962
P6096	*Nerz*	1963
P6097	*Puma*	1962
P6098	*Gepard*	1963
P6099	*Hyane*	1963
P6100	*Frettchen*	1963
P6101	*Ozelot*	1963

Displacement: 190 standard
225 full load
Length (oa): 140ft
Beam: 23.5ft
Draught: 7.5ft
Machinery: Four diesels on four shafts
12,000bhp for 40kts
Armament: Two 40mm guns (2 × 1) TTs
Two 21-inch (2 × 1)

Frettchen

The Typ 142 was an immediate, improved follow-on series to the Jaguar/Typ 141 (qv) whose production ceased in 1960. Although of similar size, the 142s have a 20% increase in displacement due to improvements in both weapons and sensors. Even so, the basic design is now 20 years old and, close akin to the S-boat of World War II, contrasts unfavourably with newer torpedo-armed FACs such as the Swedish Spica, of similar size. It is worthy of note that those European fleets that operate FACs in quantity, still run torpedo-armed boats in an apparently guided-missile dominated world. The reason is that the modern, wire-guided torpedo is of very great range and accuracy and is very difficult to detect and counter. Only two tubes are carried by the 142s (firing over the counter), in contrast to the four or six shipped by the 141s and firing unguided torpedoes in classic fashion. Fire control is effected by HSA-built WM17 whose associated antennas occupy the dome above the bridge.

Although not small craft by any means, the 142s have only a pair of 40mm guns as surface armament. This was probably because more potent weapons were not available at that time but it must inevitably affect their survivability compared with later boats. The machinery outfit is the same as that fitted in the 141 but, although the extra displacement has incurred a two-knot penalty, their 40kts speed is more than adequate to operate with the later, but slower, GM craft bearing in mind that, being smaller, they would be earlier affected by deteriorating weather conditions. As a lower degree of automation is built into these earlier designs the crew is at about 40, of the same strength as the later, and far more complex, classes. Construction is of wood on light alloy frames

Jaguar/Typ 141 FAC (torpedo)   West Germany

Displacement: 160 tons standard
185 full load
Length (oa): 140ft
Beam: 23.5ft
Draught: 7.5ft
Machinery: Four diesels on four shafts
12,000bhp for 42kts
Armament: (as built) Two 40mm guns (2×1)
Four/Six 21-inch TTs (4×1 or 6×1)
Disposals: P6069 *Albatros* (scrapped); P6084 *Alk* (scrapped); P6074 *Bussard* (scrapped); P6091 *Dommel* (scrapped); P6088 *Elster* (scrapped); P6072 *Falke* (to Greece); P6066 *Fuchs* (scrapped); P6073 *Geier* (to Greece); P6089 *Reiher* (scrapped); P6068 *Seeadler* (to Greece); P6076 *Sperber* (scrapped); P6085 *Storch* (to Turkey); P6063 *Tiger* (to Turkey); P6082 *Weihe* (scrapped); P6062 *Wolf* (to Turkey); P6083 *Kranich* (scrapped); P6060 *Leopard* (scrapped); P6065 *Löwe* (to Turkey); P6061 *Luchs* (scrapped); P6067 *Marder* (scrapped); P6064 *Panther* (scrapped); P6086 *Pelikan* (to Turkey); P6090 *Pinguin* (to Turkey); P6071 *Greif* (to Greece); P6075 *Habicht* (to Greece); P6087 *Häher* (to Turkey); P6058 *Iltis* (scrapped); P6059 *Jaguar* (scrapped); P6070 *Kondor* (to Greece); P6077 *Kormoran* (to Greece)

The first postwar German Schnellboote were the Silbermowe-type boats of the early 1950s (see under Greece) and their close adherance to the designs of the late war demonstrated that the builders, Lürssen, had not yet re-established an innovative design team. Only six of these were built, however, before the run was curtailed in 1956 and a new and much improved type introduced. It was to prove an extended class, planned at 40 but, in the event, the final 10 hulls were modified to the Zobel class (qv). 32 were built by Lürssen at their Vegesack facility and eight by the Rendsburg yard of Krogerwerft.

With their raised-forecastle hulls, they carried the stamp of earlier designs but, where predecessors had forward tubes beneath the forecastle deck and firing through doors, the extra 23ft of hull in the Jaguars permitted both pairs of TTs to be sided abaft the break in the hull and angled outboard. Although noted for their dryness forward, both Jaguar and Zobel groups have dodgers rigged aft semi-permanently, which suggests a lot of free water in a seaway.

The hulls are of wood planking on steel frames, with light alloy superstructure, and represent a transition between the older, flat-sectioned, high-speed craft and the modern trend toward greater displacement and superior sea-keeping. Built before the formation of MTU by amalgamation of marine engine builders, the Jaguars fell into two groups, 20 powered by 20-cylinder Daimler-Benz engines and 10 by 16-cylinder Maybachs. Officially, the D-B powered boats are sometimes referred to as Typ 140s. Increase of shp of one-third over that of the Silbermöwes required a fourth engine and shaft

— whether this was a matter of engine availability/dimensions or just because the propellers used could not absorb more than 3,000shp each is not clear.

The 40mm aft is an improvement over the earlier boat's 20mm and the forward gun is recessed into the forecastle deck to lower its centre of gravity and improve view forward from the wheelhouse. If mines are carried (up to four) the after TTs have to be landed.

None of the class remains under the German flag, though Greece and Turkey operate seven each, having already scrapped some for spare parts. Others were especially built to the same design for Turkey and Saudi Arabia.

Typ 206 Patrol Submarine   West Germany

		Launched	Completed
S192	*U13*	1971	1973
S193	*U14*	1972	1973
S194	*U15*	1972	1973
S195	*U16*	1972	1973
S196	*U17*	1972	1973
S197	*U18*	1972	1973
S198	*U19*	1972	1973
S199	*U20*	1973	1974
S170	*U21*	1973	1974
S171	*U22*	1973	1974
S172	*U23*	1974	1975
S173	*U24*	1973	1974
S174	*U25*	1973	1974
S175	*U26*	1973	1975
S176	*U27*	1973	1975
S177	*U28*	1974	1975
S178	*U29*	1973	1975
S179	*U30*	1974	1975

Displacement: 420 surfaced
600 submerged
Length (oa): 160ft
Beam: 15ft
Draught: 13ft
Machinery: Two diesel-generator sets powering one propulsion motor One shaft
1,500bhp for 10/17kts
Armament: Eight 21-inch TTs

In this age of the nuclear submarine it is often thought, erroneously, that the diesel-electric (conventional) boat is outdated but, in fact, she is complementary to their operations and not displaced by them. The place for the nuclear fleet submarine is unrestricted blue water, where she can use her speed, deep diving abilities and virtually unlimited range to maximum effect; once in shallow inshore waters, however, she is immediately at a disadvantage compared with the purpose-built patrol submarine, which is compact and silent. The latter's hull tends to be short and of maximum diameter, offering a minimum target for her quarry's active sonar. She lacks the noisy, pressurised-water cooling pumps of the 'nuke' and all her machinery is resiliently mounted; cruising quietly with her large diameter propeller turning slowly, her enemy's passive sonar also has a poor target whilst her own, untroubled by self-induced noise, can 'hear' the better. She operates by patient stalking of a target, her active systems being used only for the final attack phase. Placed across an enemy's lines of approach and departure, the patrol submarine offers a formidable threat.

A good example of this type of boat is the German Typ 206, developed from the Typ 205 and with 30% greater submerged displacement. Visually, the fin profile is different and a bow fairing has been added, encompassing the passive surveillance sonar array and adding buoyancy forward to improve characteristics in the surfaced conditon. Also mounted, with two others in the fin fairing, is the passive ranging transducer; target range can be established by triangulation and its speed by time-lapse methods without betraying the boat's presence through active ranging. For final stages of an attack, a trainable active sonar array is mounted in the forward end of the fin. Hydrophones at either end

U24

complement the passive sonars. Painstakingly-acquired attack data is of no use without an adequate means of attack and a powerful battery of eight TTs forward can fire the large Seal wire-guided torpedo, small homing torpedoes or eject mines.

Current practice is to the single-hulled submarine having all ballast tanks carried inboard, ie no saddle tanks. Batteries are carried low in lieu of solid ballast. A pair of diesels are coupled to generators which, in turn, power the single propulsion motor which turns the single shaft surfaced and submerged. The diesels are designed to accommodate the fluctuating input air pressures for the 'snorting' conditon. The 206 design is being developed further as the 750-ton Typ 210 for the mid-1980s. Three slightly-modified 206s have been built in the UK under licence for Israel.

Typ 205 Patrol Submarine   West Germany

		Launched	**Completed**
S180	*U1*	1961	1964
S181	*U2*	1962	1962
S188	*U9*	1966	1966
S189	*U10*	1967	1967
S190	*U11*	1968	1968
S191	*U12*	1968	1969

Displacement: 370 tons surfaced
450 submerged
Length (oa): 1,425ft
Beam: 15ft
Draught: 13ft
Machinery: Two diesel-generators powering two propulsion motors, coupled to one shaft
1,500bhp for 10/17kts
Armament: Eight 21-inch TTs

West Germany recommenced submarine construction in the late 1950s, bound by treaty limitations to designs of under 450 tons displacement. In an era when submarines tended to displace about three times this figure, it might have appeared a crippling limitation but it was turned to advantage in pioneering the small, tubby boat better suited to operations within the NATO framework rather than on the earlier oceanic scale.

With a length/breadth ratio of less than 10:1, the resulting single-hulled Typ 205 contrasted strongly with the then current boats, very slender and with external ballast tanks. Though propelled by only a single screw, she proved very agile and packed no less than eight TTs in the blunt forward end. After tubes were dispensed with as torpedoes can now run under guidance and it is not necessary to aim the whole boat along the firing track.

Where the earlier Typ XXI had ejected torpedoes from the tubes with compressed air, carefully regulated so that the water filling the tube forced the air back into the boat, without the production of a telltale bubble, the new boats adopted the simple, swimout principle, where the torpedo is run up in the flooded tube and leaves under its own power. If mines are to be laid from the same tubes, some form of ejection still has to be provided. Space has been saved by the elimination of the large torpedo-loading hatch forward. By trimming the boat by the stern, torpedoes can be passed into the hull through the upper pair of tubes.

The small size of the 205, together with the shallow water in which it is designed to operate, combine to make her a poor target for an escort's sonar. It was felt that she would be vulnerable to both magnetic mining and detection by airborne MAD and special amagnetic steels were produced for their construction. These turned out to have inferior metallurgical properties and, although *U1* and *U2* were rebuilt in conventional plate, *U3-8* were

U10

U11

scrapped owing to the cost. *U3* had been lent to Norway in 1962-4 to train crews for the 15 Typ 207s (qv) then building in Emden.

U9-12 were constructed of improved materials and still serve, together with the rebuilt *U1* and *U2*. Two improved 205s were built by Denmark as the

Narvhalens (qv). Both 205s and 207s are likely to be replaced by the Typ 210, now under development. A heavily-modified Typ XXI built in 1944, scuttled in 1945 and salvaged in 1957 is operated by the Bundesmarine as a floating testbed. She is named *Wilhelm Bauer* but is in no way a front line warship.

Typ 209 Patrol Submarine   West Germany

Displacement: 1,050 surfaced
1,250 submerged (typical)
Length (oa): 180ft (typical)
Beam: 20.5ft
Draught: 18ft
Machinery: Four diesel-generators powering single propulsion motor.
One shaft 10/20kts
Armament: Eight 21-inch TTs

The 209 was produced as an export submarine design and has proved very successful, being found in the navies of Argentina, Colombia, Ecuador, Greece, Peru, Turkey and Venezuela, with Uruguay expressing interest and possibly some being built for Iran. None serves with the West German Navy but, as it is an obvious development of the Types 205 and 206, it will almost certainly influence the design of the projected 750-ton Typ 210. Larger than earlier boats from the IKL stable, it is found in the navies of Argentina, Colombia, Ecuador, Greece, patrols (up to 50 days' duration) and deep diving to about 750ft. There are slight variations in length and displacement according to the requirements of purchasing navies.

They are of single-hulled, single screw construction with a relatively large fin, characteristically rectangular in profile with a narrow finned projection running aft from the top edge, housing the diesel exhaust. No less than eight telescopic masts retract into the fin; from forward to aft these accommodate: SLAM anti-helicopter missile launcher (if fitted), search periscope, 'snort' induction mast, UHF and HF communications antennas, ECM, attack periscope and radar antenna.

Four MTU generator sets are housed two thirds aft, with a separate machinery control room immediately forward. The single propulsion motor is placed as far aft as possible, driving the shaft axially through the centre of the after trim and ballast tanks. Good weight distribution is achieved by generating power remotely from the motor and only a short shaft is required. In addition the motor speed and is low and can be accurately controlled, driving a large diameter, low speed (and, therefore, quiet) propeller.

Control room and communications centre are situated directly below and the fin. Accommodation is forward of this and separated by a WT bulkhead from the torpedo room right forward. This space houses eight tubes, loaded through the caps, and having stowage below the accommodation for six spare torpedoes. Batteries are large and placed right at the bottom of the hull over about half its length and accounting for about 20% of the boat's displacement. They are charged by the main diesel generators and force-cooled for high demands (up to about 22kts can be made submerged for a very limited period).

The usual range of passive and active sonars is fitted, together with a Thomson-CSF fire control. An Omega low frequency navigation system, is also installed. Hulls can be produced in prefabricated sections for shipment to a customer for final assembly. The diving planes are situated low down, forward and the high speed hull has cruciform control surface ahead of the propeller. A high level of automation has been built in, keeping crew down to only 31.

Vosper Mk 1 Corvette

Ghana

		Launched	Completed
F17	*Kromantse*	1963	1964
F18	*Keta*	1965	1965

Displacement: 435 standard
550 full load
Length (oa): 177ft
Beam: 28.5ft
Draught: 12ft
Machinery: Two diesels on two shafts
7,000bhp for 20kts
Armament: One 4-inch gun
One 40mm gun
One triple-barrelled Squid AS mortar

This elegant little pair of ships represent the smallest of a long series marketed by the UK firm of Vosper Thornycroft and currently extending up to the 424ft Mk 10s built for Brazil (see *Warships of the World: Escort Vessels*). A strong resemblance has been kept between each class, the next largest extant being the Nigerian Mk 3s (qv).

Ghana's seaboard is about 400 miles of the former Gold Coast. Somewhat featureless and without many ports it is noted for its heavy offshore swell. For policing this stretch, usually against illicitly-run small craft, large complex ships are not necessary and the Mark 1s strike the correct balance of design to act as leaders to a group of ex-British small craft now approaching retirement.

The steel hull is flush-decked with a full-width bridge house. A feature of the smaller VT designs is the bulwark forward with a series of mercantile type freeing ports at the after end. Superstructures are continuous and topped by a low, well-proportioned funnel exhausting the two Maybach diesels, built under licence by Bristol Siddeley. A low, lattice mast supports the large antenna of the Plessey ASW1 surveillance radar and a Decca type navigation set. The old, hand-worked 4-inch gun is adequate for the job and, aft, a 40mm Bofors pattern gun superfires a Squid AS mortar, for which a hull-mounted sonar is provided. Both were refitted in the UK in 1974-5. Another of the type serves under the Libyan flag.

Ford Seaward Defence Boat

Ghana

		Completed
P13	*Elmina*	1963
P14	*Komenda*	1962

This pair are similar to the British Ford class SDBs (qv) and were built in the UK to Ghanaian account. They differ from the RN units in having a two-shaft layout, powered by a pair of 16-cylinder MTU diesels.

Algerine Corvette

Greece

		Completed
M12	*Armatolos* (ex-HMS *Aries*)	1943
M58	*Machitis* (ex-HMS *Postillion*)	1943
M64	*Navmachos* (ex-HMS *Lightfoot*)	1943
M74	*Polemistis* (ex-HMS *Gozo*)	1943
M76	*Pyrpolitis* (ex-HMS *Arcturus*)	1943

All Canadian-built units of the British Algerine class of ocean minesweeper (qv). They differ in having the original single 4-inch gun replaced by a pair of American pattern 3-inch 50s. They are officially listed with M flag superior pennants but are classed as Corvettes and occasionally are used for auxiliary duties, with an A number.

Combattante III FAC (missile) Greece

		Completed
P50	*Antiploiarhos Laskos*	1977
P51	*Plotarhis Blessas*	1977
P52	*Ipoploiarhos Troupakis*	1977
P53	*Ipoploiarhos Mikonios*	1977

Four standard Combattante IIIs built by CNM Cherbourg. Full details in French section.

Ipoploiarhos Troupakis

Combattante II FAC (missile) Greece

		Completed
P54	*Ipoploiarhos Batsis* (ex-*Calypso*)	1971
P55	*Ipoploiarhos Arliotis* (ex-*Evniki*)	1972
P56	*Antiploiarhos Anninos* (ex-*Navsithoi*)	1972
P57	*Ipoploiarhos Konidis* (ex-*Kymothoi*)	1972

Four standard Combattante II class FACs built by CMN Cherbourg. Full details in French section.

Six more have since been ordered of which the first two are to be built by CMN, for an early 1979 delivery, and the remainder in Greece. They are reported to have a modified armament of six Norwegian Penguin SSMs, one 76mm OTO-Melara and two 40mm guns. This would seem to be a little on the light side for such a large hull (compare with Israeli Saar and Norwegian Storm classes) and introduces a new missile and gun calibre to complicate logistics. With this class, the nomenclature of FACs appear to have changed from its earlier classical names to those of Greek naval personnel who have distinguished themselves.

Asheville FAC (gun) Greece

		Completed
—	(ex-USS *Beacon*, PG99)	1969
—	(ex-USS *Green Bay*, PG101)	1969

These are two standard US-built Asheville class patrol gunboats (qv), transferred in 1977. No new names or pennant numbers had been announced at the time of writing (1978), over a year later, which may indicate problems with commissioning eg the GE gas turbine is a type new to the Greek Navy. No missiles are fitted but, as the type has performed well with Standard SSMs for the US Navy, they could well be armed with four Penguins without too much difficulty.

Esterel 32m FAC (missile)   Greece

Kelefstis Stamou

		Completed
P28	*Kelefstis Stamou*	1975
P29	*Diopos Antoniou*	1976

Displacement: 80 full load
Length (oa): 105ft
Beam: 19ft
Draught: 5ft
Machinery: Two diesels on two shafts
2,700bhp for 30kts
Armament: One 40mm gun (aft)
One 20mm gun (forward)
Four SS.12M SSMs

This handsome pair of all-wood boats was ordered to Cypriot account but transferred to Greek. Rather more simple than the average run of Greek FACs they are capable of cruising better than 1,500 miles at 15kts, making them ideal for patrolling the extensive coasts of the Aegean on fishery protection or similar duties. Only basic communication and navigation electronics are fitted but a nominal stopping power is provided by the four SS.12Ms, pairs on two mounts forward of the wheelhouse and controlled optically.

Brave FAC (missile)   Greece

		Completed
P19	*Aiolos* (ex-*Pfeil*, P6193)	1962
P20	*Astrapi* (ex-*Strahl*, P6194)	1962

Displacement: 95 standard
110 full load
Length (oa): 99ft
Beam: 25ft
Draught: 7ft
Machinery: Three Proteus gas turbines on three shafts
12,750bhp for 55kts
Armament: Two 40mm guns (2 × 1)
Four side-launched 21-inch torpedoes

Both of these boats were constructed in the UK, by their designers Vospers, to German account. Two Brave class boats had recently been completed for the Royal Navy as the first designed with all-gas

turbine propulsion. Of composite, wood on metal construction, they had a flat, planing hull and their three Proteus engines could drive them at 55kts in calm conditions. As the German taste in FACs has always been for the slower, displacement type of hull with an accent on range and seakeeping, it was the more surprising when they acquired two. Both were completed in 1962 and only the ex-*Strahl* is truly a Brave boat, the ex-*Pfeil* being a modified design known to Vosper as a Ferocity. The major difference lies in having only two GTs and shafts in place of three, which incurs a speed penalty of barely five knots and allows a slightly smaller hull. Designed as interchangeable gun or torpedo boats they served only five years under German colours; having had no observable influence on subsequent German boats, they were transferred to Greece in 1967. Similar boats still serve under the flags of Denmark, Libya and Malaysia. See also notes under UK Cutlass class.

Jaguar FAC (torpedo)   Greece

		Completed
P196	*Hesperos* (ex-*Seeadler*, P6068)	1958
P197	*Kataigis* (ex-*Falke*, P6072)	1958
P198	*Kentauros* (ex-*Habicht*, P6075)	1958
P199	*Kyklon* (ex-*Greif*, P6071)	1958
P228	*Lelaps* (ex-*Kondor*, P6070)	1958
P229	*Skorpios* (ex-*Kormoran*, P6077)	1958
P230	*Tyfon* (ex-*Geier*, P6073)	1958

Standard German-built Jaguar class FACs (qv), these seven are the survivors of 10 boats transferred from the West German Navy in 1976/7. The remaining three, ex-*Albatros* (P6069), ex-*Bussard* (P6074) and ex-*Sperber* (P6067) were neither renamed for commissioned into the Greek Navy but broken up for spares. The five surviving 116ft Silbermöwe class FACs have been deleted by the Greek Navy.

Tjeld FAC (torpedo)

Greece

		Completed
P21	*Andromeda*	1967
P23	*Kastor*	1967
P24	*Kyknos*	1967
P25	*Pigassos*	1967
P26	*Toxotis*	1967

Five standard Norwegian Tjeld class FACs (qv) — sometimes known as the Nasty class — built by Batservis to Greek account. A sixth unit, *Iniohos* (P22), was completed at the same time but was disposed of in 1972.

Typ 209 Patrol Submarine

Greece

		Completed
S110	*Glavkos*	1971
S111	*Nereus*	1972
S112	*Triton*	1972
S113	*Perseus*	1972

These four were the first of the German Typ 209s (qv) to be built and are similar to the later boats. A further four are under construction by the parent yard, Howaldtswerke, Kiel.

Ex-US Patrol Submarines

Greece

		Completed
S86	*Triaina* (ex-USS *Scabbardfish*, SS397)	1944
S114	*Papanikolis* (ex-USS *Hardhead*, SS365)	1944
S115	*Katsonis* (ex-USS *Remora*, SS487)	1946

Though generally similar, these three vary in detail by viture of differing postwar modification programmes. *Triana* is a Balao class submarine which was not Guppy-ised postwar but was rebuilt externally. She has a distinctive step in the forward side of the fin, due to a low external con. *Papanikolis* is also a Balao class boat but was one of 29 given the Guppy IIA conversion. Her profile is clean of any real projections.

Katsonis is a Tench class boat, commissioned postwar and subsequently given the later Guppy III conversion. Externally she differs from the other two by having the three distinctive domes of the PUFFS ranging sonar spaced along her upper deck. The three were transferred in 1965, 1972 and 1973 repectively and fuller details may be found under the US section.

Guinea/Guinea Bissau

Formerly French Guinea, this state has a coastline of near 200 miles in West Africa, as does the adjacent Guinea Bissau (formerly Portuguese Guinea). Complex and shallow river estuaries with many islands are a feature of the shore and create a need for basic patrol craft. Both states have turned to the Communist bloc for these. Guinea is believed to operate the following:

Six Shanghai II class FAC (gun) (qv) transferred from China in 1973-6.

Two P6 class FAC (qv) transferred from the Soviet Navy and probably no longer torpedo-armed.
Two Mo-VI gun-armed derivatives of the P6 transferred in 1972 from the Soviet Navy.

Guinea Bisau has one P6, again probably gun-armed and from the same source. The operational status of these units at any time is doubtful.

Petya Corvette

India

P68 *Arnala;* P69 *Androth;* P73 *Anjadip;* P74 *Andaman;* P75 *Amimi;* P77 *Kamorta;* P78 *Kadmath;* P79 *Kiltan;* P80 *Kavaratti;* P81 *Katchal;* P82 *Kanjar;* P83 *Amindivi*

Twelve Soviet Petya II class corvettes (qv) standard except for reduced electronics fits. Transferred piecemeal between 1969 and 1975.

Nanuchka GM Corvette

India

K71	*Vijay Durg*
K72	*Sinhu Durg*
K73	—
K74	—

Downgraded versions of the Nanuchka class (qv), purpose-built in the Soviet Union and delivered in 1977-8. Two more may be following the first four. Only two, separate canister launchers are carried per side, virtually identical with those carried by the Osa II class FACs. It would thus appear that they carry four SS-N-2A modified Styx missiles and not the six SS-N-9s fitted in the Soviet units. With a Band Stand air search radome fitted, together with a (discreetly covered) Pop Group apparently on the forward superstructure, an SA-N-4 point defence launcher may well be fitted beneath the foredeck silo cover but this must remain doubtful as it is not a Russian habit to export its latest hardware.

Osa I/II FAC (missile) India

Osa I: K82 *Veer;* K83 *Vidjut;* K84 *Vijeta;* K85 *Vinash;* K86 *Nipat;* K87 *Nashat;* K88 *Nirbhik;* K89 *Nirghat.*
Osa II: K90 *Prachand;* K91 *Pralaya;* K92 *Pratap;* K93 *Prabal;* K94 *Chapal;* K95 *Chamak;* K96; K97

Apparently standard Osa I and II class FACs (qv). The Osa Is were transferred in 1970-1 and the Osa IIs in 1976. Three Osa Is reported destroyed during the Indo-Pakistan war of 1971; whether these were of, or in addition to, those listed is not clear. Note 'corvette' flag superior.

Foxtrot Patrol Submarine India

S20 *Kursura;* S21 *Karanj;* S22 *Kanderi;* S23 *Kalvari;* S40 *Vela;* S41 *Vagir;* S42 *Vagli;* S43 *Vagsheer*

Standard Soviet-built Foxtrot class submarines (qv)

S20-23 transferred from Russian fleet in 1968-70 and the remainder during 1973-5. As Russia disposes of more of her aging fleet of conventional submarines, others may be transferred in addition.

Albatros Corvette Indonesia

Pattimura

		Completed
801	*Pattimura*	1958
802	*Sultan Hasanudin*	1958

A pair of Ansaldo/Livorno-built corvettes, identical to the Italian Albatros class but slightly scaled-up. About 20ft longer 950/1,200 tons displacement and with propulsive power increased from 5,200 to 7,000bhp.

Kronstadt Patrol Craft Indonesia

810 *Tjutjut;* 811 *Katula;* 812 *Tohok;* 813 *Palu;* 814 *Pandrong;* 815 *Sura;* 816 *Kakap;* 817 *Barakunda;* 818 *Sembilang*

About 12 Russian Kronstadt class patrol craft (qv) were transferred in 1958. Some have been scrapped and probably only a few of those listed above are still active. The example shown appears to have been rearmed with a Hedgehog AS mortar forward. The displaced 85mm gun has been moved aft and two twin Russian pattern 30mm guns (possibly from scrapped Komar FACs) are staggered in the waist after the fashion of a Shanghai II.

PSMM-type FAC (missile)   Indonesia

Four PSMMs (qv) of American design are reported to have been delivered from a Korean yard. It is not known if they have had Harpoon SSMs fitted.

Komar FAC (missile)   Indonesia

610 *Kepaplintah;* 602 *Kelamisani;* 603 *Sarpawesesa;* 604 *Pulanggeni;* 602 *Kalanada;* 608 *Surotama;* 609 *Sarpamina;* 611 *Nagapasa;* 612 *Griwidjaja*

About 12 standard Komar class FACs (qv) were transferred from the Soviet Union 1961 and 1965. All survivors now of doubtful value.

PC-type Patrol Craft   Indonesia

805 *Hui* (ex-USS *Malvern*, PC580); 806 *Torani* (ex-USS *Manville* PC581); 807 *Tjakalang* (ex-USS *Pierre* PC1141)

Three survivors of a group of PCs built 1941-4 and transferred from the US Navy in the late 1950s.

Probably in poor condition, with original armament replaced by 37mm and 25mm guns of Russian origin. See notes under French Le Fougueux class.

Jaguar FAC (torpedo)   Indonesia

652 *Beruang;* 653 *Matjan Kumbang;* 654 *Anoa;* 665 *Hariman*

Four Jaguar class FACs (qv) built by Lürssen to Indonesian account between 1959 and 1960. Four others have been stricken.

Typ 209 Patrol Submarine   Indonesia

Two standard Typ 209s (qv) were ordered from West Germany in 1977.

Whiskey Patrol Submarine   Indonesia

403 *Naggabanda;* 410 *Pasopati;* 412 *Bramastra*

Believed to be the only units remaining from 14 Whiskey A class submarines (qv) transferred from

Russia in the early 1960s. Two remain active by virtue of spare parts supplied from the West; Russian components no longer being made available.

Bayandor Corvette

Iran

Bayandor: note pennant number now 81.

		Laid Down	Launched	Completed
81	*Bayandor* (ex-F25; ex-PF103)	1962	1963	1964
82	*Naghdi* (ex-F26; ex-PF104)	1962	1963	1964
83	*Milanian* (ex-F27; ex-PF105)	1967	1968	1969
84	*Kahnamuie* (ex-F28; ex-PF106)	1967	1968	1969

Displacement: 900 standard
1,135 full load
Length (oa): 275ft
Beam: 33ft
Draught: 10ft
Machinery: Two diesels on two shafts
5,600bhp for 20kts
Armament: Two 3-inch guns (2×1)
Two 40mm guns (1×2)
Two 25mm guns (1×2)

These little ships are interesting in being one of the very few examples of American-built warships designed for export and having no equivalent in the USN. The first pair were the first new warships of any size acquired by the Iranian Navy at the beginning of its expansion during the 1960s and were funded by the Mutual Aid programme, which accounts for the early PF (patrol frigate) categorisation. They compared interestingly with the smaller Italian Albatros design, which came from the same source.

Of distinctly un-American appearance, the ships have a flush-decked hull with the single-block superstrucutre based on a full-width deck house. There is a very mercantile-looking bridge front, the whole topped-off with a widely-braced pole mast, bearing the large antenna of an SPS-6 search radar, so long the feature of American destroyers, together with a commercial Raytheon navigation radar antenna; some have an SPS-10 and 12 in place. A single funnel exhausts the two diesels, its after side cranked, almost Japanese-style.

As built, the armament included a 3-inch 50 in an open mounting at either end of the superstructure, the forward one superfired by a Hedgehog AS spigot mortar and the after one by a twin 40mm mounting. Submarines are less a problem in the Gulf than local craft engaged in illicit trades, so the Hedgehog was removed and a Russian built twin 25mm gun mounting substituted. DC racks and projectors (K-guns) were retained. A second identical pair was completed in 1969 on the same terms.

All are now due for a mid-life long refit and will probably each get an OTO-Melara 76mm forward together with updated electronics. The DCs are of doubtful use and could be shed in favour of a triple Mk 32 AS TT bank. In the present petro-dollar euphoria, even a pair of Harpoon SSMs would not be surprising despite the ships' low speed. Two similar vessels serve under the flag of Thailand.

Combattante II FAC (missile)

Iran

Shamshir

		Completed
P221	*Kaman*	1977
P222	*Zoubin*	1977
P223	*Khadang*	1977
P224	*Peykan*	1977
P225	*Joshan*	1978
P226	*Falakhon*	1978
P227	*Shamshir*	1978
P228	*Gorz*	1978
P229	*Gardouneh*	1978
P230	*Khanjah*	1978
P231	*Neyzeh*	1979
P232	*Tabarzin*	1979

A class of 12 basic Combattante IIs (qv) all built by the parent company, CMN, Cherbourg. They are the only examples so far to be armed with Harpoon SSMs, mounted in two pairs angled out in the customary amidships position. They differ also in having an HSA fire control in its characteristic 'egg' enclosure in place of the more usual French electronics. A 76mm OTO-Melara is mounted forward and a 40mm gun aft but no TTs are fitted. The machinery has been up-rated from 12,000 to 14,400bhp.

BH7 Hovercraft/SES   Iran

Six BH7s (qv) have been delivered by the British Hovercraft Corporation, two Mk 4s in 1970-1 and four Mk 5s in 1974-5. All carry a light automatic armament and the Mk 5s in addition are fitted for the carriage of unspecified SSMs, possibly a single Harpoon on either side. It would be difficult to envisage their purpose on what is primarily a fast assault craft, bent more on evading surface forces rather than attacking them; with this in mind, a short-range deterrent such as the little SS.12M could prove adequate.

Note the two twin Sea Killer II SSM launchers on this BH-7 (mockups).

Tang Patrol Submarine   Iran

		Laid Down	Launched	Completed
101	*Kusseh* (ex-USS *Trout*, SS566)	1949	1951	1952
102	*Nahang* (ex-USS *Wahoo*, SS565)	1949	1951	1952
103	*Dolfin* (ex-USS *Tang*, AGSS563)	1949	1951	1951

Three standard Tang class submarines (qv) transferred from the US Navy in 1978. Their function is to give basic training for crews to man planned new construction. Six Typ 209s are reported to have been ordered from West Germany with an option on 10 more, but, with the current unrest in Iran against over-rapid 'westernisation' some of these plans may well suffer. Earlier rumours of interest in nuclear submarines can safely be discounted.

Iraq

Unlike Iran, which has a coastline over 1,000 miles in length and dominating the whole eastern side of the Persian Gulf and its approaches in the Strait of Hormuz and the Gulf of Oman, its neighbour Iraq has only a nominal 30-mile coast, bordered by the strategically important Shatt-al-Arab. This major waterway conveys the waters of the combined Tigris and Euphrates rivers to the sea and gives access to the up-river oil refineries so vital to the Iraqi economy.

Naval requirements are restricted to a number of shortish-range smaller warships capable of quick delivery of a punch heavy enough to deter any force with ambitions toward blockading this exit. In the 20 years since the overthrow of the monarchy the country has 'gone left' in its loyalties and its navy consists entirely of craft from Russian sources. These, at present, are believed to comprise:

Six to eight Osa I class FAC (missile) (qv) transferred between 1972 and 1974.

Six to eight Osa II class FAC (missile) (qv) transferred between 1974 and 1976.
About 10 P6 class FAC (torpedo) (qv) remaining of 12 transferred between 1959 and 1962.
Three SO-I class patrol craft (qv) transferred in 1962.

It is reported that these forces will be boosted shortly by 10 missile 'frigates' probably the export version of the Nanuchka corvette (qv) being supplied also to India.

New construction Corvettes   Israel

Displacement: c850 tons
Length (oa): 253ft
Beam: 30ft
Draught: 11ft
Machinery: One gas turbine 24,000bhp
Two diesels CODAG configuration on two shafts
40+kts
Armament: Two 76mm guns (2 × 1)
Six 35mm guns (3 × 2)
Four Gabriel II SSMs
One twin 375mm AS rocket launcher
Helicopter

Two corvettes are known to be building to the above specification, with options on several more. Their high speed points to a command function within a group of FACs, the ships being large enough to house the electronics for attack data processing and sharing. In addition longer range surveillance and target acquisition radars can be carried together with a small helicopter. As will have been noted under the Reshef entry, the new Harpoon SSMs will have a capability well beyond the range at which the craft

can detect a target although the missile, once launched, runs under an internal guidance system not easy to jam, switching to active homing only for the final phase. The helicopter would not, therefore, have any mid-course correction function but is probably multi-function, it can be used for positively identifying targets before missile launch (an obvious point but all too often overlooked); it can be used (and has been) to fly low over an FAC formation to offer a target to an incoming Styx-type missile and, having lured it clear of the formation, jinking hard to allow the missile to overshoot and get lost; lastly it can be used to give AS support. This latter point is important as Israel's likely enemies have numerous submarines, deployed close to the country's rather restricted sea approaches. Some of the Reshefs carry sonar and a few DCs but are little more than a gesture; the new corvettes will carry sonar and an AS mortar, with the helicopter available to carry either sensors or weapons. The single gas turbine is a General Electric LM2500, as standardised by the US Navy in current flotilla ships.

Reshef FAC (missile)   Israel

Reshef

		Completed
—	*Reshef*	1973
—	*Keshet*	1973
—	*Romah*	1974
—	*Kidon*	1974
—	*Tarshish*	1975
—	*Yaffo*	1975

Displacement: 415 standard
450 full load
Length (oa): 191ft
Beam: 25ft
Draught: 7.5ft
Machinery: Four diesels on two shafts
10,600bhp for 32kts
Armament: Two 76mm guns (2×1)
Two 20mm guns (2×1)
Four Harpoon SSMs (2×2)
Six Gabriel I and II SSMs (6×1)

Six Reshefs were completed to the above specification, the Harpoon SSMs being a later addition. The design corresponds closely to the West German Typ 143 and the French-designed Combattante IIIs but, if reports can be believed, are of considerably lower propulsion power, transmitted on only two shafts.

Their outfit of six Gabriel missiles included both Mark Is (880lb launch weight/14-mile range), and Mark IIs (1,100lb/26 miles), giving the equivalent Exocet-armed boats the edge. The addition of Harpoon will give ability out to about 120 miles, assuming that the programming data is available and giving a clue to the function of the 850-ton corvettes at present under costruction. It is worthy of note that the fire control system was Israeli-built by an industry now acquiring considerable expertise.

Built of steel the Reshefs are very strong and seaworthy and their range (4,000 miles at 17kts) has enabled them to cross the Atlantic and circumnavigate the African continent with the aid of RAS for deployment in the Red Sea and Gulf of Aqaba.

Three more of the class are being built in Israel to South African account, the latter country constructing a further three. Six more 'improved Reshef' have been ordered by the Israeli navy. Their length, at over 200ft, makes them the largest FACs to date. The first, reportedly named *Nitzahon*, was launched in 1978 with a similar armament to the earlier boats but an increased speed of 34kts.

Saar FAC (missile)   Israel

		Completed	
311	*Mivtach*	1968	**Displacement:** 220 standard
312	*Miznach*	1968	250 full load
313	*Mizgav*	1968	**Length (oa):** 147.5ft
321	*Eilath*	1968	**Beam:** 23ft
322	*Haifa*	1968	**Draught:** 8ft max
323	*Akko*	1968	**Machinery:** Four diesels on four shafts
331	*Saar*	1969	14,000bhp for 40kts
332	*Soufa*	1969	**Armament:** Varies but usually; Type I
333	*Gaasch*	1969	One 40mm gun and eight Gabriel I launchers
341	*Herev*	1969	Two 40mm guns and five Gabriel Is
342	*Hanit*	1969	Three 40mm guns and four TTs
343	*Hetz*	1969	Type II
			One 76mm gun and either five or six Gabriel Is

Although of a Lürssen design, all of the class were built by CMN, Cherbourg. The reason for this was purely political but was one of the first examples of collaboration between the two companies which has since led to very successful derivatives. Lürssen has since built three more to the same design for Ecuador, but armed with Exocet SSMs, Lürssen's far-eastern partners have built six gun-armed versions for Malaysia and three more have come from Singapore for Thailand, armed to a similar specification as the Israeli boats. The great differences in these armament fits emphasises the flexibility of the modern FAC.

The first group of boats was ordered with a light and orthodox armament of three Italian-pattern 40mm guns, one forward and two abaft the bridge structure, together with four single fixed TTs, sited right aft, for firing the small 324mm (12.75-inch)

homing torpedo of the American Mk 46 type. Type II boats, ordered in 1966, specified the OTO-Melara 76mm gun forward. After delivery, the boats were progressively fitted with the home-built Gabriel SSM. Type Is lost the after two 40mm guns and TTs replaced by two triple Gabriel launchers, trainable in azimuth, together with a pair of fixed, forward-firing launchers flanking the forward gun. Type II boats carry either two triple or one triple and one twin launcher amidships. In addition, the Type Is carry a small sonar set and, presumably, can accommodate depth charges representing, until the completion of the new corvettes, the only AS potential in the naval forces. The greater part of the electronic fit is of Israeli origin. Like the Reshefs, the steel-hulled Saars have shown themselves to be capable of long, open-water passages.

Typ 206 Patrol Submarine   Israel

		Completed
—	Gal	1977
—	Rahav	1977
—	Tanin	1977

Displacement: 500 surfaced
650 submerged
Length (oa): 160.8ft
Beam: 15.8ft
Draught: 12.5ft
Machinery: Two diesel-generators powering one drive motor
Single screw 2,500shp for 11/17kts
Armament: Eight 21-inch TTs

These three submarines are not truly Typ 206s, as built for the Bundesmarine, but the closely-related IKL500 design of Ingenieurkontor Lübeck and built under licence by Vickers in the UK. They differ externally in having a lower forward extension to the fin but, otherwise, the Typ 206 notes are relevant. An addition to the German boat's outfit is a retractable British SLAM launcher, firing marinised Blowpipe missiles to deter helicopter attack.

Both Modified T class ex-British submarines have now been disposed of and it is interesting, in view of the longish experience that the Israelis have now had in this direction, that they have so little AS potential in their surface ships, considering their potential opponents.

de Cristofaro Corvette   Italy

Pietro de Cristoforo

		Laid Down	Launched	Completed
F540	*Pietro de Cristofaro*	1963	1965	1965
F541	*Umberto Grosso*	1962	1964	1966
F546	*Licio Visintini*	1963	1965	1966
F550	*Salvatore Todaro*	1962	1964	1966

Displacement: 900 standard
1,020 full load
Length (oa): 263ft
Beam: 33.5ft
Draught: 9ft
Machinery: Two diesels on two shafts
8,400bhp for 23kts
Armament: Two 76mm guns (2 × 1)
One single-barrelled AS mortar
Two triple AS TTs

Some six years after the completion of the Albatros class corvettes (qv) an improved type was laid down for the same purpose, ie coastal escort duties. With a slight increase in hull dimensions, a raised forecastle was added to improve seakeeping. The armament shows a very considerable improvement with the 40mm guns replaced by the then-current 76mm gun of the Brescia Allargato pattern, a 62-calibre weapon similar to the later OTO-Melara Compatto, with the lower rate of fire of 60rpm compared with 85. It also weighs 12 tons compared with the Compatto's 7.5 tons.

Coastal escorts require also the means to detect and attack submarines. Their small size prohibits the helicopter now de rigeur with larger AS vessels but they would normally operate within the range of

shore-based aircraft. The class carries an American SQS-35 hull-mounted sonar for general and shallow water use, backed-up a towed VDS of the SQS-36 pattern, handled by the prominent hydraulic crane on the quarterdeck and capable of detection of submerged targets below the water layers of varying temperature and salinity for which the Mediterranean is noted. Where the older ships were equipped with outmoded forward-firing Hedgehog AS mortar, the de Cristofaros have a single-barrelled Menon mortar mounted abaft the diminutive funnel. Its barrel is elevated permanently at 45 degrees and it fires its automatically-loaded 350lb AS rockets out to ranges variable between 500 and 1,000yd by varying the amount of propellant gases allowed into the barrel. Two triple TTs are also carried for the launching of AS torpedoes. An Elsag fire control is ued for AS work and an Orion for guns.

Three of the class have Fiat high-speed diesels but *Visintini* has Tosi diesels. With only limited life left in the Albatros class hulls, the de Cristofaros will be on their own by about 1983 but the extensive building plans for the Marina Militare do not include a successor, although there has been talk of a CODOG corvette. Hydrofoils are being constructed but cannot be seriously considered as straight replacements for corvettes.

Albatros Corvette   Italy

		Laid Down	Launched	Completed
F542	(ex-PCE1626) *Aquila* (ex-HMS *Lynx*)	1953	1954	1956
F543	(ex-PCE1919) *Albatros*	1953	1954	1955
F544	(ex-PCE1920) *Alcione*	1953	1954	1955
F545	(ex-PCE1921) *Airone*	1953	1954	1955

Albatros

Displacement: 800 standard
950 full load
Length (oa): 250ft
Beam: 31.5ft
Draught: 9.5ft
Machinery: Two diesels on two shafts
5,200bhp for 19kts
Armament: Two 40mm guns (2 × 1)
Two triple AS TTs
Two Hedgehog AS mortars

Eight of this class were built in Italian yards with American funding (hence the early PCE classification). Four were of Danish account and one for the Netherlands the latter being transferred back after only five years of service, becoming the Italian *Aquila*). As one of the Danish ships was also discarded at an early age it would seem that the scantlings may be too light to suit northern conditions. The design was later 'stretched' for the Bergamini class escorts (see *Warships of the World: Escort vessels*) and later modified further to become the de Cristofaro corvette.

Single block superstructure is built on to a full-width deckhouse, on a flush-decked hull with a pronounced sheer forward and a characteristically Italian boat bow. There is no funnel, the twin Fiat diesels exhausting through a mack.

Originally, two 76mm Brescia guns were fitted, the forward one superfired by the Hedgehog and the after by a twin 40mm mounting. This armament was replaced in the early 1960s by two single 40mm guns, one forward and one in the after superimposed position. At the time it is said that new OTO-Melara pattern 76mm weapons are still satisfactorily serving a variety of other Italian ships, one can only surmise that the design is rather tender.

As a simple coastal escort capable of series production, the Albatros would appear to have been adequate but now has outdated weaponry and sensors. The class is now relegated to a primarily training role. Two further units, slightly scaled-up, were completed for Indonesia in 1958 as the Pattimura class (qv).

Apé Corvette

Italy

	Laid Down	Launched	Completed
A5328 (ex-F567) *Apé*	1942	1942	1943

Displacement: 670 standard
770 full load
Length (oa): 212.5ft
Beam: 28.5ft
Draught: 9ft
Machinery: Two diesel on two shafts plus two cruising motors
3,400bhp for 15kts
Armament: Two 40mm guns (2 + 1)

Disposals:
F578 *Baionetta;* F549 *Bombarda;* F569 *Chimera;* F575 *Cormorano;* F547 *Crisalide;* F563 *Danaide;* F568 *Driade;* F548 *Farfalla;* F577 *Fenice;* F572 *Flora;* F576 *Folaga;* F571 *Gabbiano;* F566 *Gru;* F561 *Ibis;* F562 *Minerva;* F574 *Pellicano;* F573 *Pomona;* F564 *Scimitarra;* F579 *Sfinge;* F565 *Sibilla;* F570 *Urania.*

Apé's A pennants signify that she is now used as an auxiliary (support ship for divers) rather than as an effective fighting ship. She is interesting, nevertheless, in being the last survivor of a 22-strong class which, commenced in 1942, were Italy's first frigate-style ships. Prewar assessments had shown that any likely submarine threat could be contained by the standard torpedo-boat designs such as the Climene, Orsa and Partenope classes of the late 1930s. These were really small destroyers, closely related to equivalent German types and mounted a balanced armament. As things turned out, the assessment was wrong. The Royal Navy used small destroyers successfully in the Mediterranean because they required nimbleness to survive air attack but were also faced with a submarine threat that they could cope with. On the other hand, as

British surface ships had to contend with such a high level of enemy air activity, the Royal Navy tended to use many small submarines in a strike role and these the Italian torpedo boats could not contain.

AS ships require capacity rather than speed and the slim, high speed hull of the small destroyer, devoted largely to machinery, was unsuitable. The four Orsas of 1938 moved somewhat in the right direction with a greater beam and a 20% reduction in power and their influence on the Ape class was considerable. Although shorter, they retained the long forecastle and characteristically isolated bridge/funnel placement. The main departure was in the adoption of diesel propulsion for a modest 18.5kts, no longer attainable. An interesting addition was a pair of 150hp electric motors which could be clutched on either shaft to give silent running at about 6kts for stalking a submerged target. They originally carried only DCs but were later equipped with Hedgehog AS mortars. Some had AS TTs for a while. Postwar gun armament has been confirmed to only two/three 40mm weapons. *Ape* herself will be retained only as long as she is useful in training.

Sparviero Hydrofoil (missile)   Italy

		Completed
P420	*Sparviero*	1974
—	*Nibbio*	1979
—	*Falcone*	1979
—	*Astore*	1980
—	*Griffone*	1980
—	*Gheppio*	1980
—	*Condor*	1981

Displacement: 63 tons
Length (oa): 80.5ft (foils extended)
Beam: 40ft (foils extended)
Draught: 14.5ft (boating mode)
Machinery: Foilborne — GT (4,500bhp) driving water-jet
Hullborne — Diesel driving retractable propeller
Max speed 50kts
Armament: One 76mm gun

Though many Italian yards offer FAC designs, few have had much luck in the export market and the MMI, like the other large western navies, operates few for its own uses. Even so as guardian of NATO's southern flank, the Italians face a considerable threat from FACs operated by other states that have acquired them without difficulty and whose responsibility in their use may be called to question. Following the highlighted need for a fast interdiction craft, the Italians joined with the West Germans and Americans in a project to produce a PHM, known as the NATO hydrofoil (see American Pegasus class). After great problems, including large cost over-runs, the European partners pulled out.

Meanwhile, a joint company, Alinavi, had been set up, combining the talents of the experienced

Messina-based Rodriquez company and Boeing, to produce a different PHM of more modest parameters. The result, much based on the earlier *Tucumcari*, was the *Sparviero* (ex-*Swordfish*) with a length of about 80ft compared with the *Pegasus'* 131ft. A smaller gas turbine, the well-proven British Proteus, could thus be used, coupled to a pump for high speed waterjet propulsion. A small diesel is also incorporated, driving a rectractable propeller for hullborne movements, when the stainless steel foils are lifted to reduce drag.

In spite of its lack of size, the *Sparviero* ships a 76mm OTO-Melara gun, looking disproportionately large, controlled by an Italian-built Elsag director. Two canister launchers are also mounted for Otomat Teseo SSMs, believed to be the early versions with a limited 30-mile range. These travel initially under autopilot control and then, after target acquisition by an active head, ascend steeply for a final dive on to target. Later marks have an improved 50-60-mile range and can be produced in an AS version, though the latter would not be carried by a hydrofoil.

After some five years of evaluation of the prototype, the class of six follow-ons was ordered. Though they are reported to have met the design requirements, the 400-mile range at 45kts emphasises that they are in no way a replacement for the modern FAC in spite of an enthusiastic lobby. They do have half the crew and they do have only a fraction of the power requirements of an FAC carrying the same armament but the latter is now a small warship in its own right and can keep the seas for extended periods when required. And that is what it is all about.

Freccia/Lampo FAC (torpedo)   Italy

		Completed
P491	*Lampo*	1963
P492	*Baleno*	1965
P493	*Freccia*	1965
P494	*Saetta*	1966

		Lampo	Freccia
Displacement:	standard	190	180
	full load	210	205
Length (oa):		139ft	151ft
Beam:		21ft	23.5ft
Draught:		5ft	5.5ft

Freccia

Machinery: Lampo
One gas turbine, two diesels, three shafts
11,700bhp from GT and diesels for 39kts
Freccia
One gas turbine, two diesels, three shafts
11,850bhp from GT and diesels for 40kts
Armament: (both)
Three 40mm guns (3×1)
Two 40mm guns and two 21-inch TTs

In view of the number of missile-armed FACs now operating in the enclosed basins of the Mediterranean, it is rather surprising that the Italian Navy, once such firm believers in speed, have not produced a wider range of examples. They would seem to have discounted their use in a NATO context and reason that enemy craft can best be countered by other means, such as the helicopter. Thus, the most modern operational designs are the two Freccias, dating from the mid-1960s, and improvements of the two Lampos that preceded them. Both types are CODAG propelled, the older having MTU diesels on the wing shafts, boosted by an Italian-built Metrovick GT and the newer with Fiat diesels and Proteus GT. Where on the Lampos the

GT exhausts through a low casing close abaft the bridge, the Freccias have a small funnel to carry the heat and noise farther away.

The earlier boats were close akin to the *Folgore* (P490) the survivor of a much modified pair dating from 1955 which, in turn, owed much to the German S-boat of World War II. Their flush hulls incorporated a spray chine but the Freccias have a low forecastle for better seakeepng, without sheer and with the line of the afterdeck continued forward as a knuckle. Only when it is realised that, in length and installed hp the Freccia equates to a Combattante II does it become apparent how much the FAC has advanced in little more than a decade, for the Italian boats carry only three 40mm in a gunboat role and surrender two of these if just two TTs are shipped.

Saetta acted for a time as trials ship to prove the Contraves Sea Killer Mk I SSM (later mounted on the Iranian Saam class frigates, see *Warships of the World: Escort Vessels*). The weapon was known also as the Nettuno and was a beam rider of about eight miles range and, for these experiments, she carried a five-cell launcher amidships. Both Freccias have also a small gun director and a lattice mast to support the improved electronics.

Sauro Patrol Submarine   Italy

		Laid Down	Launched	Completed
S518	*Nazario Sauro*	1974	1976	1978
S519	*Fecia di Cossato*	1975	1977	1978
S520	*Leonardo da Vinci*	1977	1979	1981
S521	*Guglielmo Marconi*	1977	1980	1981

Displacement: 1,450 surfaced
1,630 submerged
Length (oa): 210ft
Beam: 22.5ft
Draught: 19ft
Machinery: Three diesel-generators powering one propulsion motor Single shaft
3,650bhp for 11/20kts
Armament: Six 21-inch TTs

All Italian built submarines are, at present, produced by the Monfalcone yard of Italcantieri, which has designs for three basic types of 1,700, 1,450 and

500 tons surface displacement. While none of the first type has yet been built, four of the smallest have been produced as the Toti class (qv) and two of four of the 1,450-tonners, known as the Sauro class. They are in the upper size band of the contemporary patrol submarines but still considerably smaller than the large ex-American boats that they will replace and more suitable for operations in the constrictions of the Mediterranean. Known officially as the Type 1081, the hull is of rather slimmer form than usual although released figures would suggest that the performance is no better than that of the directly comparable French Agosta class (qv). Endurance for

Nazario Sauro

Carlo Fecia di Cossato: appearance at launch, secured to launching cradle and with temporary flotation tanks.

both is quoted as 45 days but, where the Agosta has four TTs with 20 reloads, the Sauro has six TTs (all forward) and only one reload per tube, which would seem hardly adequate for such long patrols. An attack computer is fitted.

The lines of the hull are very clean for good hydrodynamics and avoidance of flow-generated noise. All sonars are sited within the casings rather than in domes. Propeller-induced noise is kept to a minimum by adopting a seven-bladed, slow-turning screw, heavily skewed to reduce the tip loading which is a source of cavitation. The shaft is driven by a specially designed, slow-revving, double rotor motor situated right aft in a compartment separated by the switchroom from a space two-thirds aft housing three diesel generators. Submerged, the Sauros are capable of about 20kts for about one hour.

Toti Patrol Submarine   Italy

		Laid Down	Launched	Completed
S505	*Attilio Bagnolini*	1965	1967	1968
S506	*Enrico Toti*	1965	1967	1968
S513	*Enrico Dandolo*	1967	1967	1968
S514	*Lazzaro Mocenigo*	1967	1968	1969

Displacement: 525 surfaced
580 submerged
Length (oa): 151.5ft
Beam: 15.5ft
Draught: 13ft
Machinery: Two diesel-generators powering one propulsion motor One shaft
2,200bhp for 14/15kts
Armament: Four 21-inch TTs

These were the first boats designed and built in Italy subsequent to World War II and, as such, represent a radical move away from the larger ocean-going submarines previously operated by the Italian Navy. They were contemporary with the German Typ 205 (qv) which, for all its material failings seemed a better package.

A submarine's offensive capacity is still vested almost entirely in its TTs and a 205 has packed eight into the forward end of a hull somewhat shorter than that of a Toti, which has only four. While it can be argued that large salvoes are a thing of the past, the Germans, with excellent wire-guided torpedoes for both anti-ship and AS work, still deem a heavy forward battery necessary. The Toti's extra machinery power gives her a superior surface speed but a lower submerged speed, pointing to a less efficient hull, whose single screw runs in an aperture in the stern frame, forward of the rudders.

These little submarines, known officially as the Type 1075, present a very neat appearance. A prominent bow dome contains the active sonar transducers whilst those for the passive set are wrapped around the inner bow casing in a horseshoe configuration. Three pairs of small fins, equispaced along the hull, contain the elements of a passive ranging system, analogous to the American PUFFS.

Enrico Toti

Ex-American Patrol Submarines   Italy

		Laid Down	Launched	Completed
S501	*Primo Longobardo* (ex-USS *Volador*, SS490)	1945	1946	1948
S502	*Gianfranco Gazzana Priaroggia* (ex-USS *Pickerel*, SS 524)	1944	1944	1949
S515	*Livio Piomarta* (ex-USS *Trigger*, SS564)	1949	1951	1952
S516	*Romeo Romei* (ex-USS *Harder*, SS568)	1950	1951	1952

S501 and 502 are ex-American Tench class boats of an improved Balao type, later modernised to Guppy III standards. Both were transferred in 1972. S515 and 516 are ex-American Tang class submarines (qv) transferred in 1973 and 1974 respectively. With their various retrospective improvements, the two above pairs are virtually identical. Five other ex-US war-built and 'Guppied', submarines were also operated by the Italian Navy. Of these, the ex-Gato class *da Vinci* (S510) and *Tazzoli* (S511) were deleted in 1973 and the three ex-Balao class, *Morosini*, *Torricelli* and *Cappellini* (S507) went in 1975, 1976 and 1977 respectively.

Primo Longobardo alongside fleet replenishment tanker *Stromboli*.

Tang class submarine *Romeo Romei*: note configuration of after control surfaces

54

Livio Piomarta Tang class submarine.

Balao class submarine Alfredo Cappellini.

Umitaka Corvette

Japan

		Laid Down	Launched	Completed
309	Umitaka	1959	1959	1959
310	Otaka	1959	1959	1960
311	Mizutori	1959	1959	1960
312	Yamadori	1959	1959	1960
313	Otori	1959	1960	1960
314	Kasasagi	1959	1960	1960
315	Hatsukari	1960	1960	1960
316	Umidori	1962	1962	1963
317	Wakataka	1962	1962	1963
318	Kumataka	1963	1963	1964
319	Shiratori	1964	1964	1965
320	Hiyodori	1965	1965	1966

Displacement: 420/460 standard
450/480 full load
Length (oa): 197ft
Beam: 23.5ft
Draught: 8ft
Machinery: Two diesels on two shafts
3,800/4,00bhp for 20kts
Armament: Two 40mm guns (1×2)
Two triple AS TTs (some have two singles)

The 12 Umitakas are enlarged derivatives of the earlier, seven-strong Kari and Kanone class, deleted in 1977. These were 310/330-tonners (301-307) launched in 1956 and were followed immediately by the one-off 375-ton *Hayabusa* (308) whose extra hull size enabled the 4,000bhp of the twin diesels to be boosted by a de-rated 14,000hp gas turbine. Though the hull was considerably modified in form, it was still capable of no more than 26kts and the ship had only a short, experimental career.

There was a reversion to an enlarged basic Kanone class hull when the first of the Umitakas was laid down early in 1959. Though diesels of the same power were incorporated, the extra length of hull permitted improved lines which kept the speed the same at 20kts. They are simple little ships designed for operations close in among the islands where larger AS ships would be at a disadvantage. Armament is light, only a pair of 40mm guns are mounted, in a open position forward. Also forward is a Hedgehog mortar, supported aft by AS TTs, triple Mk 32s in 316-320 and two singles in the remainder. 309, 310, 317 and 318 have an enlarged bunker capacity, increasing their range from 2,000 to 3,000 miles at 12kts. Electronics, including sonar and ECM, are of American origin and dated, and the class is now too slow and poorly armed for its primary function of ASW, a job carried out more efficiently inshore by land-based helicopters.

PT11 FAC (torpedo)   Japan

		Completed
811	*PT11*	1971
812	*PT12*	1972
813	*PT13*	1972
814	*PT14*	1974
815	*PT15*	1975

Displacement: 100 tons
Length (oa): 116ft
Beam: 30ft
Draught: 4ft
Machinery: Two gas turbines and two diesels in CODAG configuration. Three shafts
11,000bhp total for 42kts
Armament: Four 21-inch TTs

Although the construction of several hydrofoils has been forecast, each of 100 tons and armed with Harpoon SSMs and the 76mm OTO Melara gun, Japan operates at present only one class of FAC, the torpedo-armed PT11 class of five craft. At first sight, the island-studded seas around Japan would seem, like the Baltic, to constitute first-class FAC country but it is evidently considered that any sea war will be largely AS in nature and fought mainly deepsea. The

PT11s probably have less a strike role than a responsibility for exercising fleet units in anti-FAC techniques.

Japan has never been an enthusiastic builder of FACs and, since the war, produced only PT1-10 of which the majority were small World War II craft PT7-8, a pair of Mitsubishi-designed boats of 1957 were 112ft in length and of comparatively high freeboard, well capable of coping with the turbulent waters of the area. From these two was developed PT10, a 105ft, triple diesel boat which was really a prototype for the five PT11s. These again have high-freeboard, all steel hulls with a low raised forecastle into which the forward 40mm is sunk, a feature closely common with the German Jaguars. The fully-enclosed wheelhouse is flanked by four 21-inch TTs, weapons close to the Japanese heart. An interestng innovation is the CODAG propulsion, embodying two JM200 GTs built by IHI and two 24W2 Mitsubishi diesels. As these drive three shafts, it is probable that the two diesels drive the centre propeller through a common gearbox, boosted by a GT on each wing shaft. Experience in the small GT-powered craft was gained with the earlier Hayabusa but, as an FAC arrangement, it would seem unique.

Uzushio Patrol Submarine   Japan

		Laid Down	Launched	Completed
SS566	*Uzushio*	1968	1970	1971
SS567	*Makishio*	1969	1971	1972
SS568	*Isoshio*	1970	1972	1972
SS569	*Narushio*	1971	1972	1973
SS570	*Kuroshio*	1972	1974	1974
SS571	*Takashio*	1973	1975	1976
SS572	*Yaeshio*	1975	1977	1978
SS573	—	1976	1978	1979

Uzushio

Displacement: 1,850 surfaced
Length (oa): 236ft
Beam: 30ft
Draught: 24.5ft
Machinery: Two diesel-generators powering one motor Single shaft
3,400/7,200bhp for 12/20kts
Armament: Six 21-inch TTs

Commenced in 1968, this class marked a great step forward in postwar Japanese submarines dropping the old-style twin-screw configuration in favour of a single-screw, high speed hull based heavily on the American Barbel class (qv) of a decade earlier, dedicated to optimum submerged performance with few concessions to surface conditions. Credited with

a good diving depth, the hull is of double skin construction where the modern trend is for single-hulled boats, short, beamy and capacious, offering a smaller sonar target.

All six TTs are sited forward of amidships and the diving planes in the fin, which is thus placed well forward. These features leave the bow unobstructed for the optimum siting of a large passive sonar array. Where the Barbels have a three-diesel generator, two-motor machinery outfit the *Uzushio* has her single screw driven by a more modern two-diesel, single-motor layout. Produced at a rate of about one per year between 1971 and 1978, the design would appear to be successful but, with the yet-unnamed SS573, the length will be increased by some 13ft and the surfaced tonnage to about 2,200.

Oshio Patrol Submarine   Japan

Michishio

		Laid Down	Launched	Completed
SS561	*Oshio*	1963	1964	1965
SS562	*Asashio*	1964	1965	1966
SS563	*Harushio*	1965	1967	1967
SS564	*Michishio*	1966	1967	1968
SS565	*Arashio*	1967	1968	1969

Displacement: 1,650 surfaced
Length (oa): 289ft
Beam: 27ft
Draught: 16ft
Machinery: Two diesel-generators powering two drive motors
Two shafts 6,300bhp for 14/18kts
Armament: Six 21-inch TTs
Two 12.7-inch AS TTs

The five Oshio class boats followed on from the Hayashios and from the same yards. Where the latter craft were tailored to near-sea operations, the Oshios were of twice the displacement for more distant work. Both classes are closely similar in appearance and very clean of protrusions on their outer skin.

Each has a fin with a rounded step on the forward side and a straight-stemmed hull with a minimum of flattening on the top of the casing. As is usual with slower submarines, the diving planes are forward to increase their effect. They have an older-style after end with twin propellers sited forward of the control surfaces.

Six 21-inch TTs are mounted forward with the interesting addition of two small-bore AS TTs aft. As this arrangment was not carried over to the Uzushios, it can only be surmised that improvements in passive sonar enabled detection and engagement of a hostile boat beyond the range of the small AS torpedoes and larger weapons could be used from the main tubes.

Hayashio Patrol Submarine   Japan

		Laid Down	Launched	Completed
SS521	*Hayashio*	1960	1961	1962
SS522	*Wakashio*	1960	1961	1962
SS523	*Natsushio*	1961	1962	1963
SS524	*Fuyushio*	1961	1962	1963

Displacement: 750 tons surfaced (521 and 522)
790 tons surfaced (523 and 524)
Length (oa): 193.5ft (521 and 522)
200ft (523 and 524)
Beam: 21ft
Draught: 13.5ft
Machinery: Two diesel-generators powering two propulsion motors, two shafts 2,300bhp
521 and 522 — 11/14kts
523 and 524 — 11/15kts
Armament: Three 21-inch TTs

Though the Imperial Japanese Navy had a powerful submarine arm during World War II the latter's achievements were comparatively poor in relation to its size. On the other hand, the opposing American boats enjoyed great success, stemming from both superior technology and more imaginative deployment. Rebuilding from scratch, postwar and under American supervision, it is hardly surprising that the new generation of Japanese warships reflected a strong outside influence, not the least in

submarine design. In 1955, the Gato class boat *Mingo* was acquired from the USN, renamed *Kuroshio* and used to train new crews. By 1960, Kawasaki's Kobe yard had completed the one-off 1,100-ton *Oyashio*, beginning a strong association whereby every Japanese submarine since has come from Kobe, being built either by Kawasaki or Mitsubishi.

Oyashio gave the necessary experience to commence a new pair, SS521 and SS522 in mid-1960. These were more modest 750-tonners, designed for coastal use and with a comparatively light armament of only three TTs, all forward. Virtually as soon as they were in the water, a new pair, SS523 and SS524 were commenced. These were two metres longer in the hull, giving a bonus of extra battery capacity and a slightly higher submerged speed. As a submarine design, these are in no way revolutionary but good, solid boats by firms 'getting their hand back in' and with generous margins of safety. They remain the Japanese navy's only small submarines.

Hayashio

North Korea

The greater part of the naval forces of the People's Democratic Republic of North Korea comes from either China or the USSR and, in spite of ideological differences between the latter states, Korea succeeds in keeping sufficiently in tune with each to receive higher technology boats from the Russian navy simultaneously with Chinese-built craft. There is now an increasing movement toward the production of warships within Korea, firstly by direct reproduction of standard imported types and, latterly, by home-designed craft.

N Korea's by no means insignificant forces are always kept in very good order and at present, believed to be composed as follows:

Three/six Sariwon class large patrol craft. These were designed and built at home in the 1960s and are 500-ton motorships with one 85mm and two 57mm guns. They were based heavily on some ancient Tral class minesweepers, acquired from the USSR in the mid-1950s.

Four Hai Nan class patrol craft transferred from China in 1975-6.
About 15 SO-I class patrol craft, of which about half were transferred from the USSR in the late 1950s and the remainder built locally as copies.
About eight Osa I class FAC (missile) transferred from the USSR.
Ten Komar class FAC (missile) transferred from the USSR.
Four Shershen class FAC (torpedo), transferred from the USSR.
60-80 P6 class FAC (torpedo) mostly of local construction.
About 20 P4 class FAC (torpedo) mostly of local construction.
About 10 Shanghai class FAC (gun) transferred from China.
About 10 Romeo class patrol submarines of which only six were Chinese built 1973-5 and the remainder constructed in Korea.
Four Whiskey class patrol submarines transferred from the USSR.

PSMM-type FAC (missile)   South Korea

Seven of these are operated (for notes, see under Asheville class) four of which were US built in the parent yard at Tacoma and three in South Korea.

Named *Paek Ku 12-19* inclusive, less 14. Four Standard SSM launchers fitted.

Asheville FAC (missile)   South Korea

One, the USS *Benicia* (PG96) has been acquired from the US Navy and renamed *Paek Ku 11* in 1971. She has been fitted for two/four Standard SSM launchers. Four more of the class are being sought,

also to be SSM-armed. South Korea also possesses about half a dozen coastal escorts of ex-American Auk and PCE types which are of little fighting value.

CPIC FAC (gun)   South Korea

Displacement: 70 tons full load
Length (oa): 100ft
Beam: 18.5ft
Draught: 6ft
Machinery: Three gas turbines (6,750hp) and two diesels (500hp) in CODOG configurations
Three shafts 45kts max
Armament: Two 30mm guns (1×2)
One 20mm gun

The CPIC was developed by the Tacoma Boatbuilding Company in the USA as a small, but fast, gun-armed patrol and interdiction craft. Besides a single 20mm weapon, the 100ft aluminium FAC is armed only with the twin 30mm Emerlec mounting, based on the Hispano HS831 cannon and engineered into a lightweight assembly capable of rapid response and a rate of fire of 600rpm from either barrel. As with the PSMM design Tacoma drew upon proven CODOG technology from the Asheville PGMs and installed three low-power Avco

CPIC type FAC (gun). This is a trials picture before armament was fitted: note distinctive GT exhausts.

Lycoming gas turbines on three shafts, with the wing shafts each capable of being driven by a 250bhp Volvo diesel for cruising economy. A drawback to the type is the large superstructure associated with gas turbine drive and giving a high silhouette. The lead boat, numbered PKM123, was built in the US and was to have been followed by seven more, built in Korea but these have been abandoned as four more of the more versatile Ashevilles have been made available for transfer from the US Navy.

Wadi Mragh Corvette   Libya

Displacement: 550 standard
630 full load
Length (oa): 202.5ft
Beam: 30.5ft
Draught: 7ft
Machinery: Four diesels on four shafts
18,000bhp for 33kts
Armament: Four Otomat SSM launchers
One 76mm gun
Two 35mm guns
Two triple AS TTs

Italian yards have so far had little luck in attracting FAC orders but these four ships for Libya demonstrate a new approach. They are hardly longer than the West German Typ 143s which are at the top end of the FAC size range, and yet are very different in appearance, with heavier scantlings and

a greater beam aimed at seakeeping rather than speed. Though installed power is about the same, the speed is reduced to some 32kts with a range well in excess of 4,000 miles at an economic speed of 14kts. They have four shafts, each driven by an MTU diesel but the builders, CNR of La Spezia, offer also two and three-shaft variants.

A large and versatile armament is fitted with the main clout residing in the four Otomat SSMs. An OTO-Melara 76mm is mounted forward and, finally, a twin 35mm Oerlikon-OTO GDM-C mounting aft, in place of the Breda 40/L70 or second 76mm earlier mooted. Hull-mounted sonar and Mk 32 TTs give genuine AS potential to a navy that is increasingly interested in submarine operation. Except for a Decca navigation radar, all major electronics are of Italian origin. The name ship commissioned in 1978 and is interesting in being representative of a type that has great potential for growth.

Vosper Mk 1 Corvette   Libya

	Launched	**Completed**
Tobruk	1965	1966

Displacement: 450 standard
500 full load
Length (oa): 177ft
Beam: 28.5ft
Draught: 13ft
Machinery: Two diesels on two shafts
3,800bhp for 18kts
Armament: One 4-inch DP gun
Four 40mm guns (4×1)

The startling contrast between this simple little ship and the four GM corvettes now being built in Italy illustrate vividly the change of stance of the Libyan navy in little over a decade. She is a repeat of the pair of Mk Is built for Ghana (qv) but with considerably lower machinery power and three extra 40mm guns. Being the first ship of any size built for the new Libyan navy, she was built to a very simple specification and included also State accommodation.

Tobruk

Combattante II FAC (missile)   Libya

A class of 10 basic Combattante IIs (qv) have been ordered from the parent yard of CMN Cherbourg for a 1979-80 delivery. They are of the so-called IIG variant and armed with four Otomat SSMs, one 76mm OTO-Melara gun forward and a twin Bofors/Breda 40L70 40mm 'Compatto' mounting aft.

Osa II FAC (missile)   Libya

At least five were transferred from the USSR in 1976-7. More, possibly 10, are expected.

Susa FAC (missile)   Libya

Susa class FAC (missile): note ship illustration is almost exactly similar to *Pahlawan* built for Brunei.

		Completed
PO1	*Susa*	1969
PO2	*Sirte*	1969
PO3	*Sebna* (ex-*Sokna*)	1969

Three Vosper-built boats virtually identical to the Danish Søløven class (qv), but with TTs replaced by small SS.12M missiles launched from frames flanking the forward end of the superstructure. The 40mm guns are in open mountings.

Foxtrot Patrol Submarine
Libya

Up to six may be acquired from the USSR with two delivered by the end of 1977. Libya's ambitions to become a serious naval power in the Mediterranean have outstripped her ability to train men and set up facilities; thus, a plan to purchase four French-built Daphné class boats has been shelved.

Spica-M FAC (missile)
Malaysia

Four FACs based on the Swedish class (qv) have been ordered from Karlskronavarvet for 1979-80 delivery. Unlike the Swedish boats, they carry four MM38 Exocet launchers and, as these are mounted aft, the bridge structure has been moved forward from its characteristic situation on the originals. The hull is also some eight feet longer and driven by three MTU diesels in place of the earlier GTs; their lower power reduces the maximum speed to 35kts. An interesting addition is a Blowpipe mounting for deterring helicopters, to the attentions of which FACs are extremely vulnerable. This optically guided missile forms also the basis of the SLAM system for submarines, as fitted in the Israeli Typ 206s. In addition to retaining the 57mm gun forward, the builders have succeeded also in accommodating a 40mm weapon aft. Why the Malaysians should seek to acquire yet another type of FAC when they already operate four Exocet-armed Combattante IIs is not known.

Combattante II FAC (missile)
Malaysia

		Completed
P3501	*Perdana*	1972
P3502	*Serang*	1973
P3503	*Ganas*	1973
P3504	*Ganyang*	1973

Four basic Combattante IIs (qv) from the CMN yard at Cherbourg. Only two MM38 Exocets are carried, together with a 57mm Bofors pattern gun forward and a 40mm weapon aft, a light armament by Combattante II standards.

Lürssen-type 45m FAC (gun)
Malaysia

		Completed
P3505	*Jerong*	1976
P3506	*Todak*	1976
P3507	*Paus*	1976
P3508	*Yu*	1976
P3509	*Baung*	1977
P3510	*Pari*	1977

This class of six boats was built by a Lürssen-affiliated yard in Malaysia and is a variant on the German-built group for Ecuador (qv). Unlike them, this class is not missile-armed but carries a comparatively light gun armament of one Bofors pattern 57mm forward and a single 40mm aft, reflecting a patrol rather than combatant function. In addition, the class has a three-diesel, three-shaft propulsion system, disposing of only 9,900bhp for a more modest 32kts.

The Malaysian navy disposes further of 22 Vosper-built 103ft patrol boats. These are capable of some 27kts and are armed with only a pair of 40mm guns. They reflect, along with other classes, the need for small but nimble craft in large numbers to police the shallow and complex Malaysian coast.

Lürssen-type 36m FAC (torpedo)

Mauritania

Two of this type were completed in 1978 by the Spanish Bazan yard. They are similar to the six Barcelo class (qv) recently built by the same yard for the Spanish Navy. Like the Barcelos, they do not normally carry TTs but have adequate stability to ship two or four 21-inch TTs like the sister craft serving with the navies of Chile and Ecuador. Normal armament is only one 40mm and one 20mm gun. Propulsion is by two diesels, generating 6,000bhp, and built under licence by Bazan to MTU design.

Azteca Patrol Craft

Mexico

		Completed
PO1	Andres Quintana Roo	1974
PO2	Matias de Cordova	1974
PO3	Miguel Ramos Arizpe	1974
PO4	Jose Maria Izazgu	1974
PO5	Juan Bautista Morales	1974
PO6	Ignacio Lopez Rayon	1974
PO7	Manuel Crecencio Rejon	1975
PO8	Antonio de la Fuente	1975
PO9	Leon Guzman	1975
PO10	Ignacio Ramirez	1975
PO11	Ignacio Mariscal	1975
PO12	Heriberto Jara Corona	1975
PO13	Jose Maria Maja	1975
PO14	Felix Romero	1975
PO15	Fernando Lizardi	1975
PO16	Francisco J. Mujica	1975
P17	Pastor Romaix	1975
P18	Jose Maria del Castillo Velasco	1975
P19	Luis Manuel Rojas	1976
P20	Jose Natividad Macias	1976
P21	Esteban Baca Calderon	1976
P22	Ignacio Zaragoza	1976

Displacement: 130 tons
Length (oa): 112ft
Beam: 28ft
Draught: 7ft
Machinery: Two diesels on two shafts 3,600bhp for 24kts
Armament: One 40mm gun
One 20mm gun

Should the Mexicans expand this class to an intended 80 it will be easily the largest in the west. The first 21 were built by a group of three Scottish yards but P22 was the first home-built unit, constructed with British assistance, as the pilot for the remainder, all of which it is intended to build in Mexico. With extensive coastlines on both the Pacific and Atlantic, fishery protection itself is a task of some magnitude but this has recently been magnified by the discovery of very extensive offshore oil reserves, representing a national asset that will require patrolling. It is this task for which the Azteca was designed, beamy and comparatively slow, intended to stay at sea. The comfortable hull is topped by a large superstructure abaft which the twin diesels exhaust through a pair of slim uptakes placed athwartships and bridged to form a base for both radar antenna and mast.

As the intended function is purely patrol, the armament is light but there is sufficient stability to increase this without problem. A 57mm or Penguin-sized SSMs could easily be accommodated although it would probably not be possible to increase the speed by very much, even by the installation of more powerful machinery.

More and more states are declaring rights to offshore continental shelf areas, 200-mile limits of plain 'exclusive economic zones' and these, particularly where they have proven mineral reserves, will need policing. Craft such as the Azteca, backed by larger and more powerful ships, will probably be built in large numbers worldwide in the years to come.

Andres Quintana Roo

Le Fougueux Patrol Craft

Morocco

	Laid Down	Launched	Completed
32 *Lieutenant Riffi*	1963	1964	1964

Very similar ship to French *Le Fougueux* (qv) but differs in having old pattern 76mm forward in an open mounting. Where the French naval units have four diesels, the Moroccan has two of slightly higher power.

Lürssen-type 58m FAC (gun)

Morocco

The Spanish Bazan yard, having recently completed the six Lazaga class (qv) are now building a further four to Moroccan account. Where the Spanish boats are only gun armed with provision for SSMs (probably Harpoon) it is possible that the new boats will carry four Exocet in addition to a 76mm OTO-Melara and a 40mm gun, with two triple AS TTs as an alternative fit. Four further Harpoon-armed boats of the same type are found under the Turkish flag.

PR72-type Patrol Craft

Morocco

Okba

	Completed
Okba	1976
Triki	1977

Displacement: 375 standard
Length (oa): 189ft
Beam: 25ft
Draught: 7ft
Machinery: Four diesels on four shafts 11,000bhp for 28kts
Armament: One 76mm gun
One 40mm gun

This pair of craft, built by the French SFCN concern, are a down-graded version of the six being built for Peru (qv) by the same manufacturer. They are large boats, as large as a Combattante III, and could easily be retrofitted with four SSMs as large as Exocet and for which the fire control has already been installed. A further pair have been funded.

Wolf Corvette

Netherlands

		Laid Down	Launched	Completed
F817	*Wolf* (ex-PCE1607)	1952	1954	1954
F818	*Fret* (ex-PCE1604)	1952	1953	1954
F819	*Hermelijn* (ex-PCE1605)	1953	1954	1954
F820	*Vos* (ex-PCE1606)	1953	1954	1954
F821	*Panter* (ex-PCE1608)	1952	1954	1954
F822	*Jaguar* (ex-PCE1609)	1952	1954	1954

Fret

Displacement: 850 standard
970 full load
Length (oa): 184.5ft
Beam: 34ft
Draught: 14.5ft
Machinery: Two diesels on two shafts
1,800bhp for 15kts
Armament: One 3-inch gun
Four/Six 40mm guns

The main strength of the Royal Netherlands Navy is organised into three task forces to work within the NATO framework, two in the North Atlantic and one in the English Channel. As the Dutch coast faces the North Sea, however, the protection of shipping moving in this area is also a responsibility and it was to discharge this that the six coastal escorts of the Wolf class were built. At the time, the Dutch fleet had only the little prewar home-built Crijnssen class

sloops and a collection of war-built minesweepers and the American offer to build and finance six small escorts was welcome. What was surprising was that they were repeats of the numerous PCEs built during the war; many of these had been already transferred abroad and the strange decision to build yet more seems to have been to create work.

In appearance, the Wolfs are similar to the earlier examples of the class but lack their diminutive funnel and have a larger boat slung under gravity davits on the port side. As built they inherited depth charges and racks as sole AS armament, but have since had a Hedgehog mortar added. They have given good service and are not scheduled for replacement until about 1984 although now very dated and not even fast enough for effective fishery protection duties. Similar, war-built PCEs (with funnels) serve still with Burma, Ecuador, South Korea and the Philippines.

Zwaardvis Patrol Submarine   Netherlands

		Laid Down	Launched	Completed
S806	*Zwaardvis*	1966	1970	1972
S807	*Tijgerhaai*	1966	1971	1972

Displacement: 2,350 standard
2,600 submerged
Length (oa): 218ft
Beam: 33ft
Draught: 25ft

Machinery: Three diesel-generators powering one propulsion motor
5,200bhp for 14/20kts
Armament: Six 21-inch TTs

Zwaardvis

These are large boats by modern standards approximating in size to the French Agostas and equally geared to distant water operations. In design, they are based heavily on that of the American Barbel class boats (qv) which incorporated the high speed hull developed from the Albacore experiments. Dimensions of the Zwaardvis class adhere closely to those of the Barbel but, though the appearance, too, is similar, it lacks the total cleanliness of the American design. The humpbacked profile of the 'teardrop' hull is characteristic, giving something of the look now associated with nuclear submarines. With the large fin also set far forward, it has been possible to mount the diving planes on it (the Barbels had theirs resited in this position, having been built with them right forward). Two distinctive, square-sectioned bulges are faired into the trailing edge of the fin and house sonar and ECM sensors. These features, together with the slightly elevated casing abaft the fin, make the class easy to recognise from most angles.

A battery of six TTs is carried forward with two reloads per tube carried inboard. Following the deep diving Dolfijn class, the Zwaardvis class is also probably well capable of similar performance, with 'swim-out' launch capability for at least some tubes. A mixture of large British-type anti-ship and American Mk 37 AS torpedoes are shipped, the latter wire-guided. A computerised M8 fire control by HSA accepts inputs from all available sensors and can cope with three simultaneous targets.

One bonus of the single teardrop hull is its great vertical depth, allowing a two-deck layout, even over the battery compartment amidships. Living conditions are considerably superior to the great majority of contemporary submarines.

Three diesel-generators power the propulsion motor for running surfaced or at 'snort-depth' and two groups of batteries are supplied for submerged navigation, water-cooled to permit over-running for short periods in the 'group-up' condition. For these limited bursts, it is likely that the maximum speed is considerably in excess of the 20kts quoted. A single, five-bladed, propeller is mounted abaft the control surfaces.

The first boat of an improved class has been ordered for delivery late-1982 and a second will be ordered shortly with a further two planned. They will be of similar length to the Zwaardvis design but less beamy. A similar machinery layout will be installed but with the more modern Pielstick diesel. It is anticipated that they will be capable of operating at even greater depths and that more extensive automation will reduce the present boats' rather large crew of 67 to about 49, thus increasing endurance and improving life-cost margins.

Dolfijn Patrol Submarine Netherlands

		Laid Down	Launched	Completed
S804	*Potvis*	1962	1965	1965
S805	*Tonijn*	1962	1965	1966
S808	*Dolfijn*	1954	1959	1960
S809	*Zeehond*	1954	1960	1961

Displacement: 1,500 surfaced
1,825 submerged
Length (oa): 261ft
Beam: 28ft
Draught: 16ft
Machinery: Two diesel-generators powering two propelsion motors Two shafts
3,100bhp/4,400shp for 14.5/17kts
Armament: Eight 21-inch TTs

Dutch submarines have never been numerous, but their designers have been highly innovative producing among other things, the snort. Having interests in the Far East, the Netherlands produced warships with an eye to colonial service and submarines tended to be on the large size. Only a handful of these O boats survived the war and these were supplemented by ex-British and, then, ex-American units. In 1949, construction of a further four boats (known as 032-35) was authorised but it

was not until 1954 that the first two were laid down as the *Dolfijn* and *Zeehond*, with the second pair being held back with the intention of redesigning them for nuclear propulsion.

The design of the class was certainly radical and based on the reasoning that a better deep-diving performance would be achieved by using small diameter, but thick, pressure hulls. To give the necessary internal volume, three were necessary, in the form of contiguous tubes with their axes parallel and disposed in a triangular fashion with a long centre section joined to two shorter flanking sections, set lower. This arrangement gives the class a unique rounded triangular cross-section.

The centreline tube is of larger cross-sectional area than the others and houses the crew, armament and most of the electronics. Each of the lower tubes contains a diesel generator, batteries, a propulsion motor and one shaft. The after body is of the old-style, twin screw layout with a single rudder

Potvis

abaft the propellers and after hydroplanes above them. Diving planes are mounted forward and are retractable. The fin followed the remainder of the boat's outer surfaces in being clean and un-fussy.

By 1960/1, when this pair was completed, it had been realised that nuclear propelled boats were rather ambitious, particularly now that the East Indies were no longer a colonial possession. A second, improved pair was therefore ordered for completion in 1965/6. All are reputedly capable of a near 1,000ft operating depth and must be regarded as successful on this point although the fact that the concept was not followed in succeeding classes suggests drawbacks with small diameter hulls.

Both pairs have been modernised and are now identical. Improvements have included an M8 fire control by HSA for the eight TTs. As the class will have to last at least until the completion of the improved-Zwaardvis class, they are to be re-engined shortly with Pielstick engines, compatible with those on the new boats.

Vosper Mk 9 Corvette   Nigeria

		Completed
F83	*Erin'mi*	1978
F84	*Enyimiri*	1979

Displacement: 820 standard
Length (oa): 226ft
Beam: 34.5ft
Draught: 12ft
Machinery: Four diesels on two shafts 20,000bhp for 29kts
Armament: One 76mm gun
One 40mm gun
Two 20mm guns
One twin-barrelled AS rocket launcher
One triple Seacat SAM system

In common with other states with new-found oil riches, Nigeria is expanding her fleet considerably to become established as the premier naval force on the African west coast. The two Mk 9 corvettes are the first yet built by Vosper Thornycroft and are of a size that represents an addition to the middle of their range. Though distinctly ships from the VT stable, with their strongly raked bows with prominent knuckle and large squat funnel, they present a much more 'built-up' appearance than earlier ships of the series. Accommodation for the large crew of 90 is largely responsible in this, a number that includes a flag officer and his staff.

For their size, the Mk 9s carry a balanced general purpose armament which, though having commonality with other ships under the Nigerian flag, comes from a wide range of countries. Forward is an Italian OTO-Melara 76mm gun, a great improvement on the ex-Royal Navy twin 4-inch DPs carried by earlier ships. This is superfired by a Swedish Bofors twin-barrelled AS rocket launcher and a twin Bofors 40mm mounting is sited aft. Two Swiss-pattern Oerlikon 20mm guns are also carried and overall gun direction is by a Dutch HSA M20 system. Right aft is sited a triple short Seacat SAM launcher whose director is alongside the large Plessey AWS-2 search radar antenna aft. The multi-national approach is maintained in the machinery space, where the two shafts are powered by four MTU diesels of West German manufacture.

Though little larger than the S-143s also being built for Nigeria, and lacking much of the FAC's glamour, the Mk 9 is a 'regular' warship of good range and should suit her owner's purposes admirably.

Erin'mi

Vosper Mk 3 Corvette Nigeria

Otobo

		Completed
F81	*Dorina*	1972
F82	*Otobo*	1972

Displacement: 500 standard
650 full load
Length (oa): 202ft
Beam: 31ft
Draught: 11ft
Machinery: Two diesels on two shafts
4,450bhp for 23kts
Armament: Two 4-inch DP guns (1×2)
Two 40mm guns (2×1)

These elegant little warships are a stretched version of the Mk 1 Keta class built for Ghana, and resemble them closely. The extra space forward permitted the

fitting of an ex-Royal Navy twin HA 4-inch Mk 19, similar to that already mounted in the frigate *Nigeria* and once very common in RN ships up to cruiser size. With the exception of this elderly, hand-worked mounting the armament and electronics fit is modern and largely compatible with that of the new Mk 9s. Both the main battery and the two 40/60 Bofors guns can be laid by the HSA M22 fire control in its familiar masthead 'eggshell' radome. Two flare projectors are also fitted. The large antenna of the Plessey AWS is still prominent aft on a diminutive mainmast. Sonar and depth charges can be carried if required. A simple propulsion system is retained in each of the two shafts being powered by a MAN diesel. There is still a major general purpose role for these ships to fulfil though Nigeria is now tending toward modern, high technology warships.

Typ 143 FAC (missile) Nigeria

Three Typ 143 FACs were ordered from Lürssen in West Germany in 1977 and the data for this class is valid as the design for the 143 'follow-ons' is still progressing and the last of the West German craft was, itself, completed only in 1977. Reports that the SSM outfit will be changed to four Otomats seem odd in view that the Combattante IIIBs also under

construction are to carry Exocet, though the Otomats have nearly four times the range of the 26-mile MM38 Exocet. It would seem logical that a lighter surface armament of one 76mm and one 40mm gun be carried and with little likely use for TTs, these items are probably to be optional extras.

Combattante III FAC (missile) Nigeria

Three Combattante III FACs (qv) were ordered from CMN, Cherbourg at about the same time as the Typ 143s from Lürssen, rather puzzling in view of the very similar size and capabilities of the two classes; it is possible that the two groups have been acquired with the intention of their evaluation prior to a larger series being built. As each has already been shown to be thoroughly adequate under various flags it probably demonstrates no more than that the usual Nigerian taste for shopping in as many markets as possible, with little regard for logistics.

The only Typ III Combattantes so far completed were the four for Greece (qv) and the new boats are

designated IIIB due to their armament being modified. Though four MM38 Exocets are still carried the gun armament has been reduced by substituting a 40mm Breda mounting for the after 76mm OTO-Melara and no TTs are apprently normally shipped.

Sleipner Corvette

Norway

		Laid Down	Launched	Completed
F310	(ex-P950) *Sleipner*	1963	1963	1965
F311	(ex-P951) *Aeger*	1964	1965	1967

Displacement: 600 standard
790 full load
Length (oa): 228ft
Beam: 26ft
Draught: 8.5ft
Machinery: Four diesels on two shafts
9,000bhp for 25kts
Armament: One 3-inch gun
One 40mm gun
One Terne ASW system
Two triple Mk 32 AS TTs

Designed for inshore AS operations the two Sleipners are similar in both size and function to the West German Thetis class (qv) of a slightly earlier date. The design philosophy of the two classes varies considerably and makes an interesting comparison. For a projection of the type to date, the contemporary French A69s (see *Warships of the World: Escort Vessels*) should also be compared, having again a similar function, but larger.

Five of the Norwegian class were planned but only two survived defence cuts. Built for open Northern sea conditions, the flush-decked hull rises in a pretty sheer forward, into a prominent knuckle to reduce loose water topside. What does come aboard is cleared by the forward edge of the bridge structure which is brought out to the deck edge, almost American-style. Note the shallow draught. The superstructure is of single block construction with an open bridge above and abaft a fully enclosed wheelhouse and a large, but well proportioned funnel, exhausts the four MTU diesels coupled two-by-two to the twin shafts. The mast arrangment is interesting with a tripod lower mast bearing a surveillance radar antenna and supporting the modern equivalent of a fidded topmast, itself crowned by a DF loop.

Surface armament is light with a fully enclosed US-pattern 3-inch 50 forward with integral control radar and single 40mm gun with a folding canopy right aft. A separate optical director is sited atop the bridge. Unlike the Germans, the Norwegians prefer their AS weapon aft. This is the home-produced Terne in its rather bulky, stabilised mounting capable of placing six-round salvoes of 265lb AS rockets out to 1,000yd every 45sec. It receives attack data from its own active, home-built sonar but searches are conducted by an American-pattern SQS-36 passive sonar. Backup is provided in two triple Mk 32 AS TTs atop the after superstructure and depth charges can be carried.

With an updated armament, the Sleipner type of corvette represents an economic and efficient ship, near-ideal for EEZ policing, providing also a perfect training platform for crews and excellent experience for early commands. It would be good to see a series of such vessels under the White Ensign.

Sleipner

Hauk FAC (missile)   Norway

Hauk: note Penguin SSMs and after TTs not yet fitted.

	Completed
P986 *Hauk*	1977
P987-999 Ordered 1975	

Displacement: 120 standard
150 full load
Length (oa): 120ft
Beam: 20.5ft
Draught: 5.5ft
Machinery: Two diesels on two shafts
7,000bhp for 35kts
Armament: Six Penguin Mk 2 SSM launchers
Two 21-inch TTs
Four 21-inch TTs
One 40mm gun
One 20mm gun

A class planned at present to be 14-strong, the Hauk is a direct development of the Snogg design. This latter class was completed in 1970-1 and the Swedish Navy then ordered a modified boat as prototype for a projected class of its own. This was completed in 1972 as the *Jägaren*, of which 16 follow-ons are now being built in Norway as the Hugins (qv), and it is basically the *Jägaren* design which was completed as the Hauk.

The powerful hull is topped by a GRP superstructure but the Norwegians have opted only for a 40mm gun forward in an open mounting, contrasting with the Swedish boats' fully enclosed Bofors 57mm gun. Either class can carry, in addition, either four TTs or six of the Penguin SSM in its improved Mk 2 version, of 20 miles range. The choice of a smaller gun forward means that the two forwards TTs can be carried in addition to the SSMs. If it is intended that two further TTs can be carried aft in lieu of the Penguins, it is noticeable that the hull is not notched for the purpose (compare with Snogg class). The Kongsberg MS1-80S control is in a distinctive helmet-shaped rotating housing.

With hull and machinery of proven design, the Hauks should prove excellent boats though it is noticeable that, in common with FACs of other Scandinavian navies, they tend to be shorter than the average missile-armed boat and with shorter-ranged main armament, reflecting the type of mission and smaller radius of action for which they are intended.

Snogg/Storm FAC (missile)   Norway

Rapp (Snögg class)

Traust (Storm class)

Snogg

		Completed
P980	*Snogg* (ex-*Lyr*)	1970
P981	*Rapp*	1970
P982	*Shar*	1971
P983	*Rask*	1971
P984	*Kvikk*	1971
P985	*Kjapp*	1971

Storm

P960	*Storm*	1968
P961	*Blink*	1965
P962	*Glimt*	1966
P963	*Skjold*	1966
P964	*Trygg*	1966
P965	*Kjekk*	1966
P966	*Djern*	1966
P967	*Skudd*	1966
P968	*Arg*	1966
P969	*Steil*	1967
P970	*Brann*	1967
P971	*Tross*	1967
P972	*Hvass*	1967
P973	*Traust*	1967
P974	*Brott*	1967
P975	*Odd*	1967
P976	*Pil*	1967
P977	*Brask*	1967
P978	*Rokk*	1968
P979	*Gnist*	1968

Displacement: 110 standard
135 full load
Length (oa): 120ft
Beam: 20.5ft
Draught: 5.5ft
Machinery: Two diesels on two shafts
7,200bhp for 35kts

Armament: Snogg
Four Penguin SSM launchers
Four 21-inch TTs
One 40mm gun
Storm
Six Penguin SSM launchers
One 76mm gun
One 40mm gun

Though often listed separately, these two groups of boats vary only with their weapon fits. The 20 Storms are heavily armed with six Mk 1 Penguin SSMs and a 40mm gun aft, and a Bofors-type 76mm automatic weapon forward whilst the follow-on group of six Snoggs carry a more general-purpose armament. This consists of four Penguins and two single 40mm guns, saving enough topweight to mount four TTs firing 21-inch wire-guided torpedoes, weapons entering a new era of popularity because of their reliability and high immunity to countermeasures. Each group of boats complements the other, a philosophy reflected in the navies of Denmark, Sweden and West Germany also.

The hulls are steel-built and of easy lines, with the sheerstrake of the torpedo carriers notched to guarantee launching clearances. In addition, the Snoggs present a higher profile with the superstructure a halfdeck higher and radar antennas mounted on an open lattice ahead of a separate mast bearing the communications aerials. Atop their lower deckhouses, the Storms have their director antenna housed in an inverted fishbowl radome, on a low frame. A simple two-diesel, two-shaft machinery layout has been retained though the MTU engine was adopted in favour of the previously used Deltic. It should be noted that *Storm* is the second boat of the name; the original, completed in 1963 as prototype, was scrapped and replaced.

Tjeld/Nasty FAC (torpedo)　　　　　　　　　Norway

		Completed
P343	*Tjeld*	1960
P344	*Skarv*	1960
P345	*Teist*	1960
P346	*Jo*	1961
P347	*Lom*	1961
P348	*Stegg*	1961
P349	*Hauk*	1961
P350	*Falk*	1961
P357	*Ravn*	1962
P380	*Skrei*	1964
P381	*Hai*	1963
P382	*Sel*	1964
P383	*Hval*	1964
P384	*Laks*	1966
P385	*Knurt*	1966
P386	*Delfin*	1966
P387	*Lyr*	1966
P388	*Gribb*	1962
P389	*Geir*	1962
P390	*Erle*	1962

Displacement: 70 standard
82 full load
Length (oa): 80.5ft
Beam: 24.5ft
Draught: 6.5ft
Machinery: Two diesels on two shafts
6,200bhp for 45kts max
Armament: One 40mm gun
One 20mm gun
Four 21-inch TTs (Note: A second 40mm gun can be fitted in lieu of the 20mm gun and after TTs)

Cast strongly in the mould of the World War II high speed MTB, the Tjeld is small by modern standards with an open bridge not ideally suited to northern conditions and a size and range which restricts it to use within the Leads, where its speed and small silhouette could be utilised to the full. As these waters are unusually ice-free, the double-skin Mahogany hull is not so liable to damage as those of boats employed farther south in the Baltic.

Designed by the well-known Mandal firm of Batservis as a speculative venture, the 'Nasty' prototype was evaluated by the Royal Norwegian Navy, which then built a further 20 as the Tjeld class. With a high freeboard and low superstructure the hull can be fitted as either a torpedo or gunboat, armed as noted above. For machinery the British Napier Deltic was specified; recently used in the Royal Navy's Dark class FPBs, the engine offered an extremely high power-weight ratio and a great reduction in fire risk compared with the petrol engines formerly common.

Two of the class were built for the US fleet's 'brown water navy' but have now been stricken. Four further units were Norwegian-built for the Greek navy and the class is enjoying a late revival by being built under licence in Turkey, which had acquired two boats previously operated by West Germany. Lacking both modern sensors and equipment, the class will probably disappear in the future as the new Hauk class commissions. It should be noted that the lead ship of the class repeats the name of the Tjeld (P349). Note the non-sequential pennant numbers.

Laks

Typ 207 Patrol Submarine　　　　　　　　　Norway

Utstein

S300	*Ula*	1965
S301	*Utsira*	1965
S302	*Utstein*	1965
S303	*Utvaer*	1965
S304	*Uthaug*	1966
S305	*Sklinna*	1966
S306	*Skolpen*	1966
S307	*Stadt*	1966
S308	*Stord*	1967
S309	*Svenner*	1967
S315	*Kaura*	1965
S316	*Kinn*	1964
S317	*Kya*	1964
S318	*Kobben*	1964
S319	*Kunna*	1964

Displacement: 370 standard
480 full load
Length (oa): 149.5ft
Beam: 15ft
Draught: 14ft
Machinery: Two diesel-electric sets powering one propulsion motor One shaft
1,200/1,700bhp for 13/17kts
Armament: Eight 21-inch TTs

All of the class were built by the old Rheinstahl Nordseewerke at Emden in West Germany; they carry a '207' label but are really variants on the 205s then building for the Bundesmarine (qv). The Danish Narvhalens are also closely related. It would seem that the Norwegians ordered the class on the strength of the German reputation for excellence in submarines, for the K-group (S315-9) were ordered before the Germans had completed even their first postwar boat. They were, perhaps, fortunate for, where the Germans experienced metal problems in the hulls of the early 205s, the 207s seem to have performed well and a further 10 follow-ons (S300-9) were added.

Though fitted with minimal casing topsides like the German and Danish near-sisters, the 207 has a different fin profile, with a cranked leading edge with an access door in it. All have an after extension to the fin, housing the top of the submerged escape chamber. In common with the variants, the 207's hull is of single skin construction and carries a forward battery of eight TTs.

The single screw is set above the lower rudder, abaft the upper rudder and forward of the hydroplanes for maximum effect. A crew of only 17 is required. Now becoming dated, the class is to be refitted in sequence with new sensors and batteries, and fitted for firing and control of the long range wire-guided torpedo.

Meanwhile, the Norwegian navy is interested also in the Germans' new Typ 210 project for a 750-ton patrol submarine which will probably resemble the Typ 209/Glavkos under the Greek flag (qv). It should be noted that, unlike the other Scandinavian navies, the Norwegian has deep waters close in and its submarines have a correspondingly greater emphasis on deep diving and less on minelaying.

Brooke Marine 37.5m Patrol Boat (missile) Oman

		Completed
B2	*Mansur*	1973
B3	*Nejah*	1973
B4	*Wafi*	1977
B5	*Fulk*	1977
B6	*Aul*	1977
B7	*Jabber*	1977

Displacement: 135 standard
153 full load
Length (oa): 123ft
Beam: 22.5ft
Draught: 5.5ft
Machinery: Two diesels on two shafts
4,800bhp for 27kts

Armament: B1-3
Two MM38 Exocet SSM launchers
Two 40mm guns (2 × 1)
B4-7
One 76mm gun
One 20mm gun

This class has literally gone from strength to strength and well illustrates the versatility of the modern small warship when imaginatively designed. B1-3 were ordered from the UK yard of Brooke Marine at Lowestoft in 1971, before Iran really began to expand her fleet to become the dominant Persian Gulf power. With only a brace of 40mm guns, the 123ft steel-hulled boats were armed very lightly but adequately, with their 27kts cruising speed, for normal patrol duties. They were commissioned in

Mansur

1973, proved suitable and were followed by an order for four more, B4-7, in 1974. With Iran now ordering ships to her own account, in place of acquiring used tonnage, and Iraq taking delivery of FACs from Soviet sources, possibilities larger than the average illicitly trading dhow emerged and the new boats were armed with a 76mm OTO-Melara gun, though still optically laid. In 1977, with newly-acquired flotillas of missile-armed FACs in the inventories of the aforementioned navies, B1-3, the original trio returned to their UK builders for refit and the installation of two MM38 Exocet SSMs with a British control system.

This ability to change armament and function stems from the beamy and stable hull, typically Brooke Marine, which with its gentle chine is designed and powered to keep the sea comfortably rather than for all-out attack purposes. The superstructure is compact, with a fully enclosed bridge and given lift by the inclusion of a rakish funnel that exhausts the twin Paxman Venturas.

Whether the last four boats will also be missile-fitted will probably depend on the balance of power in the Gulf. At the time of writing Saudi Arabia, with a Gulf coastline, is building two powerful Harpoon-armed flotillas in the USA and the plans of Iran seem set for change with the country's internal problems. The situation, as ever in the Middle East, remains fluid. B1 *Bushra* (1973) was swept overboard and lost from ship delivering her to Oman subsequent to modernisation.

Light Forces Pakistan

Subsequent to the Indo-Pakistan war of 1971, Pakistan took the new course of seeking Chinese help in the reconstruction of her light forces. This was predictable as India was already receiving craft from the USSR and each wished to demonstrate to the Western naval powers that it had a freedom of choice. So far transferred are:

Twelve Shanghai II class FAC (gun) in 1972-3.
Five Hai Nan class patrol craft in 1976-8.
Up to six Hu Chwan class torpedo-armed hydrofoils in 1973.

None of these carry SSMs but, with India now deploying the SS-N-2 (Styx) on a large scale, Pakistan may be obliged to reply.

Daphné Patrol Submarine Pakistan

		Laid Down	Launched	Completed
S131	*Hangor*	1967	1969	1970
S132	*Shushuk*	1967	1969	1970
S133	*Mangro*	1968	1970	1970
S134	*Ghazi* (ex-*Cachalote*)	1967	1968	1969

Four near standard French-built Daphné class patrol submarines (qv) of which the first three were built to Pakistani account and the fourth acquired in 1976, from Portugal, who is slimming her naval forces since her withdrawal from colonial territories. Half-a-dozen Type SX404 miniature submersibles are being purchased from the Italian firm of Cosmos. With a submerged displacement of under 70 tons and a length of about 52ft, they carry no offensive armament but are designed to transport up to 12 free-swimming divers for use against hostile installations and anchored shipping.

PR72 FAC (missile) Peru

The Peruvian navy which is in a phase of great expansion, has ordered (1976) six Exocet-armed PR72s from the French SFCN organisation, probably to offset similar missiles carried by craft of the flanking states of Ecuador and Chile. General data for the class can be found by reference to Morocco but, where the latter boats were down-graded versions of the PR72, the Peruvians have taken one of the full specification options.

With four SACM diesels developing 20,000bhp on four shafts, a maximum of 37kts can be realised, against a continuous rating for about 30kts. In addition to the four MM38 Exocet SSMs, a 76mm OTO-Melara gun and a twin Breda 40mm L70 are carried. The builders offer options with Otomat Mk 2 missiles and two twin Oerlikon 35mm mountings. Control is by a Vega system with Triton search radar and Pollux fire control radar. Optical laying can also be effected. The PR72 is a direct competitor to the Combattante III, with which it bears comparison.

Typ 209 Patrol Submarine Peru

		Completed
S45	*Islay*	1974
S46	*Arica*	1975

The above two submarines are standard West German Typ 209s (qv) and are to be joined by a further four, two of which were ordered in 1976 and two in 1977. The 209 has sold well in South

America, creating a 'knock-on' effect in that S45-6 were built concurrently with a similar pair for Colombia to the north. The latter state has coasts on either ocean, encouraging its northern neighbour, Venezuela to acquire two similar boats and then its southern neighbour, Ecuador, flanked also by Peru,

to follow suit. Only Peru's southern neighbour, Chile, has ordered elsewhere, ie a brace of Oberons from the UK. Considered in relation to new acquisitions by Argentina and Brazil on the Atlantic coast there are now a goodly number of modern submarines in South American waters.

Abtao Patrol Submarine

Peru

		Laid Down	Launched	Completed
S41	*Dos de Mayo* (ex-*Lobo*)	1952	1954	1954
S42	*Abtao* (ex-*Tiburon*)	1952	1953	1954
S43	*Angamos* (ex-*Atun*)	1955	1957	1957
S44	*Iquique* (ex-*Merlin*)	1955	1957	1957

Displacement: 825 surfaced
1,400 submerged
Length (oa): 243ft
Beam: 22ft
Draught: 14ft
Machinery: Two diesels (surfaced)
Two drive motors (submerged)
Two shafts 2,400bhp for 16/10kts
Armament: Six 21-inch TTs (four forward two aft)
(one 5-inch gun can be carried)

Interesting boats in being a rare example of the USA building deliberately for export. They were 'stretched' from the design of the pair of Mackerels, then being built for the US Navy and small, simple boats for the purpose of targets and training. At 243ft, they represent a considerable growth on the original 131ft design but, although since modernised in the USA, they lack propulsive power and their submerged 10kts speed is totally inadequate for modern submarine operations. Their life expectancy can be only until the last of the Typ 209s commission and, indeed, they may well bequeath their names.

Ex-US War-built Patrol Submarines

Peru

		Completed
S49	*La Pedrera* (ex-*Pabellon de Pica*; ex-USS *Sea Poacher*, SS406)	1944
S50	*Pacocha* (ex-USS *Atule*, SS403)	1944

This pair of submarines are ex-American Balao class boats (qv) Guppy-ised in the early 1950s and acquired in 1974. Large and slow by modern

standards they yet have the range and endurance to be useful in Pacific waters, and are likely to outlast the Abtao class boats.

Poland

The majority of Polish naval craft have been acquired from the USSR, the remainder are home-built. Twelve Osa I class FAC (missile) are operated and were transferred from the Soviet Navy after 1966. Up to 28 P6 type FAC (torpedo) were also acquired in the late 1950s but these have nearly all now been discarded.

Four Whiskey class patrol submarines were transferred from the USSR in the early 1960s and operate under the names: *Orzel* (292); *Sokol* (293); *Kondor* (294); *Bielik* (295) — all old-established submarine names in the Polish navy.

In addition there is a Polish-built FAC (torpedo) known as the Wisla, which is of a size with the P6s and probably intended as a direct replacement. About 15 are believed to have been built so far and relevant data is as follows:

Displacement: c75 full load
Length (oa): 82ft
Beam: 18ft

Draught: about 5.5ft
Machinery: Probably diesel, speed c35kts
Armament: Four 21-inch TTs
Two 30mm guns (1×2)

Comparable also with a Norwegian Tjeld (qv) the craft is a modern version of the classic MTB with, apparently a metal hull. Two full sized TTs overlap on either side and forward is the familiar helmet-shaped mounting of the twin Soviet 30mm gun. Unlike the average torpedo-armed FAC, the superstructure is high with a distinctive exhaust atop its after end. The size and configuration is a feature which has given rise to speculation regarding gas turbine propulsion, but this seems unlikely on so small a craft.

Daphné Patrol Submarine

Portugal

		Completed
S163	*Albacora*	1967
S164	*Barracuda*	1968
S166	*Delfin*	1969

Three near-standard French Daphné class patrol submarines (qv). Four were built in France to Portuguese account but one, *Cachalote* (S165), was sold to Pakistan in 1975.

Romania

Bordered by the Soviet Union and Bulgaria, and with a short coastline on the restricted and shallow Black Sea, Romania's naval needs are served by a limited number of small fighting ships, including rivurine craft for use on the lower Danube. Until the early 1970s, ties with the Soviets were absolute and ships acquired prior to this time were all from this source. Since then, a degree of independence has been shown including the acquisition of Chinese craft, some of which have then been copied and built in Romanian yards. Ex-Russian craft include the following:

Three Poti class corvettes, transferred about 1967. Three Kronstadt class patrol craft, transferred in the early 1950s, and now of little value.

Up to six Osa I class FAC (missile) transferred in 1964.
About 15 P4 class FAC (torpedo) transferred in the mid-1950s, about 10 still survive but in doubtful condition.

Craft of Chinese origin include:

About 20 Shanghai II class patrol craft, largely built in Romania since 1972. Most are gun-armed but a few are equipped with two Russian-pattern MBU-1200 'flat-five' AS rocket launchers forward.
At least 10 Hu Chwan torpedo-armed hydrofoils. Three were built in China in the early 1970s and the remainder were Romanian built. Construction of both classes continues.

Al Saddiq Corvette

Saudi Arabia

		Contractural Completion
511	*Al Saddiq*	1980
513	*Al Farouq*	1980
515	*Abdul Aziz*	1980
517	*Faisal*	1981
519	*Khalid*	1981
521	*Amyr*	1981
523	*Tariq*	1981
525	*Oqbah*	1982
527	*Abu Obadiah*	1982

Displacement: 720 tons
Length (oa): 234.5ft
Beam: 27.5ft
Draught: 9ft
Machinery: One gas turbine 16,500bhp for 30kts
Two diesels 3,000hp for 20kts
CODOG configuration Two shafts
Armament: Two quadruple Harpoon SSM launchers
One 76mm gun
Two triple AS TTs

For long, Saudi Arabia's marine forces consisted of light patrol craft, backed up by a trio of West German-built Jaguar FACs. With the increasing strength of other Persian Gulf states since the early 1970s came a need for reappraisal and an agreement with the USA to develop and strengthen the Saudi fleet. The 'teeth' of this new construction are contained in two classes of missile carriers from two small but excellent American builders.

From Peterson's, on the Great Lakes' Sturgeon Bay, is coming a nine-strong class of corvette of the type that will show significant growth over the next few years. Like enlarged Asheville class gunboats, their nearest equivalent would appear to be the new Israeli corvette but without its helicopter. The fine lines are a feature of this type and the length/breadth ratio compares interestingly with the tubby Russian Nanuchka of roughly similar function.

Two quadruple Harpoon SSM launchers have been specified, lightweight systems that are gaining in popularity. Besides the 76mm OTO-Melara gun and light automatic weapons, the corvettes will carry also one 81mm and two 40mm mortars, presumably with a view to providing plunging fire support from close inshore, though the hazarding of high-technology, thin-skinned ships to land-based low-trajectory fire would seem precarious.

A lightweight SQS-56 sonar, newly developed by Raytheon from smaller ships, is installed in the keel, backed up by two of the ubiquitous triple Mk 32 AS TTs, although the only submarines domiciled in the Gulf are three Iran boats ex-American and large for such confined and shallow waters. An economic CODOG machinery arrangement has been adopted with a pair of low-power diesels affording a good cruising radius and capable of switching over rapidly to a single General Electric gas turbine for rapid boost to 30kts.

Badr FAC (missile)

Saudi Arabia

		Contractural Completion
612	*Badr*	1980
614	*Al Yarmook*	1981
616	*Hitteen*	1981
618	*Tabuk*	1981

Displacement: 320 tons
Length (oa): 184.5ft
Beam: 25ft
Draught: 6ft
Machinery: One gas turbine 16,500hp for 38kts
Two diesels 1,500hp for 18kts
CODOG configuration two shafts
Armament: Two twin Harpoon SSM launchers
One 76mm gun

The US Navy has little peacetime application for FACs and, being generally unable to match European prices, American builders get little opportunity to build modern, missile-armed FACs. Thus Tacoma Boatbuilding's design for four Saudi boats will afford an interesting comparison with what has become something of a European speciality.

The boats are large, equating directly in size to a Combattante III or PR72 yet carry an armament similar to that of an Iranian Combattante II, a rather smaller craft. Though the 76mm OTO-Melara is an excellent DP weapon with an 85° elevation and firing automatically up to 85rpm it can engage only one aerial target at a time and the light automatic weaponry appears sparse at only a pair of 20mm Oerlikons (a weakness in AA defence repeated also in the larger corvettes also under construction). The Harpoon missiles carry a heavier warhead than an MM38 Exocet (510lb against 360lb) but their longer (50-60 miles) range will be hard to realise without external aid. European designs favour four-diesel, four-shaft machinery systems and this again will provide an intriguing comparison with what must be the smallest CODOG warship yet, a choice probably influenced by a necessity for commonality with the corvettes.

Jaguar FAC (torpedo)

Saudi Arabia

		Completed
—	*Dammam*	1969
—	*Khaibar*	1969
—	*Maccah*	1969

Three standard West German Jaguar class FACs (qv) built by Lürssen to Saudi account and which have formed the core of the naval force for a decade. They have all been recently updated by the builders and will now form a balanced force, with the new gun/missile boats.

P-48 Patrol Craft

Senegal

		Completed
—	*Podor*	1977
—	*Popenguine*	1974
—	*Saint Louis*	1971

Displacement: 250 full load
Length (oa): 156ft
Beam: 23.5ft
Draught: 8ft
Machinery: Two diesels on one shaft
2,400bhp for 23kts
Armament: Two 40mm guns (2 × 1)

A class of metal-hulled patrol craft distinctive by a pronounced sheer forward and a long forward extension of the superstructure. This trio is of low power and of basic armament but has plenty of potential for carrying additional firepower if ever required. A second group of three was built in France

for Tunisia (qv) and carry eight light SS.12M missiles forward but still suffer from low powered machinery. SFCN, the builders, are now offering a variant, known as the 48S, carrying eight SS.12Ms, two 40mm and two 20mm guns and 6,000bhp diesels for a 27kts speed.

Shanghai II FAC (gun)

Sierra Leone

Three of the type were transferred from China in 1973.

Lürssen-type 48m FAC (missile)　　　Singapore

		Completed
P76	*Sea Wolf*	1972
P77	*Sea Lion*	1972
P78	*Sea Dragon*	1974
P79	*Sea Tiger*	1974
P80	*Sea Hawk*	1975
P81	*Sea Scorpion*	1975

Displacement: 230 tons
Length (oa): 158ft
Beam: 23ft
Draught: 7.5ft
Machinery: Four diesels on four shafts
14,400bhp for 37kts
Armament: One 57mm gun
One 40mm gun
Five Gabriel SSM launchers

Typically Lürssen in appearance, the West German yard built the two lead boats and assisted Singapore Shipbuilidng in the construction of the remainder. Oddly, the latter yard build also the Lürssen 45m design under licence and three constructed for Thailand (qv) mount precisely the same armament on the smaller hull. In place of the usually favoured 76mm gun the weapon carried forward is a Bofors 57mm complemented by the common 40mm weapon aft. Five Mk 1 Gabriel SSMs are carried, a triple aft-facing mounting and two facing forward and flanking the bridge superstructure. A Dutch HSA fire control system is fitted and it would seem that the Gabriel launchers are not usually mounted.

Sea Dragon

Vosper Thornycroft 110ft FAC (gun)　　　Singapore

Type A		Completed
P69	*Independence*	1970
P70	*Freedom*	1971
P71	*Justice*	1971
Type B		
P71	*Sovereignty*	1971
P73	*Daring*	1971
P74	*Dauntless*	1971

Displacement: 100 standard
130 full load
Length (oa): 110ft

Beam: 21ft
Draught: 5.5ft
Machinery: Two diesels on two shafts
6,200bhp for 32kts
Armament: Type A
One 40mm gun
One 20mm gun
Type B
One 76mm gun
One 20mm gun

Sovereignty

This short, beamy design is aimed primarily at economical patrol duties and is of comparatively low power. Nevertheless they are an upgraded version of a patrol craft design which has previously been built for both Malaysia and Peru. The Type A boats, with their light armament, carry only basic electronics and have a glazed wheelhouse. The Type B boats, on the other hand, mount a Bofors TAK 76mm gun forward together with Kongsberg fire control (a similar outfit to the Norwegian Storm class). Because of its size the bridge is built a half-deck higher and is unglazed, possibly due to blast effects. The hulls are steel, with a knuckle and spray chine forward, and upperworks are of light alloy. Comfort for the 20-odd crew is enhanced by both full air-conditioning and anti-roll stabilisers. Vosper Thornycroft built the lead boat of both groups in its UK yard and the remainder in its local yard in Singapore.

Somali Republic

Whilst aligned with the Soviet bloc, Somalia was supplied with Russian-built craft as part of an exchange agreement for base rights. These included:

Up to three Osa II class FAC (missile) transferred in 1975.
Four P6 class FAC (torpedo) transferred in 1968.
Up to four Mol class patrol craft, transferred in 1976.

Reshef FAC (missile)   South Africa

Six of these are reported under construction, three by the parent yard in Israel (qv) and the remainder in South Africa.

Daphné Patrol Submarine   South Africa

		Laid Down	Launched	Completed
S97	Maria van Riebeeck	1968	1969	1970
S98	Emily Hobhouse	1968	1969	1971
S99	Johanna van der Merwe	1969	1970	1971

Three French-built Daphné class submarines that bear easily the most unlikely names of their type. Though near-standard boats, it is noteworthy that French export submarines are invariably built in civilian yards (in this case Dubigeon/Normandie) whilst those for the French Navy almost all come from naval yards. The same builders were in addition constructing two Agosta class submarines for South Africa; though one of these had been launched late in 1977 the contract was reneged by UN resolution.

Atrevida Corvette   Spain

		Laid Down	Launched	Completed
F61	Atrevida	1950	1952	1954
F62	Princesa	1953	1956	1957
F64	Nautilus	1953	1956	1959
F65	Villa de Bilbao (ex-Favorita)	1953	1958	1960

Displacement: 1,010 standard
1,135 full load
Length (oa): 248ft
Beam: 33.5ft
Draught: 10ft

Machinery: Two diesels on two shafts
3,000bhp for 18kts
Armament: One 3-inch gun
Three 40mm guns (3 x 1)
Two Hedgehog AS mortars

Atrevida

This quartette are the survivors of a class of six, of which the *Descubierta* (F63) was discarded in 1971 and the *Diana* (F66) in 1973; as these names have already been repeated by the new Descubierta class frigates (of which four are yet to be named) it may presage the demise of the remainder. As they are far from old by Spanish standards it can only be assumed that they have proved a disappointment in service; geared as they are, with Hedgehogs and no less than eight depth charge projectors, to AS warfare their modest power and speed would certainly seem inadequate to render economic a much-needed updating of armament.

Known officially as the F60 class they have exceptionally handsome hulls, somewhat unbalanced by the lack of funnel, the diesel machinery exhausting through the side. As built, they were to carry a German-pattern 4.1-inch in A position, superfired by a twin 37mm; no less than 12 20mm in quadruple mounts were to be sited in tubs aft. They have been modernised, however, and now carry a US-pattern 3-inch 50 forward, superfired by a single 40mm gun, two more of which are mounted aft. A useful feature, once common to Spanish ships, is the ability to carry mines, in this case 20. The earlier tripod mast has been replaced by a less elegant lattice, bearing the antenna of an American SPS-5B general purpose search radar. A small sonar, also of American origin, is fitted.

Lürssen 58mm FAC (gun)   Spain

		Completed
PO1	Lazaga	1975
PO2	Alcedo	1977
PO3	Cadarso	1976
PO4	Villamil	1977
PO5	Bonifaz	1977
PO6	Recalde	1977

Displacement: 275 standard
400 full load
Length (oa): 190.5ft
Beam: 25ft
Draught: 8.5ft
Machinery: Two diesels on two shafts
8,800bhp for 29kts
Armament: One 76mm gun
One 40mm gun
Two 20mm guns

The Spanish navy commonly acquires good foreign designs for its new buildings, often having the lead ship constructed in its country of origin and building the remainder in home yards. During the 1950s a class of Lürssen-designed craft were built under licence, close akin to the S-boat of World War II. That they were satisfactory was evident when a new FAC programme was recently undertaken, with two Lürssen designs being purchased.

The first of these was a large 58m craft based on the Reshef hull, termed by the Spanish the P-OO, of which the first of class *Lazaga* was completed by Lürssen in 1975 and which firm then went on to build the *Dogan*, as lead ship for a Turkish class (qv). The two groups form an interesting comparison for, where the Turks have fitted their boats with full power machinery and a powerful gun/SSM armament, the Spanish required all-weather patrol craft and have opted for a 76mm OTO-Melara forward and a single 40mm gun aft. AS TTs and depth charges can be carried but this is not usual and the decks have an under-utilised air about them although SSMs could be mounted if required. An HSA fire control tops off the bridge, which has conspicuous wings to assist in manoeuvring alongside other craft prior to boarding during fishery protection duties.

Only about 45% of the full designed power has been installed, on two shafts in place of four and developed by MTU engines built under licence by the builders, Bazan. Unused deadweight has resulted in greatly increased bunker capacity, the craft being capable of over 6,000 miles range at 17kts, 50% better than even the long-legged Reshefs. A class of four boats has been ordered from Bazan by Morocco but it is not yet absolutely certain that they will be repeats of the Lazagas.

Alcedo

Lürssen 36m FAC (gun)

Spain

Laya

		Completed
P 11	*Barcelo*	1976
P 12	*Laya*	1976
P 13	*Javier Quiroga*	1977
P 14	*Ordonez*	1977
P 15	*Acevedo*	1977
P 16	*Candido Perez*	1977

Displacement: 135 full load
Length (oa): 119ft
Beam: 19ft
Draught: 6ft
Machinery: Two diesels on two shafts
5,800bhp for 34kts
Armament: One 40mm gun
Two 20mm guns

The second Lürssen design recently acquired by the Spanish navy is the well-proven 36m craft serving already with Chile and Ecuador. Again, the leadship, *Barcelo*, was constructed in West Germany and the remainder following from the La Carraca yard of Bazan. Unlike the other classes, the Spaniards are armed for patrol duties with only light automatic weapons with optical direction, though two 21-inch TTs or SSMs could be accommodated if required. This is again a two-shaft variant, comparatively low powered by Bazan-built MTU diesels. Two further boats of the class have been ordered from the Spanish yard by Mauritania.

Agosta Patrol Submarine

Spain

Four of the type, known as the S70 class and numbered S71-74, are being constructed by Bazan's Cartagena yard for completion from 1981 onward. No French-built lead ship was acquired.

Daphné Patrol Submarine

Spain

		Laid Down	Launched	Completed
S61	*Delfin*	1968	1972	1973
S62	*Tonina*	1969	1972	1973
S63	*Marsopa*	1971	1974	1975
S64	*Narval*	1971	1974	1975

Four of the standard French Daphné class (qv) known to the Spanish as the S-60 type and all built in Spain by Bazan/Cartegena.

Narval

Ex-US Patrol Submarines

Spain

		Laid Down	Launched	Completed
S31	*Almirante Garcia de los Reyes* (ex-USS *Kraken*, SS370)	1943	1944	1944
S32	*Isaac Perel* (ex-USS *Ronquil*, SS396)	1943	1944	1944
S34	*Cosme Garcia* (ex-USS *Bang*, SS385)	1943	1943	1943
S35	— (ex-USS *Jallao*, SS368)	1943	1944	1944

Four ex-American Balao class boats (qv) of which the last three had a Guppy IIA conversion. S31 is still basically a World War II boat, capable of only 10kts submerged and in poor condition. Similarly, a fifth boat, *Narciso Monturiol*, S33 (ex-USS *Picuda*, SS382) was scrapped after machinery failure. All were transferred during 1971-4 (except S31 in 1959) but will be kept in commission only until the new Agostas commission.

Sri Lanka

Following independence in 1972, Sri Lanka (ex-Ceylon) immediately acquired five Shanghai II class FAC (gun) from China. A change of direction was evident by 1975 when a Mol class FAC (gun) was constructed in the USSR for the new navy.

Jägaren FAC (missile)

Sweden

		Completed
P150	*Jägaren*	1972
P151	*Hugin*	1977
P152	*Munin*	1978
P153	*Magne*	—
P154	*Mode*	—
P155	*Vale*	—
P156	*Vidar*	—
P157	*Mjolner*	—
P158	*Nysing*	—
P159	*Kaparen*	—
P160	*Vakoaren*	—
P161	*Snapphanen*	—
P162	*Spejaren*	—
P163	*Styrbjorn*	—
P164	*Starkodder*	—
P165	*Tordon*	—
P166	*Tirfing*	—

Displacement: 115 standard
140 full load
Length (oa): 118ft
Beam: 20.5ft
Draught: 5ft
Machinery: Two diesels on two shafts
7,000bhp for 35kts
Armament: One 57mm gun
Six Penguin Mk 2 SSM
or Four 21-inch TTs

For securing their shallow and constricted offshore waters the Swedish navy has long recognised the value of the torpedo-armed FAC. These have been supported by conventional heavier units of excellent design but it is now accepted that these would have little chance of survival in a Baltic now dominated by the missile and, as they reach their allotted span,

Hugin

they are being disposed of without replacement. It is against this background that the Swedes had built a single boat in 1972 by the Norwegian Batservis Verft for evaluation. Whilst this was being conducted the Norwegians ordered a class of 14 near-identical craft, to become the Hauk class (qv). Sixteen further units were ordered for the Swedish navy, all to be Norwegian-built, the first commissioning as the *Hugin* in 1977.

Their steel hulls are considerably shorter than those of earlier FACs and incorporate much aluminium and laminated wood; superstructure is of GRP. Of round-bilge form the lines are powerful but easily driven by only two propellers. These, interestingly, are powered by twin MTU diesels of obsolete design but which have performed well in the Plejad class for over 20 years. Armament is on a heavier scale than that of the Hauks. Six of the new

Mk 2 Penguin canister/launchers are mounted aft, capable of carrying a 250lb warhead for 15 miles. They can be removed and replaced by a second gun, four torpedo tubes or mines on the fitted rails. Depth charges can also be carried. The single 57mm gun forward is the Bofors L70 model, sealed to operate in NCB conditions and able to fire 40 rounds of ammunition at a rate of 200rpm without reloading. A wide variety of ammunition can be fired, along with chaff or flares from the racks on the sides of the gunhouse. An advanced weapon control system is fitted, developed by Philips from that on the Spica IIs and capable of tracking both surface and aerial targets for gun, torpedo or missile. Electro-optical sights are included for passive laying and a data link enables attack information to be coordinated with that from other craft.

Spica FAC (torpedo)   Sweden

Spica I		Completed
T121	*Spica*	1966
T122	*Sirius*	1966
T123	*Capella*	1966
T124	*Castor*	1967
T125	*Vega*	1967
T126	*Virgo*	1967
Spica II		
T131	*Norrköping*	1973
T132	*Nynashamn*	1973
T133	*Norrtalje*	1974
T134	*Varberg*	1974
T135	*Vasteras*	1974
T136	*Vastervik*	1975
T137	*Umea*	1975
T138	*Pitea*	1975
T139	*Lulea*	1975
T140	*Halmstad*	1976
T141	*Stromstad*	1976
T142	*Ystad*	1976

Displacement: 200 standard
230 full load
Length (oa): 135ft
Beam: 23.5ft
Draught: 5.5ft
Machinery: Three gas turbines on three shafts
12,900bhp for 40kts
Armament: One 57mm gun
Six 21-inch TTs

It is sometimes forgotten that the technology that has produced the guided missile has also considerably improved the gun and torpedo since World War II. Torpedoes have certain advantages

over missiles, not the least being a usually larger warhead delivered below the target's waterline, where it can do the most damage. They can be launched without betraying the launcher's presence and can be of very long range. Some, such as the Swedish navy's TP61, are wire-guided, responding to pulse-coded signals transmitted over a wire paid out by the torpedo. These signals cannot be readily jammed by the target, even if the torpedo has been detected, and final approach is often guided by passive homing on the target's generated noise.

The two groups of Spicas were designed around these formidable weapons and, used in combination with the new SSM-armed Jägarens, present a very real threat to anyone violating Swedish waters. As no missiles are fitted, the superstructure is set far aft to give the 57mm Bofors gun a maximum firing arc (and also a distinctive profile, which resembles the Danish Willomoes class). Hulls are beautifully seaworthy and are powerfully built of steel to withstand the pounding of short Baltic seas and the abrasive effect of the winter ice typical of the area.

The Spica I group of six craft with astronomical names proved so successful that they were followed, after a full six years, by the 12 near-identical Spica-IIs, named after smaller Swedish towns. Both groups have the same armament of gun and six TTs, and it is worthy of note that, on both the Spicas and the newly building Jägarens, the 40 or 35mm secondary armament usual on FACs is lacking. Defence against aircraft or helicopter is thus dependent entirely upon the 57mm gun and, on the Jägarens, this has a rather limited arc. They are high speed boats, with a Proteus gas turbine on each of three shafts, no cruising diesels are fitted as in the later Willomoes.

Spica (Spica I class)

Norrköping (Spica II class)

Higher superstructure, crowned by the radome of an HSA M22 system, makes the Spica I easily recognisable from a II, which has a Philips electronics fit.

It has been mooted that both groups lose their after pair of TTs in favour of two SSM launchers, these possibly of a long-range Harpoon type rather than the 15-mile Penguin Mk 2. Malaysia has ordered four lightly-armed, diesel propelled Spicas for 1979 delivery.

Plejad FAC (torpedo)

Sweden

		Completed
T107	*Aldebaran*	1956
T110	*Arcturus*	1957
T112	*Astraea*	1956

Displacement: 155 standard
170 full load
Length (oa): 148ft
Beam: 19ft
Draught: 5ft
Machinery: Three diesels on three shafts
9,000bhp for 37kts
Armament: Two 40mm guns (2 × 1)
Six 21-inch TTs
Disposals: *Plejad* (T102); *Polaris* (T103); *Pollux* (T104); *Regulus* (T105) and *Rigel* (T106) in 1976. *Altair* (T108); *Antares* (T109) and Argo (T111) in 1977

Up to the 1950s Swedish FACs were based heavily on the MTB of World War II, a type now represented only by the T42s (qv). They lacked both the range and sea-keeping qualities now required and a prototype gun/torpedo boat of larger dimensions was ordered from West Germany's Lürssen yard. This was launched in 1950 as the *Perseus* (T101), of high diesel power and sporting a small funnel. Though capable of 40kts, she was not entirely successful and discarded after proving the parameters against which 11 further boats were to be built, again in Germany. Ten feet were added to these production hulls to improve seakeeping and allow for the installation of two further TTs in what is now a peculiarly Swedish layout of a pair sided forward and a further two closely overlapping on either side, aft. These can be removed to expose minelaying rails.

The bridge structure is clean-lined and capable of

Plejad

being manned under fall-out conditions, but presents a massive profile. Open 40mm mountings have now been enclosed and can be remotely controlled. Extra antennas have demanded the bracing of the pole mast. The high power of the prototypes was reduced to only 7,800bhp for the first six production boats, delivered by a Mercedes Benz engine on each of three shafts. This was increased to 9,000bhp on the last five, T108-112.

Rather longer than later classes, the Plejad also gave Lürssens a basis for the design of the Jaguar (qv) then being prepared, the latter being shorter but beamier. Like the Jaguars, the class is being discarded but for scrap rather than transfer.

T42 FAC (torpedo) — Sweden

	Completed
T46-49	1957
T50-53	1958
T54-56	1959

Displacement: 44 tons
Length (oa): 75.5ft
Beam: 19ft
Draught: 4.5ft
Machinery: Three petrol engines on three shafts 4,500bhp for 45kts
Armament: One 40mm gun
Two 21-inch TTs
Disposals: T42-45 converted in 1977 to patrol craft. Diesel propulsion and no TTs

Virtual repeats of the T32 class of 1951-2 the little T42s are the last of the once-numerous fleet of Swedish boats built after the style of the MTB of World War II. Though having steel hulls, they are very similar in size, layout and power to the wooden-hulled British Gay class of 1954. Of limited endurance, they are also not capable of the coordinated attacks of modern craft with data links. Four have already been discarded from front-line service and the retention of the remainder is rather puzzling.

Like the British boats, the T42s have petrol engines, which present great fire hazards for the close-in fighting that might be expected of them. Where the Gays were interim boats, built before the Deltic diesel was fully evaluated, the T42s have hung on to their Isotta-Fraschini engines, long after it may reasonably be expected that diesels might have been substituted.

The hard-chine, high-freeboard hull is typical of the type, with pronounced deck camber for shedding loosewater. Unusually, the single 40mm gun is mounted in a sheltered position aft. Since the photograph was taken, the foredeck flare launcher has been exchanged for a single 12-rail mounting for 57mm projectiles, and a later radar and communications antennas fitted. Only two long TTs are carried.

T42

Näcken Patrol Submarine — Sweden

		Completed
Nak	Näcken	1977
Naj	Najad	1978
Nep	Neptun	1978

Displacement: 980 surfaced
1,125 submerged
Length (oa): 135ft
Beam: 20ft
Draught: 16.5ft
Machinery: Two diesel-generators powering the one propulsive motor Single shaft
c2,300bhp for 20/20kts
Armament: Six 21-inch TTs

Näcken: launch picture, note temporary flotation tanks.

Sweden's traditionally neutral stance envisages war on only a defensive basis and being fought largely in home waters. These are constricted and suit the small handy type of submarine which has, till now, not possessed either great range or diving powers. The new Näckens, repeating names of a trio of World War II minelaying submarines, are designed with a safe depth of 300m and a collapse depth of 500, and appear to be aimed at operations in the deeper trenches in the Skagerrak to the west.

An improved and smaller Sjöormen, the Näcken packs an eight-tube battery forward, firing either the wakeless and wire-guided M61 anti-ship torpedo or the smaller M42 AS torpedo, also wire-guided and small enough to be shipped two to a tube and 'swum-out' as required. Mines can also be carried but have to be ejected.

The picture, of *Näcken* being launched by crane, shows well the cylindrical lines and long casing (the side tanks are temporary flotation aids). The two-by-two TTs, closed by flush-fitting bow caps, are evident as is the X-configuration of the control surfaces aft. Each of these act as part hydroplane, part-rudder and, along with the fin-mounted planes, are fully

computer-controlled and giving — so the Swedes claim — superior manoeuvring and slow-speed depth keeping to the conventional cruciform layout. At the time of launch the propeller was not fitted but it is a large-diameter, five-bladed type, manufactured from a special high-damping alloy designed to reduce 'singing'; further radiated noise, from cavitation, is minimised by good design and low rate of revolution. It is driven by a double-armature motor, capable of accurate control and cooled for optimum operation, as are the main batteries. All machinery is specially mounted for minimum noise and designed to withstand the high shock levels of nearby explosions, the effect of which can be much magnified in shallow waters. A wide use of automation has kept the crew to the low 20s.

The official designation of the class is the A14 and a new type A17 is already under design, though no details have yet been announced. A recent development is the URF, a 44ft rescue submarine capable of locking on to the escape hatches of any sunken Swedish submarine. Up to 25 men can be brought up per trip from up to 500m (1,600ft) depth, even with the wreck listing up to 20 degrees.

Sjöormen Patrol Submarine   Sweden

		Laid Down	Launched	Completed
Sor	*Sjöormen*	1965	1967	1967
Sle	*Sjölejonet*	1966	1967	1968
Shu	*Sjöhunden*	1966	1968	1969
Sbj	*Sjöbjornen*	1967	1968	1969
Sha	*Sjöhasten*	1966	1968	1969

Sjöhunden

Sjöormen

Displacement: 1,125 surfaced
1,400 submerged
Length (oa): 168ft
Beam: 20ft
Draught: 16.5ft
Machinery: Two diesels driving four generators
One propulsion motor Single shaft
2,200/3,500bhp for 15/20kts
Armament: Four 21-inch TTs
Two 15.75-inch (400mm) AS TTs

In contrast with the Näckens, the Sjöormen/A11B class is depth-limited to only 500ft for operations within the Baltic. Their design owed much to the American Albacore high-speed hull, whose diagonally-mounted control surfaces were also adopted. A long casing is fitted and a large fin of distinctive shape incorporating diving planes. Operating in such shallow waters, a sunken boat is

likely to reach the bottom before passing her collapse depth and the class's survivability is enhanced by a large reserve buoyancy, expressed as the relationship between surfaced and submerged tonnages. Further, the deep tear-drop hull section allowed for comprehensive horizontal, as well as vertical, sub-division.

They can be operated by as few as 18 men, of whom as many as 40% are officers, reflecting the high technical content of both armament and machinery control. Endurance is up to three weeks in what is one of the worst possible areas for submarine operations. Only four full-size TTs are carried, in addition to two smaller tubes for firing M41 of M42 AS torpedoes. Again, great attention has been paid to machinery silence and there are four battery packs, capable of series-parallel or series connection for normal or high-speed running.

Hajen Patrol Submarine   Sweden

		Type A	**Type B**
Displacement:	surfaced	785	835
	submerged	1,000	1,110
Length (oa):		217ft	228ft
Beam:		16.5ft	16.5ft
Draught:		16.5ft	16.5ft
Machinery:		Two diesel-generators driving two propulsion motors Two shafts 1,700bhp for 16/17kts	Two diesel-generators driving one propulsion motor Single shaft 1,700bhp for 17/20kts
Armament:		Four 21-inch TTs	Four 21-inch TTs

Type A		**Completed**
Bav	*Bavern*	1959
Haj	*Hajen*	1957
Iln	*Illern*	1959
Sal	*Salen*	1957
Utn	*Uttern*	1960
Val	*Valen*	1957
Type B		
Del	*Delfinen*	1962
Dra	*Draken*	1962
Gri	*Gripen*	1962
Nor	*Nordkaparen*	1962
Spr	*Springaren*	1962
Vgn	*Vargen*	1961

The Hajen class consists of two distinct groups of boats, each six strong; the first group was completed in 1957-60 and the second, known as the A11, or Draken, class in 1961-2. Though looking very similar they differ fundamentally in the arrangement aft, with the Type As firmly based on the German Type XXI and having its twin-screw layout with small-diameter propellers. Type B has a more modern arrangement, with a single large-diameter propeller and cruciform control surfaces, detectable by the upper rudder projecting above the surface of the water. An extra 11ft has been added to length; some of this can be accounted for by refined after lines though extra internal space for improved electronics and larger batteries is also likely. Either type is powered by two Pielstick medium-speed diesels and the shaft horsepower developed by the

Hajen (now has identification letters 'Haj')

Draken (now has identification letters 'Dra')

propulsion motors (two in Type A, one in Type B) is the same, so any increase in battery volume is devoted to capacity rather than extra cells for speed.

During the two decades since the Hajens started to commission, submarine design has changed dramatically and the long, slim hull with its near 13:1 length-to-breadth ratio contrasts with the tubby Näckens of about 7:1. A large number of external fittings are also evident, interrupting clean water flow over the hull and generating unwanted,

cavitation noise. The fin is reminiscent of the early 'Guppy' boats, with a low conning position backed by a tapered fairing containing the higher periscope standards.

As Sweden's first postwar design they are limited endurance boats whose crew, at 44, is double the size of modern designs. Only four TTs are carried, all forward, with eight reserve torpedoes. Like all Swedish submarines they carry identification letters on their fins, rather than pennant numbers.

Syria

This state operates a small, but powerful, force of craft, all supplied by the Soviet Union to counter Israeli strength to the south. Though they have performed consistently badly in various encounters, their strength has been maintained and a significant new acquisition was a pair of Petya I class corvettes in 1975 and 1976.

Other craft operated include:

Six Osa I class FAC (missile) transferred in the early 1970s

About six Komar class FAC (missile) transferred about 1965.

Almost 20 P4 class FAC (torpedo) were transferred in the last 1950s but the operational value of any survivors is now low.

PSMM-type FAC (missile)

These craft are based on the American Asheville class (qv) and two are operated, one built by the lead yard of Tacoma Boatbuilding and the other a home-built copy. Another 13 were cancelled, ostensibly for financial reasons but probably an early example of the USA's change of attitude toward Taiwan prior to

Taiwan

recognising the status of Red China. Though Taiwan can build the hulls, equipment and machinery is primarily American in origin. That those built are reportedly equipped with four Otomat SSMs may indicate that the Standard MR was not made available.

Ex-US Patrol Submarines   Taiwan

		Launched	Completed
SS91	*Hai Chih* (ex-USS *Cutlass*, SS478)	1944	1945
SS92	*Hai Pao* (ex-USS *Tusk*, SS426)	1945	1946

Two ex-American Tench class boats which underwent a Guppy II (qv) rebuilding. Both acquired in 1973 but provision of spares may now be a problem.

Tanzania

Another state adept at obtaining warships from both the Soviet Union and China though, of late, preference would appear to be toward the latter. Only torpedo and gun-armed craft are operated at present, and include:

Seven Shanghai II class FAC (gun), transferred from China in 1970-1.

Four Hu Chwan class hydrofoils, transferred from China in 1975-6.
Three P6 class FAC (torpedo). These were acquired via East Germany in 1975 and probably have no TTs. Probably four P4 class FAC; again likely to be only gun-armed.

Tapi Corvette   Thailand

		Laid Down	Launched	Completed
5	*Tapi* (ex-PF107)	1970	1970	1971
6	*Khirirat* (ex-PF108)	1972	1973	1974

Two corvettes identical with the Iranian Bayandor class (qv). Also built in the US, their PF designation follows on from the earlier class.

PC-type Patrol Craft   Thailand

PC1 *Sarasin* (ex-PC495); PC2 *Thayanchon* (ex-PC575); PC4 *Phali* (ex-PC1185); PC5 *Sukrip* (ex-PC1218); PC6 *Tongpliu* (ex-PC616); PC7 *Liulom* (ex-PC-1253); PC8 *Longlom* (ex-PC570)

Seven US-built PC-boats completed 1942-4 closely similar to the French Le Fougueux (qv) built to same design. Transferred 1947-52. Eighth unit, *Khamronsin* (PC3; ex-PC609) discarded 1956.

Trad Patrol Craft   Thailand

		Completed
13	*Pattani*	1937
21	*Surasdra*	1937
22	*Chandhaburi*	1937
23	*Rayong*	1938

Displacement: 320 standard
470 full load
Length (oa): 223ft
Beam: 21ft
Draught: 7ft
Machinery: Geared steam turbines two shafts 9,000hp for 31kts (designed)
Armament: Two 3-inch guns (2 × 1)
One 40mm gun
Four 18-inch TTs (2 × 2)
Disposals: *Chumporn; Phuket; Trad* 1976
Sunk: *Cholburi; Songkhla* 1941

This extraordinarily long-lived quartet are the survivors of a class of nine built by the old CRDA yard at Monfalcone, Italy. Built in the style of the Italian 'torpedo boat', common at the time, they look considerably larger than their true size. Armament and machinery were supplied by the UK.

As built they shipped a heavier armament than at present, with a third 3-inch gun in the bandstand abaft the funnel. In addition to the two existing pairs of TTs two single tubes were also sided immediately abaft the hance. Torpedoes of this calibre are now very rare and probably in short supply; their warheads are too small to inflict fatal damage on a ship of any size, except by a very fortunate chance.

Capable on speed trials of driving the ships at 34kts on about 10,000 developed hp, the machinery must now be on its last legs. Three of the class were discarded in 1976 and the remainder must soon follow as the new FACs commission, craft with immeasurably greater firepower but requiring only half the crew. These ships and the Italian Ape are the only examples remaining of this type and their passing will signal another species extinct.

Lürssen-type 45m FAC (missile)   Thailand

		Completed
1	*Prabparapak*	1976
2	*Hanhak Sattru*	1976
3	*Suphairin*	1977

Built under licence by Singapore Shipbuilding, this trio have the same data as the Quito class Lürssens

built for Ecuador (qv) except for the weapon fit. This parallels that of the Lürssen 48mm (Sea Wolf) type produced by the same builders for Singapore, ie a 57mm Bofors gun forward, a single 40mm aft and five Gabriel I launchers, two fixed facing forward and three on a common rotating mount abaft them.

Breda 50m FAC (missile)   Thailand

		Completed
4	*Ratcharit*	1979
5	*Witthayakhom*	1979
6	*Udomdet*	1979

Displacement: 235 standard
270 full load
Length (oa): 163.5ft
Beam: 24.5ft
Draught: 5.5ft
Machinery: Three diesels on three shafts
13,500bhp for 36kts
Armament: Four MM38 Exocet SSM launchers
One 76mm gun
One 40mm gun

Though offering a plethora of FAC designs for construction, Italian yards have, so far, had little luck in acquiring orders and this class represents something of a breakthrough for the Venice yard of Cantiere Navale Breda. This is the more surprising

when it is considered that Thailand already operates a trio of locally-built Lürssen 45m FACs and these can carry an identical armament to the new boats (cf Quito class under Ecuador). Indeed, it becomes more apparent that the great competition between building yards is really about building the hull and fitting it out, for the weaponry is rapidly becoming standard, together with its layout.

Here again we see the OTO-Melara 76mm gun forward and a Breda-pattern 76-calibre 40mm right aft. Four MM38 Exocet SSM canister-launchers are set further aft than usual and the proximity of the 40mm weapon means that they are set at an unusually large angle to the centre line of the ship. The radome of a WM20 fire control radar is sited atop a low, broad-based lattice mast. Only three shafts are fitted each driven by an MTU diesel and it is interesting that the (pre-trials) data listed credits a speed higher than that of the slightly smaller Lürssen — on a lower power. 20kts can be sustained using the centre-line shaft alone.

Spica-M Patrol Boat   Trinidad & Tobago

Two much-modified Spicas are being built by the Swedish Karlskronavarvet. Only the hull is really a Spica, bearing an enlarged superstructure amidships, a 40mm gun forward and a 20mm aft. Power is limited to 4,000bhp on (probably) two shafts and a

well-proportioned funnel has been added for prestige. Only basic electronics are supplied as a condition of sale but the craft are still capable of near 30kts and could be adapted for SSMs if required.

Le Fougueux Patrol Craft   Tunisia

Sakiet Sidi Youssef

		Completed
P303	*Sakiet Sidi Youssef*	1955

A standard French-built Le Fougueux class ship (qv) constructed with US funds to their number PC1618;

the French designation was P9 with, apparently, no name. In 1957 she was acquired by the West German navy and acted as an AS trials ship under the 'name' *UW12*, finally being transferred to Tunisia in 1969.

P-48 Patrol Craft   Tunisia

		Completed
P301	*Bizerte*	1970
P302	*Horriya (ex-Liberte)*	1970
P304	*Monastir*	1975

Three French-built patrol craft identical in all important respects to those built for Senegal (qv) but carrying launchers for eight small SS.12M SSMs forward of the bridge.

From left to right: *Monastir, Bizerte, Horriya*

Lürssen 58m FAC (missile)   Turkey

		Completed
P340	*Dogan*	1976
P341	*Marti*	1978
P342	*Tayfun*	1979
P343	*Volkan*	1980?

This group of boats is broadly similar to the Spanish Lazaga class (qv) and again the lead ship was built in the parent yard of Lürssen. The Turkish craft vary greatly in both their armament and installed power, however. An OTO-Melara 76mm gun is mounted

Dogan

forward and a twin Oerlikon 35mm mounting aft. Unusually, the chosen SSMs are American Harpoons; these are far more compact than the more common MM38 Exocet and eight can be carried in two quadruple launchers. A WM27 weapon control is fitted, built by the Dutch HSA concern. Unlike the Spanish and Moroccan boats, the Dogans are built as FACs and not primarily for patrol duties and they have four shafts, each powered by an MTU diesel with a maximum power of 18,000bhp for 38kts.

Jaguar FAC (missile or torpedo)   Turkey

Melten

Group A		Completed
P321	*Denizkusu*	1967
P322	*Atmaca*	1967
P323	*Sahin*	1967
P324	*Kartal*	1967
P325	*Melten*	1968
P326	*Pelikan*	1968
P327	*Albatros*	1968
P328	*Simsek*	1968
P329	*Kasirga*	1967
Group B		
P330	*Firtina* (ex-P6086, *Pelikan*)	1962
P331	*Tufan* (ex-P6085, *Storch*)	1962
P332	*Kilic* (ex-P6065, *Löwe*)	1960
P333	*Mizrak* (ex-P6087, *Hähner*)	1962
P334	*Yildiz* (ex-P6063, *Tiger*)	1959
P335	*Kalkan* (ex-P6062, *Wolf*)	1959
P336	*Karayel* (ex-P6090, *Pinguin*)	1962

Both groups of craft are standard West German Jaguars (qv). Group A boats were built by Lürssen to Turkish account and, of these, five appear to have been fitted with four Penguin SSM launchers, right aft, in place of the after TTs. It is now reported that they have been armed with Harpoons but this is not confirmed. Penguin-armed boats believed to be P322, 325, 326, 327 and 329.

All Group B are ex-Bundesmarine and transferred in 1975-6. Their wooden hulls are feeling their age and an earlier discarded trio: *Alk* (P6084); *Fuchs* (P6066); and *Reiher* (P6089) were also transferred as a source of spare parts. All are torpedo-armed.

Tjeld FAC (torpedo)   Turkey

P337 *Girne*

In 1976 the first boat built in Turkey to the Norwegian Tjeld/Nasty design (qv) was completed and commissioned. She was named *Girne* and whether she is merely for evaluation or is the first of an extended series is not yet clear although two ex-German Tjelds have been run by the Turks prior to 1973. The last of the Norwegian craft was completed in 1962.

Asheville Patrol Gunboat   Turkey

		Completed
P338	*Yildirim* (ex-USS *Defiance*, PG95)	1969
P339	*Bora* (ex-USS *Surprise*, PG97)	1969

Two standard ex-US Asheville class PGs (qv) acquired in 1973, and their short life under American colours will be noted. Neither is missile-armed.

SAR-33 FAC (patrol)   Turkey

Displacement: c200 tons
Length (oa): 110ft
Beam: 28.5ft
Draught: 10ft

Machinery: Three diesels on three shafts 12,000bhp for 40kts
Armament: One 40mm gun
Two 12.7mm guns (1 × 2)

SAR 33-class with full strike armament.

Leadship on builders' trials before armament was fitted.

So much does Lürssen dominate the German FAC market that one tends to forget that there are several other yards in the Federal Republic equally capable of producing excellent designs. Such a yard is that of Abeking and Rasmussen just across the Weser at Lemwerder and associated normally with minesweepers or commercial craft. They completed in 1977 the lead ship of a planned class of 14 for coastal patrol duties with the Turkish Gendarmerie and it is possible that the remainder will be built under licence in Turkey. They are comparatively lightly armed for their police duties but are well capable of being rearmed and absorbed into the regular Turkish navy as necessary. Armament options which can be carried include a 76mm OTO-Melara or 57mm Bofors gun forward with two Exocet or four Penguin SSMs, or two torpedo tubes

in line with usual FAC practice. HSA fire control is also specified.

It is the craft itself that is so unusual, with lines embodying an aggressiveness all of their own. The after half of the 33m length is parallel-bodied and of flat V-form in an age when round bilges predominate. A distinctive spray deflector follows the edge of the hard chine and the bows are heavily raked, with a reverse sheer with Gallic overtones. The overall impression is that the boat would pound heavily in adverse conditions but trials reports would seem to contradict this. Unusually, French diesels are installed in the prototype, possibly for dimensional reasons, and drive the three shafts through Vee-type gearboxes. Altogether a refreshing new design which will be worth watching.

PC-type Patrol Craft Turkey

		Completed
P 111	Sultanhisar	1963
P 112	Demirhisar	1963
P 113	Yarhisar	1963
P 114	Akhisar	1963
P 115	Sivrihisar	1963
P 116	Kochisar	1965

Six patrol craft built in the 1960s to the World War II 173ft PC design (qv) and almost identical with the French Le Fougueux but lacking a funnel. All were American funded and the first five were US-built, the last, Kochisar, coming from a home yard.

Typ 209 Patrol Submarine   Turkey

Atilay

		Completed	
S347	*Atilay*	1975	
S348	*Saldiray*	1977	
S349	*Batiray*	1979	Scheduled
S350	*Yildiray*	1980	

Four standard West German Typ 209s (qv) with the difference that S349 and S350 are being built in

Turkey by the Naval Yard at Golcuk. These are the first Turkish-built submarines, by the yard that recently completed the two Berk class frigates. With FACs also now home-built there seems to be a movement toward the Spanish system of acquiring suitable good foreign designs with the lead ship also coming from its country of origin, in the case of the 209s from the Howaldtswerke at Kiel.

Ex-US Patrol Submarines   Turkey

S333 *Ikinci Inonu* (ex-USS *Corporal*, SS346); S335 *Burak Reis* (ex-USS *Seafox*, SS402); S336 *Murat Reis* (ex-USS *Razorback*, SS394); S337 *Oruc Reis* (ex-USS *Pomfret*, SS391); S338 *Uluc Ali Reis* (ex-USS *Thornback*, SS418); S340 *Gerbe* (ex-USS *Trutta*, SS421); S341 *Canakkale* (ex-USS *Cobbler*, SS344); S345 *Prevese* (ex-USS *Entemedor*, SS340); S346 *Birinci Inonu* (ex-USS *Threadfin*, SS410)

Of this group, S341 and 343 are Guppy III conversions of the US Balao class submarine transferred in 1973 with an extra 20ft section added

to increase the power by the addition of a fourth diesel motor to give a surface speed of 20kts, compared with the Guppy IIA's 17kts. Submerged propulsion machinery remained unchanged for a maximum of 15kts. It is reported that SS343, *Clamagore* and SS416 *Tiru*, are also to be acquired. The remainder are Guppy IIA conversions, all of Balao class boats except S338 and 340, which are of the improved Tench class. All were transferred between 1970 and 1973.

Since World War II Turkey has acquired and discarded submarines which largely repeat the above names. To avoid confusion these were as follows:

			Discarded
S330	*Birinci Inonu* (ex-USS *Brill*, SS330)		1973
S333	*Canakkale* (ex-USS *Bumper*, SS333)		1973
S341	*Cerbe* (ex-USS *Hammerhead*)		1973
S339	*Dunlupinar* (ex-USS *Caiman*, SS323)	sunk	1953
S334	*Gur* (ex-USS *Chub*, SS329)		1974
S344	*Hizar Reis* (ex-USS *Miro*, SS378)		1977
S331	*Ikinci Inonu* (ex-USS *Blueback*, SS326)		1973
S332	*Sakanya* (ex-USS *Boarfish*, SS327)		1974
S342	*Tergut Reis* (ex-USS *Bergall*, SS320)		1977

Island Patrol Craft   United Kingdom

		Completed
P295	*Jersey*	1976
P297	*Guernsey*	1977
P298	*Shetland*	1977
P299	*Orkney*	1977
P300	*Lindisfarne*	1978
P	*Alderney*	—
P	*Anglesey*	—

Displacement: 925 standard
1,250 full load
Length (oa): 195ft
Beam: 36ft
Draught: 14ft
Machinery: Two diesels on one shaft
4,400bhp for 16kts
Armament: One 40mm gun

Shetland: note fishery protection pennant painted on funnel casing.

Exploitation of offshore mineral resources inevitably results in a proliferation of expensive structures, vital to the national economy and vulnerable to attack, not only in war but also to extremist organisations in peace. Widely scattered over the continental shelf they are difficult to police and first reaction to an emergency would probably be by helicopter with heavier backup by warship in slower time. The Royal Navy is deficient in suitable craft between the Blackwood class frigates and the Ton class coastal minesweepers, both of which are, in any case, being phased out. A new type was, therefore, required for day to day tasks, calling for good range and seakeeping qualities. It was widely expected that a 'regular' warship along the lines of a French A69 corvette would be produced and it came as a surprise when the well-known trawler yard of Hall, Russell at Aberdeen built the Islands.

Since entering service the class has been severely criticised as being too slow, too expensive, underarmed and lacking a helicopter. The handsome, trawler-type hull with its single screw was presumably chosen for economy and the initial cost was certainly disappointingly high but speed is not a part of the ship's function as fast reaction would normally be the province of the nearest 'regular' warship or craft such as the Jetfoil (qv) should it be adopted. As for armament, it does not look impressive but it is difficult to see what extra flexibility would be gained by, say, a 76mm. The lack of a helicopter is probably the greatest deficiency as the Islands work also in fishery protection and their 16kts speed has no margin over the average free-running trawler, making apprehension difficult. (Here the Danish-built but British designed Osprey would offer much.)

In their favour, the ships are superb seaboats with a cruising range better than 7,000 miles and able to stay with it long after high speed marine exotica on foils, air bubbles and planing hulls have gone home. They make ideal first commands, and breed seamen in the best sense of the word. As if to answer critics, two more to be named *Alderney* and *Anglesey* have recently been ordered but the magnitude of the task of covering the whole EEZ will certainly require further craft of greater capability. Designed on mercantile lines, the Islands can be cheaply manned by a crew of only 24 in accommodation spacious by naval standards. A detachment of 16 marines can also be carried.

Speedy Jetfoil   United Kingdom

Artist's impression of Jetfoil.

A specially-configured 115-ton version of the American Boeing Jetfoil (qv) was ordered for delivery late-1979 in order to evaluate the type for offshore patrol and fishery protection duties. The artist's impression shows it to be very similar to the commercial model with the lower passenger deck plated-in for accommodation and the upper deck largely removed, giving space for two rigid inflatables and their lightweight derricks. Armament is normally a nominal brace of 20mm guns but Harpoon SSMs could be shipped, no doubt, if required. The example shown carries the Fishery Protection pennant over the bridge and it may well be in this field rather than in the long offshore patrols that the craft is better suited, as EEC fishing regulations become ever more complex. The results of the evaluation will be interesting.

Scimitar and Tenacity FAC

United Kingdom

Sabre

	Scimitar	**Tenacity**
Displacement: standard	—	165
full load	102	220
Length (oa):	100ft	144.5ft
Beam:	26.5ft	26.5ft
Draught:	6.5ft	8ft
Machinery:	Two gas turbines and two diesels CODAG arrangement Two shafts 9,000bhp for 40kts	Three gas turbines and two diesels CODAG arrangement Three shafts 12,750bhp for 40kts
Armament:	Normally unarmed	

		Completed
P271	*Scimitar*	1970
P274	*Cutlass*	1970
P275	*Sabre*	1971
P276	*Tenacity*	1973

Like the essentially 'blue-water' navies of France and the USA, the Royal Navy has little peacetime requirement for FACs except for exercise purposes. Design and construction expertise is, however, maintained by a booming worldwide demand for this type of craft for smaller fleets. It is this very proliferation of foreign missile-carrying FACs that compels the RN to maintain the above boats, used to simulate 'enemy' counterparts, endeavouring to get within potential launch range of the exercising ship. A trans-sonic SSM launched from horizon range gives the target a maximum of three minutes to detect and react, though the best solution is not to allow any launch in the first place. The modern shipborne gun is of a high rate of fire but of a calibre too small to be effective at sufficient range and the average FAC is too nimble and too small a target to be attractive to an SSM. A helicopter, carrying suitable radar and air-to-surface missiles, such as the Sea Skua, offers the best solution, except for a saturation attack. Once the enemy has launched, the target has to employ counter tactics such as ECM, IR decoys or rapid-bloom chaff, singly or in combination, in an effort to confuse the incoming hardware.

The trio of Scimitars that form the permanent training flotilla are twin-screw variants of the well-proven Vosper Brave design, of which examples still survive in the navies of Denmark, Greece and Libya. Where these had three Proteus GTs for 55kts, the Scimitars have a two-GT, two diesel installation in a CODAG arrangement, giving a maximum of about 40kts but also an economic cruising range of 1,500 miles on diesels alone. Space has been left for a third, centreline GT and shaft should it be required. The GTs exhaust through the transom and take in air at the after end of the main superstructure. Whilst no armament is carried in the training role, the usual range of weaponry could easily be shipped. Construction is of laminated wood on wooden frames with GRP superstructure.

Other than the Scimitars, the RN's only active FAC is the *Tenacity*, a one-off speculative craft from VT, designed to carry four Sea Killer-sized SSMs aft and of the same order of size as a Combattante II; she has the more usual FAC steel hull and light alloy superstructure. Though often used in a training role *Tenacity's* superior seakeeping and 2,500-mile cruising range makes her suitable also for Fishery Protection duties. She has three Proteus GTs on three shafts with cruising diesels on wing shafts only.

Hovercraft
Data: BH7
Weight: 50 tons maximum
Dimensions: 78.5ft×45.4ft
Machinery: One Proteus gas turbine
4,250hp for about 55kts
Armament: Normally unarmed, but light automatic weapons or SSMs can be fitted.
See photo under Iranian section

United Kingdom

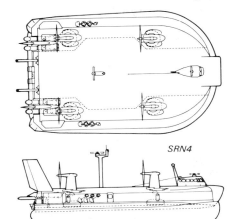

SRN4

Ever since their introduction, the hovercraft's role — if any — in the Royal Navy has been a contentious issue. Interest has centred on smallish types with flexible sidewalls, like the Russians but counter to American activity, which is geared to the rigid sidewall in an SES programme aimed at producing a frigate-sized AS vehicle. Years of evaluation in the UK have shown the SRN6 to be a useful small assault craft for personnel only though inhibited by its noise. Fitted with a forward ramp, the larger BH7 can carry both personnel and light wheeled vehicles or it can operate, like the Iranian craft, in an FAC capacity, though its smallish range, noise, large radar profile and general vulnerability would seem to make it an expensive second-best to the orthodox FAC.

More promising would seem to be a development to which the RN has not yet made any commitment, the large commercial SRN4 in the mine countermeasures role (MCM). Modern mining is a very complex business, embracing the familiar contact mine (probably best swept by commercial type trawlers with automatic winches), the magnetic and acoustic (swept usually by exploding through the influence of towed sweeps) and the pressure type.

The last-named, particularly when combined with one of the other types and with delay mechanisms, is exceptionally difficult to counter and has triggered the development of the GRP-hulled Hunt class MCMV with a price tag of £25million apiece. Located by high-definition sonars, a device on the seabed is neutralised by countermining using either divers or remotely-controlled small submersibles such as the French-made PAP. Though they have extremely low magnetic and acoustic signatures, these ships are still fair game to the pressure mine. On the other hand, the SRN4 is almost totally non-magnetic and generates little water-transmitted noise or pressure whilst hovering. Even a mine

exploding directly beneath a hovering craft does little damage due to the destructive shock wave not being transmitted to the hull.

Much larger than the BH7, the SRN4 has dimensions of about 130ft×83ft and its designed maximum of 220 tons gives a payload of 60 tons and enough fuel for a 10-hour mission. This gives her the ability to operate as a conventional towing sweeper with the Oropesa gear to counter moored mines, the Osborn acoustic sweep or the Magnetic Loop. As a hunter and disposal craft she carries the PAP104 and the French DUBM40 dipping sonar together with ancillary gear. In any of these modes the embarked gear is not permanent and can rapidly be stripped to re-establish the craft's amphibious capacity. The cost of an N4 is about two thirds that of a Hunt — it has inferior endurance but great versatility.

It would certainly appear that the hovercraft would best be employed in a low-threat environment rather than as an attack craft and the SRN4 may well be shown to have a useful inshore AS capability in addition.

Resolution SSBN   United Kingdom

Repulse

		Laid Down	Launched	Completed
S22	*Resolution*	1964	1966	1967
S23	*Repulse*	1965	1967	1968
S26	*Renown*	1964	1967	1968
S27	*Revenge*	1965	1968	1969

Displacement: 7,500 surfaced
8,250 submerged
Length (oa): 425ft
Beam: 33ft
Draught: 30ft
Machinery: One PWC reactor Steam turbines
Single shaft Speed 20/25kts
Armament: Sixteen A3 Polaris launchers
Six 21-inch TTs

Bearing some of the proudest names in the Royal Navy list, the Resolution class SSBNs are entrusted with the United Kingdom's main nuclear deterrent, a task assumed when the manned bomber became too vulnerable toward the latter end of the 1960s. Based on the range of the earlier A2 Polaris, original estimates required five of the class but financial restrictions and the availability of the longer (2,500-mile) ranged A3 made four boats an acceptable minimum; but, with one boat undergoing refit at any time, the margin is paper thin and could be reduced further by such trivia as stranding or collision. There is no back-up and even the French 'force de frappe' outnumbers it. The American Lafayettes are contemporary, with a striking similarity in both dimensions and appearance. Much has been made of the speed with which the British boats were planned and built but their average 3½-year construction times are still near twice those

of their US equivalents. Visually they differ mainly through the British practice of mounting diving planes forward rather than on the fin; their outboard ends pivot upward for reducing likelihood of damage when berthing. Though the Lafayettes have gained effectiveness by retro-fitting with the C3 Poseidon missile, there are no similar plans for the Resolutions. The A3s are fitted with excellent British-built warheads with multiple re-entry capability but are still of short range by modern standards. One propeller is fitted, powered by steam turbines drawing steam produced by heat generated by a single pressurised water-cooled reactor. Six TTs are mounted forward, for defensive use only. Each boat has to work to the maximum and two full crews are provided to take them to sea 'turn and turn about'.

There is little evidence for assuming that thought is being directed toward the successor for this near-obsolescent force. It may be that tardiness has been rewarded in that the next generation deterrent may well be carried, not by the vast ICBM, but by the small cruise missile. In the US Navy the wheel appears to be turning full circle, commencing with the crude Regulus I cruise missile, via Polaris, Poseidon and Trident, to a revolution in both size and cost in the Tomahawk, already reported to be pin-point accurate at up to 1,500 miles and capable of carrying a nuclear payload.

Swiftsure Fleet Submarine

United Kingdom

		Laid Down	Launched	Completed
S104	*Sceptre*	1973	1976	1978
S108	*Sovereign*	1970	1973	1974
S109	*Superb*	1972	1974	1976
S111	*Spartan*	1976	1978	1980
S112	*Splendid*	1977	1979	1981
S126	*Swiftsure*	1969	1971	1973
S113	*Trafalgar*	1978	—	—

Displacement: 4,200 surfaced
4,500 submerged
Length (oa): 272ft
Beam: 32.5ft
Draught: 27ft
Machinery: One PWC reactor and steam turbines
Single shaft
15,000shp for 30kts submerged
4,000bhp auxiliary diesel
Armament: Five 21-inch TTs

The Swiftsures represent a logical development of the Valiant design, showing no radical change in

propulsion or general concept. They have a far fuller form, shown externally by a constant freeboard extending much farther forward and aft, compared with the characteristically humpbacked Valiant profile. Also shorter and showing more abrupt changes of section, it is more efficient. The fin is considerably lower, as is the axis of the diving planes, which are not visible at surface trim.

Construction rate is slow at less than one per year and *Trafalgar* marks the beginning of an improved version. Expense is, of course, the prime reason but with the RN's patrol submarines the wrong side of 15 years old, great reliance will be placed on the

Sceptre

fleet boats which are totally unsuitable for many of the tasks discharged by the 'conventionals'.

Without doubt, at present, the nuclear fleet submarine is the best antidote to an enemy submarine and is also becoming an essential component of a surface task force. With the announced acquisition of the American encapsulated Harpoon missile in the early 1980s however, they will gain an enhanced anti-ship capacity to supplement their long-range wire-guided torpedoes. Should the SLCM become the chosen vehicle for the carriage of the nation's deterrent a new class of larger boats would be required in order to accommodate the vast amount of extra electronics. As it is, a comprehensive inertial navigation system is fitted, operating without need of astronomical sights. Sonars, too, are complete needing, as they do, to operate actively or passively in any plane, including upwards for operations below ice. Though not generally anywhere near as silent as a conventional boat, the fleet submarine will not usually advertise its presence by using active sonar, except on the final run-in to attack.

Valiant/Dreadnought Fleet Submarine   United Kingdom

		Laid Down	Launched	Completed
S46	Churchill	1967	1968	1970
S48	Conqueror	1967	1969	1971
S50	Courageous	1968	1970	1971
S102	Valiant	1962	1963	1966
S103	Warspite	1963	1965	1967
S101	Dreadnought	1959	1960	1963

		Valiant	Dreadnought
Displacement:	surfaced	4,400	3,500
	submerged	4,900	4,000
Length (oa):		285ft	267ft
Beam:		33ft	32ft
Draught:		27ft	26ft

Armament: (both) Six 21-inch TTs
Machinery: (both) One PWC reactor, geared turbines One shaft 20,000shp for 20/25kts

With their pioneer *Nautilus*, the Americans demonstrated the vast potential of the nuclear attack submarines, with its high speed, great endurance and continuous submerged operation. She was rapidly followed by boats which were still only nuclear propelled 'conventionals' and only with the 1956 Skipjacks came the high speed hull form. These were rapidly followed by the first SSBNs with comparable performance and strategic armament, which course was followed directly by the Soviet Navy. In order to retain its status as a front-line fleet, the Royal Navy needed to develop a counter — and this could only be another nuclear submarine.

Traditionally, British naval policy has been to react to developments rather than to initiate them, in order to avoid rendering obsolete the world's greatest fleet. But times have changed and the initiators of the maritime worlds now dominate the scene (and secure the export markets!) It was somewhat less than satisfactory therefore, to need to lean heavily on the shoulder of American technology to get Britain's first nuclear submarine to sea in a reasonable time. Though she was laid down in mid-1959, after US and Russian boats were operational, she was named *Dreadnought*, a name redolent of technological innovation and inappropriate to a vessel incorporating an American reactor and machinery, housed in a hull based heavily on that of the Skipjack. Authorised in 1956, she was completed in 1963, and saved about three years by the import of 'knowhow'. She initiated in the RN the 'new' after end, with its single, large diameter screw turning slowly abaft cruciform control surfaces.

The first follow-on Valiant had already been laid down as lead ship for a slightly larger class with a different hull shape. Though the submarine itself had taken a great step forward, its armament had not and still depended upon torpedoes fired from six tubes, all forward. Much redundancy was built into essential systems to guarantee realisation of the submarine's full potential. *Dreadnought* herself cannot really be regarded as still a front-line unit but fills a useful training role. The Valiants, too, have been surpassed by later boats but still retain a real capability, though probably against surface ships rather than other submarines.

Courageous

Oberon and Porpoise Patrol Submarine   United Kingdom

		Laid Down	Launched	Completed
S09	Oberon	1957	1959	1961
S10	Odin	1959	1960	1962
S11	Orpheus	1959	1959	1960
S12	Olympus	1960	1961	1962
S13	Osiris	1962	1962	1964
S14	Onslaught	1959	1960	1962
S15	Otter	1960	1961	1962
S16	Oracle	1960	1961	1963
S17	Ocelot	1960	1962	1964
S18	Otus	1961	1962	1963
S19	Opossum	1961	1963	1964
S20	Opportune	1962	1964	1964
S21	Onyx	1964	1966	1967
S01	Porpoise	1954	1956	1958
S07	Sealion	1958	1959	1961
S08	Walrus	1958	1959	1961

Ocelot

Displacement: 2,030 surfaced
2,400 submerged
Length (oa): 295ft
Beam: 26.5ft
Draught: 18ft
Armament: Eight 21-inch TTs
Machinery: Two diesel-generators powering two propulsion motors Two shafts
3,700/6,000bhp for 15/17.5kts
Disposals: SO2 *Rorqual* 1976; SO3 *Narwhal* 1977; SO4 *Grampus* 1976; SO5 *Finwhale* 1978; SO6 *Cachalot* 1977

'Handsome' is not a word that submarines bring to mind, but the O&P classes, with their large rectangular fins, forward hydroplanes and generally clean lines, come close to it. Externally they are identical, differences between the groups being mainly in electronics and the O's GRP or light alloy tophamper. They are the only 'conventional' submarines designed and built since World War II and thinking at their completion was in line with that of the Americans, ie that all follow-ons would be nuclear-propelled. Recent years have seen altogether a new appreciation of the patrol submarine, however, with its silent operation and great cost effectiveness and it would seem more than likely that both fleets will again construct diesel-electric boats. In today's high-technology warfare, silence means that the enemy's passive sonars cannot easily detect their target

which, in turn, has its own passive sensors rendered the more effective by a lack of self-induced noise.

As conventionally-propelled boats are air-breathing, they are now better termed 'submersibles' as to recharge batteries and renew internal air, they need periodically either to surface or to run at snort depth. For surface operation they retain the ship-shaped hull, compared with the fleet submarine's blunt cylinder designed for optimum submerged performance as true submarines. Two Admiralty Standard Range diesels each drive a generator which powers the motor to turn each shaft, a flexible system which permits simultaneous charging of batteries and needs no main gearing.

Eight TTs are carried, six forward and two aft, firing either long or short ranged torpedoes, ejecting mines or capable of launching the encapsulated Harpoon once it has been introduced. A further possible weapon is the SLAAM (submarine launched AA missile); based on the successful Blowpipe missile, a group can be housed around a rectractable mounting and fired from periscope depth at a helicopter, which today represents a grave threat to the submarine.

The Os have proved attractive export submarines, built for Australia (6), Brazil (3), Canada (3) and Chile (2). Though good for a 25-year span, the Porpoises have been dealt with savagely by successive defence cuts.

100

Pegasus Patrol Hydrofoil (PHM) USA

		Scheduled to be Completed
PHM1	*Pegasus*	1977
PHM2	*Hercules* (ex-*Delphinus*)	1982
PHM3	—	1981
PHM4	—	1981
PHM5	—	1981
PHM6	—	1982

Displacement: 240 tons full load
Length (oa): 131ft (foils extended)
147.5ft (foils retracted)
Beam: 28ft (foils extended)
28ft (foils retracted)
Draught: 23ft (foils extended)
6ft (foils retracted)
Machinery: Foilborne
Waterjets powered by one gas turbine
18,000shp for 48kts
Hullborne
Waterjets powered by two diesels
1,600bhp for 12kts
Armament: One 76mm gun
Eight Harpoon SSM launchers (2×4)

Southern NATO countries realised in the late 1960s that the Styx-armed Osa and Komar FACs, then coming forward, posed a grave threat to their surface ships in the enclosed waters of the Mediterranean. It was partly to counter this threat that a proposal was made to build an SSM-armed hydrofoil of standard design acceptable to all navies concerned. The hoped-for multi-national approach was limited finally to West Germany and Italy providing some of the funding for the craft, to be built in the US by the experienced Boeing Marine Systems. Unfortunately

the estimates for the development phase were over-optimistic and the prototype, *Pegasus*, incurred cost overruns on a scale that stimulated Italy to pursue an independent course and make the Germans think again about the 12 Exocet-armed versions that they had required (known as the Typ 162).

Since the issue of the contract in 1971, the case for the PHM in an anti-FAC role has been weakened by improved air-to-surface missiles and high-definition radars which have evolved the helicopter into a potent enemy of the small warship which, usually, is not well equipped to deal with it. Hydrofoils, too, are fragile things and less able than the average FAC to absorb punishment, and the 76mm gun is really for self-defence and for use against 'soft' targets.

Construction is of welded aluminium alloy and the craft can proceed either hullborne at low speed or foilborne at high speed. The foils are retractable and fully submerged when in use; a canard arrangement has been adopted, where the after foil is about twice the area of the forward, which provides both sensing and steering. In both modes, propulsion is by water-jet, obviating the problems of operating marine screws via complex transmission when foilborne. When hullborne, two small MTU diesels each drive a water jet with steerable nozzles and reversing buckets. For high speed foilborne operation a single, well-proven LM2500 gas turbine drives a pump which propels water through a third nozzle at a rate of about 90,000gal/min, having been drawn up the hollow after struts. The PHM can ride smoothly in Sea State 5 and the design owes much to the earlier Tucumcari.

SSM armament is exceptionally heavy in a craft its size, being two quadruple Harpoon lightweight launchers, though the prototype carried a dummy

Pegasus

assembly on the starboard quarter and a single canister to port for live firing trials. An RBOC (Rapid Bloom Offboard Chaff) launcher is also carried, with the total armament package under the control of a Mk 94 system a US-built version of the HSA WM28.

Flexibility of design offers variants in both the ASW and AAW fields, though with unspecified armament. A high level of automation is included to keep the minimum crew to only 21, permitting a five-day endurance, though UNREP can extend this.

Jetfoil Hydrofoil   USA

Jetfoil: note extreme steadiness and lack of wake in conditions of heavy swell.

Weight: 114 tons
Length (oa): 90ft
Beam: 30ft
Draught: 17ft (foils extended)
6ft (foils retracted)
Machinery: Two waterjets powered by two gas turbines
Speed 45kts

Though Boeing's Jetfoil 929 hydrofoil does not serve with the US Navy, one is being constructed for the Royal Navy and others serve commercially across the world; the example shown operated between London and Zeebrugge. The craft offers an interesting contrast to the Pegasus PHM in that it is designed as

a true foil-borne platform with an L/B ratio of only 3:1 compared with the PHM's 'ship' shape, yet still capable of cruising at up to 45kts. This generously proportioned rectangular plan gives great scope for armament, carrying a helicopter with ease for an ASW role. It is extremely manoeuvrable being capable of turning at cruising speed in about $6\frac{1}{2}$ lengths at a rate of six degrees per second, ie a reverse turn in a half minute. Crash stops can be achieved in little over four lengths. Foils are equippped with 'mechanical fuses' to minimise damage consequent upon collision with heavy floating debris. Two Allison 501-K20A gas turbines each power a Rocketdyne R-20 water-jet pump.

Small SES Test Vehicles   USA

SES-100B

SES-100A

	SES-100A	SES-100B
Tonnage:	100 gross	100 gross
Length (oa):	82ft	78ft
Beam:	42ft	35ft
Machinery:	Four GTs of 12,000hp	Three GTs of 13,500hp
Armament:	Unarmed	Unarmed
Speed:	75+kts	75+kts

The American designation SES (Surface Effect Ship) corresponds to the British rigid sidewall hovercraft, a type preferred to that evaluated by the RN with flexible skirts, eg the BH7, which is categorised as an ACV or Air Cushion Vehicle. As early steps in the development of the frigate-sized 2000 SES now under design (see *Warships of the World: Escort Vessels*) the US Navy had built two smaller craft, each close in size to the British BH7, but not really designed for quantity production. Both were completed in 1972 as two separate solutions to the same specification, the 100A by Tacoma

Boatbuilding to a Aerojet design and the 100B by Bell Aerospace. Each has the rigid sidewall for maximum longitudinal stability and strength with the 'air bubble' retained at either end by flexible skirting.

It will be noted that their quoted tonnages are in mercantile gross tons, a measure of their volume rather than their weight but each has a payload of 10 tons mass. Further, installed power is far removed from the equivalent British craft. Where the BH7 disposes of 4,250hp from a single Proteus, driving the craft at a maximum of 55kts by means of a single large airscrew, the Americans are far more powerful. The SES 100A has four Avco-Lycoming GTs of 12,000hp driving three lift fans and two waterjets for forward motion; the 100B has three Pratt & Whitney GTs of 13,500hp with propulsion by two high-speed marine screws and lift provided by no less than eight small fans powered by three small GTs each of 500hp. The former craft is credited with a 76kts maximum speed and the latter with an incredible 82+kts.

Asheville Patrol Gunboat (PG) USA

		Completed
PG92	*Tacoma*	1969
PG93	*Welch*	1969

Displacement: 225 standard
240 full load
Length (oa): 165ft
Beam: 24ft
Draught: 9.5ft
Machinery: One gas turbine 14,000shp
Two diesels 1,500shp
CODAG configuration Two shafts
40kts max or 16kts on diesels alone
Armament: One 3-inch gun
One 40mm gun
Disposals: PG84 *Asheville*, disarmed civilian training ship, 1977; PG85 *Gallup*, disarmed for environmental patrols, 1977; PG86 *Antelope*, disarmed for environmental patrols, 1978;PG87 *Ready*, disarmed civilian training ship, 1977; PG88 *Crockett*, disarmed for environmental patrols, 1977; PG89 *Marathon*, disarmed civilian training ship, 1977; PG90 *Canon*, disarmed for environmental patrols, 1977; PG 94 *Chehalis*, disarmed for

research, 1975; PG95 *Defiance*, to Turkey, 1973; PG96 *Benicia*, to South Korea, 1971; PG97 *Surprise*, to Turkey, 1973; PG98 *Grand Rapids*, disarmed for research, 1977; PG99 *Beacon*, to Greece, 1976; PG100 *Douglas*, disarmed for research, 1978; PG101 *Green Bay*, to Greece, 1976

Born from a lack of suitably-sized patrol craft during the Cuban crisis, the Ashevilles were designed by contract with Gibbs and Cox of New York against a requirement for an agile, shallow-draught vessel capable of surveillance and interdiction with an ability to render support as well as defend herself. Construction is of aluminium alloy with a composite GRP superstructure, the hull designed for high speed and propelled by a CODAG installation of an LM1500 GT and two Cummins diesels, the latter used alone for cruising economically with a 1,700-mile range.

Among the first postwar patrol craft of any size, they date from the period immediately before the installation of SSMs became general and they compare interestingly with later FAC designs. That these attractive little ships could be updated was

Asheville

demonstrated by PG86, 87, 98 and 100 later being armed for a time with two single Tartar SSM launchers aft and PG96 with a single Standard MR launcher. The hull has a fine forward entry and pronounced knuckle forward. A high-ish profile is given by the compact, two-tier superstructure with a nicely-proportioned funnel exhausting the GT, flanked by two miniature stacks for the diesels.

Forward is a single 3-inch gun in a Mk 34 mounting exclusive to the class, with its own Mk 64 fire control, linked to the SPG-50 radar outfit. Right aft is a 40mm gun (a combination very common in current FACs) and paired 50-calibre MGs flank the funnels, reminders of the close-in fighting for which the class was designed, enhanced by the carriage also of two mortars.

Though only two of the class are still active in the US Navy, all are extant, either transferred abroad or to civilian organisations. A close derivative of the PG is the PSMM (multi-mission patrol ship) built by Tacoma Boatbuilding, which yard constructed most of the Ashevilles). None of these latter craft has been acquired by the US Navy but serve under the flags of Indonesia, South Korea, and Taiwan. Similar in size they offer a wide range of options in both machinery and armament, the latter designed to include SSMs for the outset. The Indonesian boats carry four Harpoon launchers and have the similar machinery layout of the Ashevilles except for having an LM2500 GT which gives a 45kts speed. Those for South Korea have a unique layout of six small Avco-Lycoming GTs on two shafts and carry four Standard MR missiles. Finally, the Taiwan units have three GTs on three shafts and ship four Otomat missiles.

Ohio SSBN   USA

Artist's impression of *Ohio*.

	Laid Down	Launched	Completed
SSBN726 *Ohio*	1976	1977	1979
SSBN727 *Michigan*	1977	1978	1980
SSBN728-9			1981
SSBN730			1982
SSBN731-8 planned			

Displacement: 16,500 surfaced
18,700 submerged
Length (oa): 560ft
Beam: 42ft
Draught: 35.5ft
Machinery: One PWC reactor and steam turbines
One shaft
Armament: 24 launchers for Trident I SLBMs
Four 21-inch TTs

Of 41 existing American SSBNs only the Benjamin Franklin/Lafayette classes are being updated to deploy the C3 Poseidon missile, the remaining 10 boats becoming obsolescent and requiring replacement from the early 1980s. Thus, in 1974, was placed the contract for the first of the new Ohio class, designed around the large, 4,000-mile C4 Trident I missile; the bulk of 24 launch tubes has determined the enormous diameter and length of the hull, swollen further by the need for a large new type reactor (the S8G) to drive it. Each Trident I is believed to carry up to 12 independently-targeted heads to saturate the target area's defences.

With a length similar to that of a Spruance class DD, these submarines will be the world's largest to date and need plenty of deep water for successful operation. So vast is the Soviet Union however that, even with a 4,000-mile strike range, the launching vessel would sometimes need to enter shallow water in the northern Indian Ocean or the Kara/Barents Seas to reach the heartland. This is a dangerous procedure with the Russian Fleet improving its AS hardware and techniques and, with this in mind, the 6,000-mile Trident II is under development. When operational this later missile will also enable certain foreign advanced SSBN bases to be phased-out, together with their expense and political problems.

Painstaking attention has been paid to noise reduction in the Ohios and, charged with the task of avoiding detection, their only sonar is the large BQQ-5, capable of operating only in the passive mode for the purposes of early warning. Should self-protection be absolutely necessary for survival, each boat carries four TTs, though it should be remembered that these could launch not only torpedoes but also the anti-ship Harpoon or nuclear-tipped Subroc.

Patrols are conducted entirely submerged and accurate positional knowledge is of paramount importance, both for safe navigation and continuous up-dating of target coordinates. Two inertial systems are thus fitted, detecting all velocities and accelerations which are continuously computed to give a pinpoint readout. Hull construction is particularly powerful, with ballast tanks acting as a second skin around the pressure hull proper. The new pattern reactor is expected to last the life of the boat on only two charges of fuel.

Originally, a class of 10 was to have been constructed in a purpose-built 'ship facility' over a four-year period but cost escalation (an Ohio costs nearly half as much as a Nimitz class CVN) has attenuated the programme somewhat though an extra three units have since been authorised. Both the price tag and the unwieldly size of these craft have stimulated an in-depth study into a cheaper and more convenient system and the class may well be the ultimate SSBN.

Benjamin Franklin/Lafayette SSBN   USA

Lafayette

Benjamin Franklin

		Laid Down	Launched	Completed
SSBN616	Lafayette	1961	1962	1963
SSBN617	Alexander Hamilton	1961	1962	1963
SSBN619	Andrew Jackson	1961	1962	1963
SSBN620	John Adams	1961	1963	1964
SSBN622	James Monroe	1961	1962	1963
SSBN623	Nathan Hale	1961	1963	1963
SSBN624	Woodrow Wilson	1961	1963	1963
SSBN625	Henry Clay	1961	1962	1964
SSBN626	Daniel Webster	1961	1963	1964
SSBN627	James Madison	1962	1963	1964
SSBN628	Tecumseh	1962	1963	1964
SSBN629	Daniel Boone	1962	1963	1964
SSBN630	John C. Calhoun	1962	1963	1964
SSBN631	Ulysses S. Grant	1962	1963	1964
SSBN632	von Steuben	1962	1963	1964
SSBN633	Casimir Pulaski	1963	1964	1964
SSBN634	Stonewall Jackson	1962	1963	1964
SSBN635	Sam Rayburn	1962	1963	1964
SSBN636	Nathaniel Greene	1962	1964	1964
SSBN640	Benjamin Franklin	1963	1964	1965
SSBN641	Simon Bolivar	1963	1964	1965
SSBN642	Kamehameha	1963	1965	1965
SSBN643	George Bancroft	1963	1965	1966
SSBN644	Lewis and Clark	1963	1964	1965
SSBN645	James K. Polk	1963	1965	1966
SSBN654	George C. Marshall	1964	1965	1966
SSBN655	Henry L. Stimson	1964	1965	1966
SSBN656	George Washington Carver	1964	1965	1966
SSBN657	Francis Scott Key	1964	1966	1966
SSBN658	Mariano G. Vallejo	1964	1965	1966
SSBN659	Will Rogers	1965	1966	1967

Displacement: 7,250 standard
8,250 submerged
Length (oa): 425ft
Beam: 33ft
Draught: 31.5ft
Machinery: One PWC reactor Two sets steam turbines
One shaft 15,000shp for 20/30kts
Armament: Sixteen launchers for Poseidon SLBMs
Four 21-inch TTs

Though listed officially as separate classes, the difference between the two groups is minimal, confined mainly to the post-636 boats being equipped with much quieter machinery though, for reasons unspecified, the crew has been increased from 140 to 168 — as this is a distinctly retrograde step from the point of view of endurance, it can only be assumed that they are also more complex. The class is very similar to the British Resolutions, being built around identical weapon systems but differing externally in their fin-mounted diving planes (an exception is 626, with forward planes and large bow sonar dome). Where the British boats have retained their original armament, however, the Americans have updated continuously. Thus, the first eight laid down originally carried the A2 Polaris and the remainder the A3. Then, early in 1969, only two years after the last commissioned, the first was taken in hand for conversion to the C3 Poseidon, which also required the new Mk 88 fire control in place of the earlier Mk 84, to take account of the extra range. This extensive programme was completed only in 1978 yet, in 1979, SSBN657 will undergo a pilot conversion to deploy the Trident I; after evaluation, a further nine conversions are planned. This is possible because the length of the Trident I is only marginally greater than that of the Poseidon and the great 42ft diameter of the new Ohios is geared to the retrofitting of the larger Trident II. It is worthy of note that the crew of the far larger Ohio is only 133.

The number of units in the class is tailored to the number of warheads required to be deployed, bearing in mind that a number will always be unavailable due to being on passage, under refit or modernisation etc. With the number built the necessary patrol duration was set at two months, continuously submerged, with two separate crews operating the boats in rota.

It is an interesting exercise to note how successive major Russian surface ships' designs have been stimulated by increasing the range of American ICBMs. SSBN625 was the last to commission with the 1,500-mile A2 Polaris and, to range on major targets in the Soviet Union, could operate no further out than the well defined deep-water trenches of the Norwegian Sea or the line Japan-Kamchatka. These areas could be covered by the then current 3,800-ton Kashin class but the introduction of the 2,500-mile A3 Polaris in 1964 was speedily answered by the laying-down of the 6,000-ton Kresta Is, classified 'Large AS ships': these carried no major AS system, though the SS-N-14 was being rapidly developed for use in the Kresta IIs, post-1968. The Poseidon programme was then commenced and Russian counter-thought went off at a tangent with the 14,000-ton Moskva class helicopter carriers. With the advent of the Trident development in the early 1970s came also the design of the Kievs, at once a significant threat to any submarine worldwide and a final stepping stone to promoting the Soviet Union to the range of naval air powers at a time when the West is abandoning the large carrier concept.

Ethan Allen SSBN

USA

		Laid Down	Launched	Completed
SSBN608	Ethan Allen	1959	1960	1961
SSBN609	Sam Houston	1959	1961	1962
SSBN610	Thomas A. Edison	1960	1961	1962
SSBN611	John Marshall	1960	1961	1962
SSBN618	Thomas Jefferson	1961	1962	1963

Displacement: 6,950 surfaced
7,900 submerged
Length (oa): 410ft
Beam: 33ft
Draught: 32ft
Machinery: One PWC reactor Two steam turbines
One shaft 15,000shp for 20/28kts
Armament: Sixteen launchers for Polaris A3 SLBM
Four 21-inch TTs

The quintette of Ethan Allens are slightly smaller versions of the Lafayettes, which were later derivatives of the same diameter hull but with an extra 15ft section worked-in to the parallel mid-body. Both types have a similar pressurised water-cooled S5W reactor which provides the necessary thermal energy to produce steam for a pair of steam turbines which, in turn, put 15,000hp on to the single shaft. Externally, the Allens are virtually indistinguishable from the later class, in spite of their having been updated to carry the A3 Polaris in place of the A2 for which they were designed.

Due to their age they will not be given the Poseidon conversion but will be phased out after the George Washingtons as the second half of the Ohio programme is realised, by which time they will be over 20 years of age. The Allens are far more robustly constructed than the Washingtons, permitting deeper operations with consequent enhanced immunity from detection.

Ethan Allen

George Washington SSBN   USA

		Laid Down	Launched	Completed
SSBN598	*George Washington*	1957	1959	1959
SSBN599	*Patrick Henry*	1958	1959	1960
SSBN600	*Theodore Roosevelt*	1958	1959	1961
SSBN601	*Robert E. Lee*	1958	1959	1960
SSBN602	*Abraham Lincoln*	1958	1960	1961

George Washington

Displacement: 6,025 surfaced
6,900 submerged
Length (oa): 382ft
Beam: 33ft
Draught: 29ft
Machinery: One PWC reactor Two steam turbines
One shaft 15,000 for 20/29kts
Armament: Sixteen launchers for Polaris A3 SLBM
Six 21-inch TTs

In about 1958, the Russians commissioned the first of their nuclear-propelled Hotel class SSBNs; their three SS-N-4 (Sark) missiles of only 30 miles range look puny today but, at the time, mounted in a vehicle capable of virtually unlimited submerged cruising, formed a threat that needed not only to be countered but matched. The A1 Polaris was nearing readiness and it was resolved to get it to sea in the shortest possible time. By the time the first Soviet boat was completed, the Americans were under way with a programme for five (it was even planned to put A1s into the nuclear-propelled cruiser *Long Beach*, then about to be laid down).

To cut design time, the incomplete hull of the Scorpion (SSN589) of the Skipjack class (qv) was lengthened by a new parallel mid-body section, long enough to accommodate 16 vertical launch tubes in two parallel rows of eight. The Russian Sark missiles were of a length that could nowhere near be accommodated vertically in the hull and had to be enclosed within the deeper envelope of the fin, thus limiting their numbers, but the Polaris could be housed by increasing the freeboard abaft the fin with a casing that still has a rather makeshift air about it.

Between 1963 and 1967 the Hotels were updated by a conversion to the 700-mile Serb missile but the Americans retained their superiority by the introduction of the 2,500-mile A3 Polaris, for which the Washingtons were modified during 1964-7. By the latter date the full 41-boat Polaris fleet was complete, a highly creditable achievement considering that only four yards were involved, and three of those built 38 units. The average time for these extremely complex craft has remained constant at little over 24 months apiece.

Inevitably, as a prototype class, the Washingtons have been eclipsed by succeeding groups. Their machinery arrangement was successful and remained largely unchanged for the later designs but they suffered from a depth-limitation, and shallow-running submarines are the more easily detected. As the Trident-armed Ohios come forward in numbers, the Washingtons will be phased out and there are no plans to undertake any further modifications for Poseidon.

Their nomenclature dropped the Fish names of earlier boats for famous names in American history, a change that was to last only until the Ohio type was recognised as important enough to carry the State names formerly carried by battleships (but now, most confusingly, also by nuclear-propelled cruisers).

Los Angeles SSN   USA

		Laid Down	Launched	Completed
SSN688	*Los Angeles*	1972	1974	1976
SSN689	*Baton Rouge*	1972	1975	1977
SSN690	*Philadelphia*	1972	1974	1977
SSN691	*Memphis*	1973	1976	1977
SSN692	*Omaha*	1973	1976	1977
SSN693	*Cincinnati*	1974	1977	1978
SSN694	*Groton*	1973	1976	1978

Los Angeles

		Laid Down	Launched	Completed
SSN695	*Birmingham*	1975	1977	1978
SSN696	*New York City*	1973	1977	1978
SSN697	*Indianapolis*	1974	1977	1979
SSN698	*Bremerton*	1976	1978	1979
SSN699	*Jacksonville*	1976	1978	1979
SSN700	*Dallas*	1976	1978	1979
SSN701	*La Jolla*	1976	1979	1980
SSN702	*Phoenix*	1977	1979	1980
SSN703	*Boston*	1977	1979	1980
SSN704	*Baltimore*	1978	1979	1980
SSN705	—	1978	1980	1981
SSN706	—	1979	1980	1981
SSN707	—	1979	1980	1981
SSN708	—	1979	1981	1982
SSN709	—	1980	1981	1982
SSN710	—	1980	1981	1982
SSN711	*San Francisco*	1977	1979	1980
SSN712	—	1978	1980	1981
SSN713	—	1979	1980	1982
SSN714	—	1979	1981	1982
SSN715	—	1980	1981	1983
SSN716-18		1980-81	1981-82	1983-84
SSN719 Approved				
SSN720-25 Proposed				

Memphis

Displacement: 6,000 surfaced
6,900 submerged
Length (oa): 360ft
Beam: 33ft
Draught: 32.5ft
Machinery: One PWC reactor Two steam turbines
One shaft c30,000shp for 30+kts submerged
Armament: Four 21-inch TTs

A class large not only in numbers (32 funded, eight proposed) but also in dimensions, being barely shorter than the George Washington class SSBNs and with a bulkier cross section. Much larger than the preceding Sturgeons they have also twice their power from their S6G reactor, a modified surface-ship unit that accounts for much of the LA's extra length and which confers a maximum speed probably nearer 34kts than 30. Much research for the class was performed by the one-off *Glenard P. Lipscomb* (SSN685) with much the same dimensions but a lower-powered reactor driving, interestingly, a turbo-electric plant. The latter was long a favourite in American battleships, eliminating the main gearing which, at that time, gave much trouble; its lack in a submarine cuts noise considerably but, nevertheless, the LAs have reverted to the more common (and more compact) steam turbine. Commencing in 1974 the *Lipscomb's* experiments in noise reduction were a continuation of those begun in the *Tullibee* (SSN597) as far back as 1960.

At a time when successful interdiction is believed best performed by the small, silent boat it seems a retrograde step to introduce a large, fast submarine (for speed means noise) and one cannot help concluding that they are intended for a wider role. Though rather smaller, the Soviet Victors of 1968 onward are credited with a very high submerged speed, whose probable over-estimation was enough to trigger American reaction. The LAs were exceptionally long in gestation and their appearance coincided with that of the Tomahawk cruise missile. Their 'armament' of four TTs seems absurdly small until one considers that arsenal of sophisticated weaponry which they can launch. These tubes are mounted slightly forward of the fin, leaving the whole bow section available for the massive BQQ-5 sonar array, normally used passively. Long range detection can also be effected by a towed array, whose sensors can be positioned independently of thermal layers in the water and far removed from self-generated noise. Finally a new BQS-15 active attack sonar is fitted.

The Tomahawk SLCM, at 21ft, is longer than the 17½ft anti-ship torpedo but can be launched from the same tube in an encapsulating jacket, shed once clear of the surface. Once in the air, its fold-out wings convert it into a small, sub-sonic aircraft, flying on a pre-programmed flight-path at low altitudes and difficult to detect. Used tactically, it can carry a conventional payload over a bewilderingly complex 250-mile flight path but, with simpler programming, it can run a strategic 1,500 miles to plant a nuclear warhead. It is a weapon of great potential and confers on the attack submarine the ability to strike shore targets to considerable depth when operating independently in forward areas.

Another important role of the attack submarine is to 'kill' an enemy SSBN; here the BQQ-5 is a clue, as it was developed from the BQQ-2 system which was closely associated with Subroc, capable of putting a nuclear depth charge or homing torpedo on to a submerged target up to 30 miles distant. Attack submarines are being increasingly used as escorts to a surface task force and, in addition to the usual range of torpedoes, carry also the encapsulated Harpoon missile. Where the former detonates up to 500lb of explosive against the target below its waterline, the latter strikes her topsides — a less lethal position but the effect of a half-ton of machinery arriving at Mach 0.9 is usually conclusive to a frigate-sized ship.

With fully-computerised command and fire control and a reactor core-life of up to 13 years, the LA represents a formidable fighting machine but, with unit costs already soaring beyond the one-third billion dollar mark and of a size that must invite question she, like the Ohio class must surely represent the end of her particular line of development.

Sturgeon SSN   USA

		Laid Down	Launched	Completed
SSN637	*Sturgeon*	1963	1966	1967
SSN638	*Whale*	1964	1966	1968
SSN639	*Tautog*	1964	1967	1968
SSN646	*Grayling*	1964	1967	1969
SSN647	*Pogy*	1964	1967	1971
SSN648	*Aspro*	1964	1967	1969
SSN649	*Sunfish*	1965	1966	1969
SSN650	*Pargo*	1964	1966	1968
SSN651	*Queenfish*	1965	1966	1966
SSN652	*Puffer*	1965	1968	1969
SSN653	*Ray*	1965	1966	1967
SSN660	*Sand Lance*	1965	1969	1971
SSN661	*Lapon*	1965	1966	1967
SSN662	*Gurnard*	1964	1967	1968
SSN663	*Hammerhead*	1965	1967	1968
SSN664	*Sea Devil*	1966	1967	1969

		Laid Down	Launched	Completed
SSN665	Guitarro	1965	1968	1972
SSN666	Hawkbill	1966	1969	1971
SSN667	Bergall	1966	1968	1969
SSN668	Spadefish	1966	1968	1969
SSN669	Seahorse	1966	1968	1969
SSN670	Finback	1967	1968	1970
SSN672	Pintado	1967	1969	1971
SSN673	Flying Fish	1967	1969	1970
SSN674	Trepang	1967	1969	1970
SSN675	Bluefish	1968	1970	1971
SSN676	Billfish	1968	1970	1971
SSN677	Drum	1968	1970	1972
SSN678	Archerfish	1969	1971	1971
SSN679	Silversides	1969	1971	1972
SSN680	William H. Bates (ex-Redfish)	1969	1971	1973
SSN681	Batfish	1970	1971	1972
SSN682	Tunny	1970	1972	1974
SSN683	Parche	1970	1973	1974
SSN684	Cavalla	1970	1972	1973
SSN686	L. Mendel Rivers	1971	1973	1975
SSN687	Richard B. Russell	1971	1974	1975

Displacement: 3,650 surfaced
4,650 submerged
Length (oa): 292ft
Beam: 31.5ft
Draught: 29ft
Machinery: One PWC reactor Two steam turbines
One shaft 15,000shp for 20+/30+kts
Armament: Four 21-inch TTs

The 37-strong Sturgeon class are developments of the preceding Thresher design, using the same machinery layout and, therefore, slightly slower. There exists also the one-off Narwhal (SSN671), a somewhat larger boat built to investigate a reactor cooled by convection means, another attempt at reduction of radiated noise, this time by circulating pumps. In appearance, they resemble the Thresher type but have a more lofty fin, possibly to improve control characteristics whilst conferring the advantage of longer periscopes and antennas. Units numbered 678 onward are 10ft longer in the hull to accommodate the more comprehensive electronics which now demand so much of a submarine's capacity. The four TTs are housed well aft to allow space in the bow for the 15ft diameter sphere which contains the BQS-6 sonar, the active component of the BQQ-2 sonar suite; the complementary passive arrays of the BQR-7 are mounted on either side of the forward hull. Upon major overhaul, each of the class is being updated to the BQQ-5 system.

Another interesting fitting is the BQS-8 sonar, whose sensors are visible as two small domes atop the casing, aft. This is a high definition, upward-looking unit, aimed principally at navigating safely under the ice, which can extend in irregular masses to considerable depths below a surface field but which is used as a means for concealment by the SSBNs that are the prime target of the attack submarine. The sharp 'eye' of the BQS-8 can also be used to detect the presence of moored mines. In connection with ice navigation, the fin-mounted diving planes are strengthened and capable of pivoting into a vertical alignment to assist in

Sturgeon

fracturing thinner ice through which the submarine can surface. Weapon control is also comprehensive and being updated on opportunity. Again, the four TTs are capable of launching a full range of weaponry, AS and Mk 48 anti-ship torpedoes, Subroc, Harpoon and eventually, the Tomahawk SLCM.

Permit SSN

USA

		Laid Down	Launched	Completed
SSN594	*Permit*	1959	1961	1962
SSN595	*Plunger* (ex-*Pollack*)	1960	1961	1962
SSN596	*Barb* (ex-*Pollack*; ex-*Plunger*)	1959	1962	1963
SSN603	*Pollack* (ex-*Barb*)	1960	1962	1964
SSN604	*Haddo*	1960	1962	1964
SSN605	*Jack*	1960	1963	1967
SSN606	*Tinosa*	1959	1961	1964
SSN607	*Dace*	1960	1962	1964
SSN612	*Guardfish*	1961	1965	1966
SSN613	*Flasher*	1961	1963	1966
SSN614	*Greenling*	1961	1964	1967
SSN615	*Gato*	1961	1964	1968
SSN616	*Haddock*	1961	1966	1967

Displacement: 3,750 surfaced
4,300 submerged
Length (oa): 278.5ft
Beam: 32ft
Draught: 25ft
Machinery: One PWC reactor Two steam turbines
One shaft 15,000shp for 20+/30+kts
Armament: Four 21-inch TTs
Loss: SSN593 *Thresher* 1963

With the Permit (late Thresher) class, the nuclear attack submarine passed from its introductory phase, but the variations within the group demonstrate the various lines of thinking that were still being explored, underlined by the exceptionally long building times for some units. Though built on

Thresher

experience won with the earlier Skipjacks, they are roomier, lacking the extreme high-speed 'teardrop' hull. SSN613-5 have loftier fins than their classmates, together with a hull some 14ft longer to accommodate modified machinery and additional safety features consequent upon the loss of *Thresher* with all hands. The extra size puts 200 tons on the submerged displacement.

Various means have been discussed by which radiated submarine noise can be reduced and an early attempt was in the lone *Tullibee* (SSN597) of 1960. A slowish hunter-killer design, her reactor powered a turbo-electric installation to reduce requirements for noisy reduction gearing. As a submarine she lacked sufficient versatility and no more were built but the quest for silence had begun. Within the Permit class that was constructed in their place one, the *Jack* (SSN605), was selected for a further experiment with contra-rotating propellers. These were turned by concentric shafts driven by steam turbines of opposite rotation. The gain in quietness and efficiency was bought at the expense of complexity and a hull 18ft greater in length; it has not been repeated though she retains the system.

From the outset the class was designed to deploy the Subroc missile and they are still considered sufficiently modern to update the extensive BQQ-2 sonar fit to the newer BQQ-5 and the torpedo fire control from the Mk 133 to the Mk 117. Harpoon and Tomahawk will follow, in addition to the more conventional torpedo armament. This includes both the Mk 37, an 11ft, 1,400lb weapon with active and acoustic passive homing, and the controversial 20-mile ranged Mk 48, a 19ft monster of near 3,500lb launch weight and both wire-guided and self-homing. It is designed to follow the deep diving submarine target as well as a surface ship and has a unit price approaching two-thirds of a million dollars. In spite of various questions regarding its 'bang-per-buck' ratio, it has been recognised as a superb weapon, and some 1,700 have been built or are under construction.

Skipjack SSN   USA

		Laid Down	Launched	Completed
SSN585	*Skipjack*	1956	1958	1959
SSN586	*Scamp*	1959	1960	1961
SSN590	*Sculpin*	1958	1960	1961
SSN591	*Shark*	1958	1960	1961
SSN592	*Snook*	1958	1960	1961

Displacement: 3,075 surfaced
3,500 submerged
Length (oa): 252ft
Beam: 31.5ft
Draught: 29ft
Machinery: One PWC reactor Two steam turbines
One shaft 15,000shp for 20/30+kts
Armament: Six 21-inch TTs
Loss: SSN589 *Scorpion* 1968

The small, humpbacked profile of the Skipjack with an apparently over-sized fin and vestigial casing, heralded a new breed of nuclear submarine whose high speed hull — described as an 'elongated teardrop' was developed directly from experiment on the prototype *Albacore* (AGSS569). This craft was commissioned in 1953 to test a near-ideal shape, a smooth solid of revolution with only one propeller (and this abaft the cruciform control surfaces) and diving planes shifted back from the conventional bow position to the fin structure. Now used almost universally, this configuration was only one of those borne by the *Albacore* during her trials, during which she was also used to evaluate diagonal cruciform control surfaces (now used by Swedish submarines qv) divebrakes, auxiliary control flap on the fin's

trailing edge and contra-rotating propellers. Finally de-commissioned in 1972, *Albacore* has an assured place in submarine history.

The Skipjacks, too, are very fast craft, eclipsed probably only by the Los Angeles class but the penalty was an extremely fine after end which meant, among other things, no after TT armament. Six tubes were placed forward in the bow position occupied by sonar in later classes. Now lacking advanced electronics and the ability to deploy modern weaponry, the class cannot be regarded as front line, particularly as they are incapable of the deep submergence of later boats. Their machinery was particularly successful, introducing the pressurised watercooled S5W reactor, which powered all succeeding classes up to the Ohio and Los Angeles, which have the S8G, derived from a surface ship unit. All other machinery was doubled-up and a pair of small motors were installed as a 'get-you-home' measure, powered either by batteries or two diesel generators.

The undoubted success of the class was clouded somewhat by the total disappearance in 1968 of the *Scorpion* (SSN589). She had been the second of the name as the first hull was 'stretched' to become the leadship of the George Washington class SSBNs.

Skate SSN   USA

		Laid Down	Launched	Completed
SSN578	*Skate*	1955	1957	1957
SSN579	*Swordfish*	1956	1957	1958
SSN583	*Sargo*	1956	1957	1958
SSN584	*Seadragon*	1956	1958	1959

Displacement: 2,550 surfaced
2,850 submerged
Length (oa): 267.5ft
Beam: 25ft
Draught: 22ft

Machinery: One PWC reactor Two steam turbines
Two shafts 13,000shp for 15/20kts
Armament: Eight 21-inch TTs (six forward and two aft)

Skate

The four Skates date from the period immediately following the commissioning of the pioneer *Nautilus* (SSN571) and thus incorporate few lessons derived from her operation; having once established the feasibility of the nuclear submarine, the Americans were anxious to capitalise on their lead with series production. Some 50ft was saved on overall length but the design was frozen before the full results of the *Albacore* trials had been assessed and the class perpetuates the old-style hull, with full length casing, 'ship' bow and twin screw propulsion after the fashion of Guppy-modified World War II submarines. It will also be noted how much smaller the hull is in cross-section compared with later high-speed classes.

Nautilus had been equipped with an S2W reactor,

the only one built; it was developed rapidly into the S3W for the first two Skates and then further to the S4W for the second pair. Variations are marginal and consist primarily of changes in layout and operation. As a monitor of progress in reactor development, *Nautilus* 'steamed' some 62,000 miles on her first fuel core; *Skate* doubled this distance, her fuel charge lasting three years; the latest fleet submarines are planned to extend to some 10 years, possibly 'refuelling' only once during their life span.

The class is now obsolescent, with dated electronics, an inability to handle latest weaponry and a depth-limitation. Where *Nautilus* will be preserved as a permanent exhibit the best that the Skates can anticipate is a spell as a training flotilla once they pay off.

Halibut/Triton/Seawolf SSN   USA

		Halibut	Triton	Seawolf
Pennant No:		SSN587	SSN586	SS575
Laid Down:		1957	1956	1953
Launched:		1959	1958	1955
Completed:		1960	1959	1957
Displacement:	standard	3,850	5,950	3,750
	submerged	5,000	6,650	4,250
Length (oa):		350ft	447.5ft	338ft
Beam:		29.5ft	37ft	28ft
Draught:		21.5ft	24ft	23ft
Machinery:		One reactor	Two reactors	One reactor
		Two st turbines	Two st turbines	Two st turbines
		Two shafts	Two shafts	Two shafts
		13,000shp	34,000shp	15,000shp
		for 15/20kts	for 27/20kts	for 20/30kts
Armament:		Six 21-inch TTs	Six 21-inch TTs	Six 21-inch TTs

Three further nuclear submarines appear on the US navy list; all are 'one-offs' and dated to the extent that their only useful function is now research. The newest is the *Halibut*, designed to deploy a pair of 1,000-mile Regulus II cruise missiles. When this weapon was cancelled, she carried for some years five of the earlier 550-mile Regulus I together with their launchers, in an enlarged forebody, a cleaner arrangement than that of the conventionally-propelled Graybacks (qv). Regulus I was abandoned in 1965 and the submarine was, for a time, lacking a specialised function until nominated for research with Deep Submergence Rescue Vehicles (DSRV). These are miniature submersibles which can be carried either by a parent submarine or surface ship and mate with the escape hatch in a sunken

submarine, though other, auxiliary functions are possible.

She was originally to have received conventional diesel-electric machinery but, in the event, was fitted with an S3W reactor from the early Skate programme and carried the unique SSGN classification until her Regulus armoury was landed. Now overlarge, slow and dated, *Halibut* is in reserve. Slightly older is the *Triton*, the world's largest submarine until the Russian Delta IIs arrived about 1972. Designed to accompany a carrier force in the capacity of long-range radar picket she shares, with the Russian Whiskey 'Canvas Bag' (qv), an elongated fin into which a large surveillance antenna can be aligned and retracted. To achieve the high speeds required of her duties, she was fitted with two S4G

Seawolf

reactors and remains the only US submarine so equipped. Her great hull was still based on the Guppy principles and lacks the submerged efficiency of later craft so, most unusually, her surface speed is considerably higher than that when submerged; indeed she resembles in many ways the infamous British K boats of World War I. Originally classified SSRN, she apparently did not fit in too well with theory and no further units were built. She has been in reserve since 1969 and it would seem unlikely that she will see any further peacetime service.

The third boat of the trio is the *Seawolf*, built concurrently with Nautilus and commissioning in 1957 as the world's second nuclear submarine. As an alternative to the pressurised water-cooled reactor, she was fitted with an S2G unit which relied on sodium in its liquid state to effect the cooling. This highly corrosive medium produced so much trouble that the complete assembly was replaced by a modified Nautilus unit in 1959. She has remained in service in the capacity of research vehicle, latterly with small submersibles but her twin screw form is old fashioned and she has little offensive potential. Her overall appearance, indeed, makes an interesting comparison with that of the Sabalo at the head of the section dealing with ex-World War II submarines.

Barbel Patrol Submarine (SS)   USA

		Laid Down	Launched	Completed
SS580	*Barbel*	1956	1958	1959
SS581	*Blueback*	1957	1959	1959
SS582	*Bonefish*	1957	1958	1959

Displacement: 2,150 surfaced
2,900 submerged
Length (oa): 219.5ft
Beam: 29ft
Draught: 28ft
Machinery: Three diesel-generators Two motors
One shaft 3,150shp for 15/25kts
Armament: Six 21-inch TTs

If the present all-nuclear submarine policy is maintained the Barbels will be the last of a long line of American diesel/electric submarines. Laid down shortly after the nuclear-propelled Skate class, they were able to incorporate the modified Albacore high speed hull, with its clean lines and single screw. Externally, they may be taken for nuclear boats but are betrayed by the diesel exhaust aft. Their diving planes were originally placed forward, as on Albacore, but were later moved to their present position on the fin and in line with the Skipjacks, then entering service.

Expected to have about 25 years useful life, the Barbels would seem to have been successful and the class would probably have run to a far greater number but for the influence of the Rickover school, which pushed through its 'all-nuclear' ideas. Recent years have seen something of a renaissance of the conventionally-propelled submarine, in western European fleets particularly, as their advantages over the nuclear craft become apparent. These include extreme silence and better cost effectiveness; used on missions where their limitations are taken into account they still have a future.

Due to their fine after end, the Barbels carry their full battery of six TTs forward and this armament and the size of their hull make an interesting contrast with, say, a Typ 206 or a Nacken. The latter are small submarines with a large forward battery of TTs and aimed at near-water patrols in heavily-populated waters; American submarines, on the other hand, need size for their long-range operations across the oceans that flank their country. A major innovation in the class was the centralisation of all control and attack functions into a single area, since universally adopted.

Barbel

Darter Submarine (SS/SSG)   USA

	Darter	Grayback	Growler
Pennant No:	SS576	SS574	SSG577
Laid Down:	1954	1954	1955
Launched:	1956	1957	1957
Completed:	1956	1958	1958
Displacement: surfaced	1,700	2,650	2,550
submerged	2,400	3,650	3,500
Length (oa):	268ft	334ft	317.5ft
Beam:	27ft	27ft	27ft
Draught:	19ft	19ft	19ft
Machinery: (all)	Three diesel-generators		
	Two motors 5,600shp		
	Two shafts		
Armament:	Eight 21-inch TTs	Eight 21-inch TTs	Six 21-inch TTs
Speed:	19.5/14kts	20/14kts	20/15kts

Shorter derivatives of the Tang class, the Darters were little advanced when the possibilities offered by the nuclear *Nautilus* (commissioned 1954) and the high speed *Albacore* (commissioned 1953) convinced the policy-makers that future designs should combine their attributes. The Darter class was, therefore, limited to only three units, followed closely by the Barbels (qv) which bridged the changeover to the high speed nuclear Skipjacks. Only *Darter* herself was completed as originally intended, looking similar to the Tangs with a long casing of high freeboard with the three conspicuous asymmetric domes of the BQG-4 (PUFFS) sonar but with squarer fin profile.

The last two of the class were halted for conversion for the carriage of two Regulus II missiles. While not identical, the two conversions were very similar, each boat being severed on the ways for the insertion of an extra section in the midbody. Forward of the fin the casing was widened and a high forecastle resulted from the plating-in of a pair of cylindrical, pressure-tight containers, some 11ft in diameter and over 50ft in length, for the storage and preparation of two missiles. Each cylinder is sealed by a domed, watertight door (one is seen open in the illustration) and rails lead aft to where the single launcher was located, forward of the heightened fin.

The increased size of hull was necessitated by the added control and navigation electronics and the extra crew to operate the system. All TTs were retained but the submerged performance of the submarines had been seriously degraded by their bloated forebodies and this armament was now primarily defensive.

Regulus II, of course, was never to be operational but both vessels deployed the Mark I until 1964, when the programme was abandoned. Both were de-commissioned apparently with no future until it was appreciated that their large capacity could be used to advantage in amphibious warfare, where troops or swimmers could be carried for clandestine operations, techniques pursued avidly by the Japanese during World War II. Accordingly, *Grayback* was taken in hand in 1967 for further conversion. All Regulus fittings were stripped, a further new hull section installed and accommodation for up to 70 troops with their equipment or swimmers with their 'delivery vehicles' installed. She was also re-engined and fitted with new electronics, being re-rated LPSS from the previous SSG. The near 100% cost-overrun prevented a similar conversion on the *Growler* in reserve since 1964 and, oddly, still retaining her SSG classification.

Grayback

Tang Patrol Submarine (SS)   USA

Tang, early appearance: for later configuration see
Romeo Romei (Italy).

		Laid Down	Launched	Completed
AGSS563	Tang	1949	1951	1951
AGSS565	Wahoo	1949	1951	1952
AGSS567	Gudgeon	1950	1952	1952

Displacement: 2,100 surfaced
2,700 submerged
Length (oa): 287ft
Beam: 27ft
Draught: 19ft
Machinery: Three diesel-generators Two motors
Two shafts 5,600shp for 16/16kts
Armament: Eight 21-inch TTs
Disposals: *Trigger* (SS564) to Italy, 1973; *Trout*
(SS566) to Iran, 1978; *Harder* (SS568) to Italy,
1974; *Tang* and *Wahoo* were slated for transfer to
Iran in 1979/80 but this will probably be cancelled

At the close of World War II German submarine
technology was far in advance of that of the Allies
but, as the latter had already constructed large fleets
during the war, no immediate and radical change
was apparent. It was early in 1949 before the
Americans laid down the first of a new Tang class,
based closely on the German Typ XXI, with clean
lines and an expanded battery capacity to improve
submerged speed from the then-customary 10, to
about 16kts. All of the earlier clutter periscopes
standards, guns, rails, bitts, etc, were either removed
or faired in; even the forward planes were made
retractable. A further major difference was in the
adoption of a hull some 40ft shorter than in earlier

boats and, in a vessel as volume-critical as a
submarine, savings had to be made, particularly in
view of the space demands of the extra batteries.

Thus, only two TTs were fitted aft (none at all was
first mooted) and a new, and highly compact, diesel
plant installed. In place of the earlier three or four
conventional in-line engines powering two propeller-
shafts through a gearbox, a 16-cylinder 'pancake'
diesel was fitted having four banks, each with four
horizontal cylinders, disposed radially. They set such
new records for unreliability that only the first four of
the class were so equipped and these were soon
replaced by three of the more usual 1,500bhp
Faibanks-Morse diesels, with the penalty that an
extra nine-foot section needed to be let into the hull.

During the FRAM modernisation of the 1960s, the
class was again lengthened and given improved
equipment and facilities to extend its useful life. The
illustration of *Tang* shows her state immediately
prior to this last reconstruction; for their subsequent
appearance, with the prominent PUFFS dome, see
the picture of the Italian *Romeo Romei* (ex-*Harder*).
Tang was re-classified AGSS in 1975 for use in
acoustic research, on her planned transfer to Iran,
the only remaining boat, *Gudgeon* was due to take
her place.

War-built Patrol Submarine (SS)   USA

	Balao class	Tench class
Displacement: surfaced	1,525	1,575
submerged	2,425	2,500
Length (oa):	311.5ft	312ft
Beam:	27ft	27ft
Draught:	17ft	17ft
Machinery: (both)	Diesels (6,500bhp) for surface propulsion	
	Motors (2,750hp) for submerged propulsion	
	Two shafts Speed 20/10kts	
Armament:	One/two 5-inch gun	One 5-inch gun
	Two 40mm guns	Two 40mm guns
	Ten 21-inch TTs	Ten 21-inch TTs

117

Sabalo (Balao class)

As the Pacific moved toward war in the late 1930s, the latest types of US submarine was the *Tambor*, whose basically adequate design formed the basis of the rapid expansion programmes instituted in 1939. Firm believers in the benefits of series production, the Americans commenced with the 72-strong Gato class, built in only four yards. Laid down between 1940 and 1943, these were 1,525-ton boats with a powerful battery of 10 TTs, six forward and four aft, and mostly armed with a 3-inch gun and a brace of 40mm, though some carried 5-inch, a short-barrelled, 25cal weapon. As operations were carried out largely on the surface, a high speed of 21kts was built in with 6,500bhp diesels, disposed in two separate spaces, as opposed to the earlier class's one, to improve compartmentation.

The American submarine proved to be one of the prime reasons for the downfall of Japan, an island power dependent absolutely upon a large merchant fleet whose protection she largely ignored. Submarine construction continued apace and, though 19 Gatos were lost to the enemy, they were more than adequately replaced by the very similar follow-on types, the Balao class, of which 124 were built and 10 lost. Indeed, so many were built that it was rumoured that suitable 'fish' names had given out and new ones were being invented. Like the Germans, the Americans built with all-welded, prefabricated sections and construction times were often better than nine months.

The last 18 Balaos were cancelled in 1944, when an improved version, known as the Tench class, was commenced. Again very similar these were capable of deeper diving, down to 600ft and, although no less than 116 were ordered, only 23 were completed, due to the close of hostilities.

After the war, when the new German boats, particularly the Typ XXI, were examined, it was apparent that a different philosophy existed. Where virtually all earlier boats had been configured for surface operation and were, in effect, surface ships capable of submerging, these newcomers were cleaned of all protuberances that would interfere with a smooth flow over the hull, which was now shaped for optimum performance in the submerged condition, packed with batteries to exploit its speed

potential and equipped with a Schnorkel (Snort) air tube, through which the boat could ventilate and recharge batteries without surfacing. Obviously posing a grave threat to surface ships, often themselves slowed by weather conditions, they were fortunately too late to affect the course of the war.

The impact of this new approach was such as to guarantee that no further boats of the 'old' type were again constructed and that a class of boat heavily based on the Typ XXI would be built by most of the major naval powers and, lastly, that a large programme of modification would be initiated to update the large fleets of war-built submarines.

The American programme was known as Guppy (Greater Underwater Propulsive Power) and 47 boats were rebuilt, 18 Tench and 29 Balao class, whilst a further five Tench class received Snort gear. Not all of the reconstructions were similar and are known as Guppy I, IA, II, IIA and III. To generalise, however, they can be categorised as Type III and the rest; all had their original 2,750hp electric motors replaced by a new pair of twice the power but only the Type III retained all four diesels. Together with other improvements, this resulted in a 326ft hull with a 20/15kts speed and a surfaced displacement of 1,975 tons. The remainder have hulls of differing lengths but typically 20ft shorter, with a surface displacement of 1,840 tons. They have retained only three of their original four diesels, so that their speed is 18/15kts; for the penalty of two knots on the surface, more internal space can be devoted to electronics, particularly sonar. Other variations were in battery size and number and in the control centre but the situation became further confused when, at a later date, some boats underwent FRAM modernisation in addition.

Though many of the Guppy submarines still serve under many flags, they are well due for replacement (a reason for the success of a well-designed boat such as the Typ 209) and none is left in the US navy. Probably the last war-built submarine disposed of by the Americans was the *Sealion*, sunk as a target in March 1977. The Balao class boat *Sabalo* (SS302), shown in the illustration, is typical of the Guppy conversions.

Petya Corvette USSR

Petya II class corvette.

Unit: c46-50, names not known
Displacement: 950 standard
1,100 full load
Length (oa): 269ft
Beam: 30ft
Draught: 10ft
Machinery: Two gas turbines c3,000shp for 30kts
Two diesels c5,000bhp for 16kts three shafts
Armament: Petya I
Four 76mm guns (2×2)
Four MBU-2500 AS launchers
Five AS TTs (1×5)
Petya II
Four 76mm guns (2×2)
Two MBU-2500A AS launchers
Ten AS TTs (2×5)

The coastal approaches to the USSR are shallow and, in the event of hostilities would need to be patrolled by NATO submarines in the disruption of inshore shipping and shipborne operations. Further, in the early 1960s, the first western submarine-borne ballistic missiles were of short enough range to demand launching from comparatively close-in to achieve any useful penetration. Both contingencies could be met by a strong force of AS corvettes and the first class of these was the *Petya*, first observed in 1962. Surprisingly, they were gas turbine propelled, predating even the early Kashins, but this power is used for high speed boost prior to attack, normal running being on the diesels coupled to the centreline shaft. The GTs work wing shafts independently.

The hull is of low freeboard with a sharp sheer forward, an arrangement which must have still proved wet, for a short bulwark was added right forward at a later date. Wetness not only reduces

visibility for the watchkeepers, it causes equipment to fail and can prove lethal in icing conditions in northern waters. A monoblock bridge structure is provided, abaft which is a low funnel/air intake of characteristic profile and almost square plan, divided along its centreline and devoted to the GTs. The diesels exhaust on either side near the waterline and it has become general practice to disguise the discolouration at these points by painting the hull black from there aft.

There exist three separate types of Petya, all of which have four 76mm guns in two twin gunhouses. These are DP weapons with an 85° elevation and a rate of fire of about 60rpm/barrel; they are radar-laid by the single Hawk Screech director atop the bridge. All three variants also mount a quintuple 400mm AS TT bank abaft the funnel. In the Petya I, these are backed up by four MBU-2500 AS rocket launchers, the older 'flat-pack' versions with 16 barrels and a 1.5-mile range. Two of these are mounted on the step forward of the bridge and two right aft. The Petya IIs have the later 12-barrelled MBU-2500A, two of whose radial mountings are again sited before the bridge but the after ones have been exchanged for a second bank of TTs.

A recent addition has been the further modification of about 10 Type Is to Type III, losing their after MBUs to a low deckhouse containing a VDS installation. The difference in profile between these and the later Mirka type should be noted. Some of the Types I and II are equipped with mine rails, running down either side from the midship TTs and terminating at the wide, flat transom. A dozen basic Petya Is were transferred to India but are different having a triple bank of long 21-inch TTs in place of the small calibre AS tubes.

Mirka Corvette USSR

Mirka II class corvette.

Units: c20, names not known
Displacement: 1,000 standard
1,100 full load
Length (oa): 269ft
Beam: 30ft
Draught: 10ft
Machinery: Two gas turbines c30,000shp for 30kts
Two diesels c6,000shp for 20kts
Armament: Mirka I
Four 76mm guns (2×2)
Four MBU-2500A AS launchers
Five 400mm AS TTs (1×5)
Mirka II
Four 76mm guns (2×2)
Two MBU-2500A AS launchers
Ten 400mm AS TTs (2×5)

Built between 1964 and 1969, the Mirkas were an unsatisfactory attempt to improve on the Petya, construction of which was later resumed. The problem seemed to centre on the very hot GT exhaust gases from the Petya's low funnel and the Mirka design tried to exploit the compactness of these engines by moving them right aft and releasing the higher volume centre section for other uses. This course required the after end to be increased in height by about five feet over its full width and, as the run aft appears finer than that of the Petya hull, a distinctive hard knuckle has resulted on either quarter. Atop this low structure are two prominent air intakes, facing aft to reduce salt spray ingestion. In the squared transom are two flapped exhaust apertures, similar to those in GT-propelled FPBs; these have obviated the need for a funnel, though travelling on GTs at low speeds in a following sea

could be a problem. The GTs are sited above the propellers, which they drive through a Vee gearbox; as there are only two shafts (compared with the Petya's three) the cruising diesels must drive through the same gearboxes. It will be seen from the picture that the diesels exhaust from a point much further forward than in the Petyas. By suppressing the funnel the single mast can be sited almost amidships, where the antennas are subjected to less violent ship movement, leaving a gap between it and the bridge structure which makes for an easily recognisible profile.

Again there are two versions, known as the Mirka I and II; except that each has MBU-2500A AS rocket launchers, their weapon fits are identical with those of the Petya I and II. The raised poop rendered almost impossible the laying of mines or the carriage of a VDS and, as the class was terminated at about 20 units in favour of further Petyas, it would seem that they are deemed less than successful. Nevertheless, it is of interest to compare them with their counterparts of 40 years ago, the British Flowers, which reintroduced the corvette as a type. Similar in displacement, their length/breath ratio was only about 6:1 compared with the Russian's 9:1 and their 2,750hp triple expanders drove them at about 16kts compared with the 30+ of the contemporary classes. Even at 20kts, the latter has also a superior range and an incomparably more powerful armament. Only in the matter of seakeeping could they be called inferior. No western fleet has matched the current Russian enthusiasm for the AS corvette and only the French A69 is really comparable, though the Danish KV72 is closer from the machinery aspect.

Poti Corvette

USSR

Units: c65, names not known
Displacement: 500 standard
650 full load
Length (oa): 195ft
Beam: 27ft
Draught: 9ft
Machinery: Two gas turbines c2,400shp for 34kts
Two diesels c8,000bhp Two shafts(?)
CODAG configuration
Armament: Two 57mm guns (1×2)
Two MBU-2500A AS rocket launchers
Four 400mm AS TTs (4×1)

Built thoughout the 1960s the Poti is really a diminutive of the Mirka and aimed at inshore AS operations. Its similar raised poop emphasises the low freeboard aft of amidships from which the hull

rises forward in a pronounced sheer that flattens out on the forecastle; no forward bulwark is fitted. Two MBU-2500As are mounted forward on different levels and are staggered either side of the centreline, presumably to reduce mutual interference when firing. Each mounting has 12 barrels, fired sequentially and rapidly to place their projectiles in a fixed pattern out to a maximum range of over three miles. They can be both trained and elevated, and are reloaded automatically from below with the barrels in a vertical position. Four fixed AS TTs are angled out from the waist of the ship; no reloads are provided. The Hercules hull-mounted sonar that is carried is a set found in a wide variety of Soviet ships but there is no room for a VDS which would, in any case, be of doubtful value in shallow water.

For defence against surface ships and aircraft a

twin 57mm mounting and its Muff Cob director are placed amidships. They are sited here to allow the MBUs a clear zone forward but it has done nothing for their effective firing arcs. Some early units may still carry the old-pattern twin 57mm gunhouse and the 'flat-pack' MBU-2500 launchers, though these will probably be replaced during major refits.

Somewhat unusually, the Poti appears to be a four-shaft ship with a CODAG machinery arrangement. It can only be assumed that the power of the diesels was sufficient to make it advantageous to run them in combination with the GTs. This makes for complex gear arrangements which, may, in turn, account for the quadruple shafts. As with the larger Soviet corvettes, a Strut Curve air surveillance radar is provided in addition to a navigation set. A few Potis have been transferred to Bulgaria and Romania.

Grisha Corvette   USSR

Units: c32, names not known
Displacement: c850 standard
c950 full load
Length (oa): 236ft
Beam: 33ft
Draught: 10ft
Machinery: One gas turbine c12,000shp
Two diesels c16,000shp
CODAG arrangement Three shafts c32kts
Armament: Grisha I
One twin SA-N-1 launcher
Two 57mm guns (1×2)
Two MBU-2500As
Four 21-inch TTs (2×2)
Grisha II
Four 57mm guns (2×2)
Two MBU-2500As
Four 21-in TTs (2×2)
Grisha III
One twin SA-N-1 launcher
Two 57mm guns (1×2)
Two MBU-5500As
Four 21-in TTs (2×2)
Sextuple 23mm guns

This workman-like little escort appeared in 1969 and lies in size between the Poti and the Petya/Mirka and continues the trend of the former toward beamier hulls. Still searching for the ideal combination of GT and diesel, the Russians have here tried again, with a three-shaft arrangement which reduces gear complexity by having a prime mover on each, with the diesels powering the wing shafts. These diesels have been much increased in power and the GT is used in combination, developing only about 40% of the total shp (cf 75% in Poti, 70% in Mirka and nearly 85% in Petya). The GTs intakes and exhaust are again through a low, square, funnel offset to port with the diesels exhausting through the side to avoid long internal trunking from their separate space.

Dryness has been improved by the incorporation of a full-width deckhouse below the bridge and a high forecastle whose freeboard incidentally provides the volume for the 'pop-up' twin SA-N-4 launcher, whose silo cover is prominent. As on all Soviet corvettes, the anchors are stowed in pockets to reduced the pounding in a head sea. The addition of the point-defence missile is a significant step forward as earlier classes were rather vulnerable to air attack. Associated with the SA-N-4 is the Pop Group director often, as in the picture, coyly shrouded (it is clearly visible on the picture of the Nanuchka corvette). A Strut Curve radar provides for air surveillance.

Only Types I and III carry an SAM system, all have a twin 57mm mounting aft but the Grisha II has a second forward in place of the SA-N-4 and is believed to be police-manned for coastwatch duties. Adjacent to the after 57mm mounting on Types I and II is the associated Muff Cob director and forward of it is a large hinged plate; as the funnel is too far forward for its hot GT exhaust to damage the antenna it is unlikely that the plate is a heat shield, so its likely function is to protect exposed bridge personnel from microwave radiation when the director is active on a forward bearing. The Type III has an enlarged deckhouse aft, housing the sub-structure of a sextuple Gatling-type 23mm gun a last-ditch defence against incoming SSMs that have evaded both the SA-N-4 and ECM. A Bass Tilt radar is mounted atop a small house forward of it and at such an elevation that the hinged flap is not necessary; this radar can, presumably, also serve the guns as no Muff Cob is fitted. All three types carry a brace of MBU-2500A AS rocket launchers, mounted at a more comfortable distance forward of the bridge than previously. Each is equipped also with paired, trainable TTs on either side; these are the large-bore 21-inch tubes capable of launching a wide variety of torpedoes. To wring the last ounce of offensive capacity out of these small boats, the designers have also added min rails and depth charge traps. A keel-mounted sonar is carried though some have a small VDS — truly *multum in parvo*.

Grisha I class corvette: note extreme liveliness of ship in spite of very moderate sea with no breaking crests.

Nanuchka Corvette

USSR

Units: c20 names not known
Displacement: 750 standard
950 full load
Length (oa): 195ft
Beam: 40ft
Draught: 9ft
Machinery: Six (?) diesel on three shafts
28,000bhp for 32kts
Armament: Two triple SS-N-9 launchers
One twin SA-N-4 launcher
Two 57mm guns (1×2)

Designed as a stable platform for the SS-N-9 (Siren) missile, the Nanuchka stands at present in a class by herself. Of the same length as larger western FACs, she appears far more imposing with the beamy (L/B about 5:1) hull topped by a massive superstructure of a height governed largely by the requirement to see over the flanking triple missile launchers. Surprisingly, in view of the Russian experience of GT-propelled corvettes, a multi-diesel propulsion system has been chosen with two diesels on each of three shafts; where four diesels on two shafts would seem to have been more tidy. It is unlikely that such a hull could be driven any faster by higher installed power. Of a size ideal for all-weather use in the smaller seas such as the North Sea, Mediterranean or Far Eastern waters, the Nanuchka used in a group attack would provide a major headache for an escort commander.

The SS-N-9 seems still unique to this class and the new Sarancha and little has yet been published on it, though its launcher would suggest a length of about 30ft (compared with the Exocet's 17ft). Known as Band Stand, the guidance radars are housed under a conspicuous dome, flanked by smaller domes but, as an SSM of this size would be expected to have a maximum range of 150 miles, a mid-course correction would be required from an aircraft or submarine to realise the system's full potential. No helicopter is carried. The blast deflectors abaft the launcher have been filled-in in later units, such as that shown, to provide a triangular extension on either side of the superstructure.

Forward is the now-familiar circular cover to a retractable SA-N-4 launcher and the leading face of the superstructure below the Pop Group director, is also configured for blast deflection. As these craft are intended to work in narrow seas where aircraft would hold sway, the designers have taken pains to provide a good AA armament, an area in which most FACs are highly deficient. In addition to the SA-N-4, a twin 57mm gunhouse is sited right aft, together with its Muff Cob director. With a maximum range of about 5,000m and a rate of fire of about 120rpm/barrel, these weapons could get off about 40 aimed shots with pre-fragmented ammunition at, say, an incoming Exocet, assuming that Muff Cob has the necessary reaction time and discrimination.

An interesting feature of the Nanuchka is what she does not carry: no TTs, AS weaponry or mine rails. With the one-of-everything mentality of Soviet designers, this could point to a small payload in spite of the hull's apparent stability and the slow building rate of 2/3 per year is unusual. As the Komars proved the Styx for the Osas, so we may yet see that the Nanuchkas precede another SS-N-9-armed class. Six down-graded units are being delivered to India, armed only with four SS-N-11 missiles and guns.

Kronstadt Patrol Craft

USSR

Units: Over 150 built between 1950 and 1956; none now believed to be active in the Soviet fleet.
Displacement: 320 standard
390 full load
Length (oa): 170ft
Beam: 21ft
Draught: 9ft

Machinery: Three diesels on three shafts
3,600shp for 22kts
Armament: One 85mm gun
Two 37mm guns (2×1)
Later units had two MBU-1800 AS rocket launchers forward in lieu of the 85mm gun

Though the Kronstadts have probably passed from the ranks of the Soviet fleet, many still serve under the flags of friendly (or once-friendly) states. As the last was laid down in the mid-1950s, all are now elderly but the sheer versatility of the design still guarantees employment over a wide range of duties. Hard to classify precisely, the type had its genesis in the American 173ft steel-hulled 'submarine chasers' transferred during World War II. These PCs spawned the Russian-built Artillerist class of the immediate postwar years, of which the Kronstadts were slightly enlarged follow-ons.

Flush-decked, with an easy sheer at either end, they appear larger than their tonnage would suggest by virtue of the large funnel and substantial super-structure. Intended for AS operations close inshore, the early units had only DCs but soon gained an MBU-900 four-barrelled AS rocket launcher in a fold-flat mounting on the port side. A few lost their forward gun to a pair of MBU-1800 five-barrelled launchers, a great improvement but reducing their defensive armament considerably. An interesting contrast is seen in the Kronstadt in the Indonesian section with a Hedgehog of US origin forward, one of the original 37mm guns (less shield) aft and two twin 25mm mountings in the waist. Originally all had the almost obligatory mine rails aft, with a capacity of about 10 mines. The machinery layout is rather odd with three diesels on three shafts, rather over-complex and probably forced on the designers by availability of engines.

Besides AS work, their shallow draught and simple design have made them popular with 'emergent' navies without major support facilities in both patrol and escort roles. Examples may still be found under the flags of Albania, China, Cuba, Indonesia and Romania.

SO-I Patrol Craft   USSR

Units: 60-70 left of about 150 built between 1956 and 1966
Displacement: 210 standard
250 full load
Length (oa): 138ft
Beam: 21ft
Draught: 7ft
Machinery: Three diesels on three shafts
c6,000shp for 28kts
Armament: Two/four 25mm guns (1/2×2)
Four five-barrelled MBU-1800 AS rocket launchers
Two 400mm AS TTs (in some)

Though assumed to be a follow-on class to the Kronstadt, the SO-I lacks the former's versatility and is firmly geared to seaward AS defence. Again like the Kronstadt, the design was inspired by US craft transferred during World War II, in this case the 95-ton SC type. Superstructure is minimal, with a bridge house and small deckhouse only, separated by a gap which probably accommodates machinery access hatches.

The foredeck is dominated by the four MBU-1800s, whose 20 barrels are seemingly designed for a quick, 'saturation' kill, for magazine capacity cannot be on a scale to satisfy such a battery for more than a few salvoes. As built, the SO-Is each had a twin 25mm gun mounting forward and aft but, in some boats, the latter has been landed in favour of two 400mm TTs angled out on either beam and, apparently, blocking the short lengths of mine rails. No obvious means are available for the stowage of reloads. Depth charges are carried aft, the racks being shorter in the torpedo-armed boats.

The steel hull is prominently belted aft and the three diesels exhaust through the side, which is painted black in this area. A small Tamir sonar is carried in the hull but radar is confined to the Pot Head, whose antenna is flanked by those of IFF sets. With far superior craft, such as the Potis available it is surprising that so many SO-Is are still retained and many more operate with the fleets of Algeria, Bulgaria, Cuba, Egypt, East Germany, Iraq, North Korea and South Yemen, with some possibly in Vietnam.

Komar FAC (missile)   USSR

Units: c100 built between about 1958 and 1961; none left under Soviet flag
Displacement: 75 standard
85 full load
Length (oa): 87ft
Beam: 21ft
Draught: 5ft
Machinery: Four diesels on four shafts
4,800shp for 40kts
Armament: Two launchers for SS-N-2 (Styx) SSM
Two 25mm guns (1 × 2)

When the SS-N-2 (Styx) missile became operational in the late 1950s it found the Western navies ill-prepared in countermeasures and the Russians exploited the position by commencing a crash programme of conversions of P6 FAC hulls to get as many missiles to sea in the shortest possible time. Known as the Komar class, about 100 had been rebuilt by the end of 1961, when they were superseded by the purpose-designed Osa I. Two launchers were sited right aft, their size requiring sponsons to be added to the hull. Crude by today's standards, the arrangement consisted of fixed launch rails carrying the missile, which was protected by an open-sided tube of flattened section. This added mass was considerable and meant the sacrifice of the twin 25mm mounting normally carried aft, and the shifting aft of the forward gun and super-structure to reduce pounding forward, leaving a characteristically long forecastle. A widely-braced lattice mast was added to bear the antenna of the Square Tie target acquisition radar, flanked by the High Pole IFF antennas.

Retaining the P6 machinery arrangement of four diesels on four shafts, the Komars were good for 40kts in favourable conditions but extremely vulnerable to aerial attack from astern. Their Styx missiles were originally good for only about 10 miles under radio control but gave the West a fright until ECM caught up; the improved SA-N-2A more than doubled the range and relied more on passive homing devices, notably IR. None of this impressively fast programme of craft is left under Soviet colours but many still serve in Algeria, China, Cuba, Egypt, Indonesia, North Korea and Syria.

Osa FAC (missile)

USSR

Units: c220 boats were built during the 1960s
Displacement: 160 standard
205 full load
Length (oa): 123ft
Beam: 28ft
Draught: 6ft
Machinery: Three diesels on three shafts
c10,000shp for 35kts
Armament: Four launchers for SS-N-2B (Styx)
SSMs
(later boats possibly carry SS-N-11)

The Osa was the world's first purpose-designed missile-armed FAC and the Komar programme was abandoned as the new boats began to come forward in 1961. With a much larger steel hull, the Osa could carry four Styx and keep the sea the more easily. Over 100 are still active under the Russian flag and a similar number have been transferred abroad, with China producing large numbers of copies. Between them they represent a high proportion of the world's missile-armed FACs but their threat is now waning with increasing age and vulnerability of the SS-N-2B to jamming. This latter fact probably stimulated the introduction of the improved version, known as the SS-N-11.

The impact of the Styx on Western thinking was considerable with the loss of the *Eilat* in 1967 and then the events of the Indo-Pakistani conflict ramming the lesson well home. Relying on their overwhelming carrier-borne aerial striking power, the Western navies had concentrated on the development of SAMs to counter the Soviet aircraft armed with stand-off weapons to the almost total neglect of SSM production. The sudden incursion of potentially hostile SSMs coincided with the accelerated reduction in western flightdecks, and the realisation stimulated an urgent programme for the production of similar weapons. Had there been a war at about this time, the NATO fleets would have been found lacking.

The Osas are conventional, with a slightly flattened forward sheer and pronounced hard chine. All of the four canisters are aligned fore-and-aft with the after ones firing over the forward. They are a great improvement on those of the Komars, protecting their contents and enabling a pre-flight warming, essential in Northern conditions. On the early Osas, the launchers were slabsided; later craft, labelled Osa IIs (see under Libya for illustration) carry round-section, ribbed canisters which may be associated with the later, improved versions of the missile. Defensive firepower has been greatly improved, with a twin 30mm at either end, the position and height of the after mounting varying accordingly to the configuration of the launchers. A Drum Tilt director is conspicuous on its tower aft.

Three diesels are fitted, each powering one shaft, and of higher power than previously used. There are indications that they are of short life, possibly due to poor maintenance. Osas have been transferred extensively to the navies of sympathetic states, many of which are politically unstable, with all that that implies. Recipient flags to date are: Algeria, Bulgaria, China, Cuba, Egypt, East Germany, Finland, India, Iraq, Libya, North Korea, Poland, Romania, Somalia, Syria and Yugoslavia.

Osa I class FAC (missile).

Stenka FPC

Units: 60-70 built since late 1960s; names not known
Displacement: 180 standard
220 full load
Length (oa): 125ft
Beam: 28ft
Draught: 6ft
Machinery: Three diesels on three shafts
c10,000shp for 35kts
Armament: Four 30mm guns (2×2)
Four 400mm AS TTs (4×1)

A replacement for the SO-I type patrol craft, the Stenka is based on the standard Osa hull, with the addition of a low bulwark forward and anchors in hawses on either bow. The superstructure is large for the size of hull and is prominently ribbed externally, a feature that would seem to encourage ice formation in adverse conditions. An enclosed wheelhouse has an open bridge abaft it and the whole has the appearance of being designed for rapid sealing in fallout areas. The gun armament is on the same scale as that in the Osas with the associated Drum Tilt mounted in a near-identical position aft. Missiles have been exchanged for four fixed AS TTs, singly mounted aft, where depth charge traps are also sited. Presumably all carry a hull-mounted sonar but some have a VDS of the small type usually carried by the Ka-25 (Hormone) helicopter.

As on the Osa a Square Head interrogator radar antenna is mounted fore and aft of the mast but the majority mount a Pot Drum search antenna at the masthead, only a few being equipped with the improved Square Tie of the Osas. The shrouded fitting on the bridge roof in the example shown is not normally present. It would seem probable that the machinery layout has also been inherited from the FACs but this is by no means certain. An unusual feature is the motor boat in low davits, reflecting the coastal function of the class.

An 'export' variant known as the 'Mol' has been supplied to Sri Lanka, Somalia, and (possibly) Ethiopia. It carries no TTs and only optically-laid guns. Radars are the elderly Pot Head and a High Pole answering IFF antenna.

A derivative of the same class is the Turya, a hybrid hydrofoil of the same philosophy as that which produced the P8. By adding this extra lift forward, the weapon fit has changed dramatically, with four sided full-calibre 21-inch TTs and the great bulk of a twin 57mm gunhouse aft. To avoid weight forward, only a paired 25mm is fitted. Hull, electronics and general fittings are otherwise much as those on the Stenka, though the speed has been augmented to better than 40kts.

Shershen FAC (torpedo)

Units: c90 built between 1962 and mid-1970s
Displacement: 155 standard
170 full load
Length (oa): 116ft
Beam: 24ft

Draught: 5ft
Machinery: Three diesels on three shafts
c12,000shp for 38+kts
Armament: Four 30mm guns (2×2)
Four 21-inch TTs (4×1)

Another variant on the basic hull Osa, the Shershens would seem to be designed to complement these missile boats in a similar fashion to, say, the Swedish Spicas and Jägerens or the Typ 143s and 148s of the Bundesmarine. Where the earlier Komar had stemmed from the torpedo-armed P6 hull, the process was here reversed. A Shershen, in fact, looks very much like an Osa, with the long, continuous deckhouse flanked by anti-ship TTs rather than missile canisters. Without the latter items, it has been possible to move the after 30mm mounting further forward, leaving space right aft for DC racks and two short mine rails, though whether both weapons could be carried simultaneously is doubtful.

The large TTs are timely reminders that these weapons are carried also by almost every Soviet warship of any size at a time when Western

equivalents seem to almost abandon them for anti-ship use. Elsewhere, the modern long-range, wire-guided torpedo is the virtual preserve of submarine and FAC. The electronics fit virtually parallels that of the Osa and Stenka, but with only one Square Head antenna. This set complements the two High Pole aerials on the spreader to provide both interrogation and identification for IFF purposes in the high-speed, hair-trigger war of flotilla attack, instantaneous discernment between friend and foe is absolutely vital.

Around 50 Shershens are believed to be under the Soviet flag, with a like number shared between the fleets of Bulgaria, Egypt, East Germany, North Korea, and Yugoslavia, with a pair possibly with Vietnam.

P6 FAC (torpedo)   USSR

Units: Several hundred built in 1950s and early 1960s
Displacement: 65 standard
75 full load
Length (oa): 84ft
Beam: 20ft
Draught: 5ft
Machinery: Four diesels on four shafts
5,400bhp for 40+kts
Armament: Four 25mm guns (2 × 2)
Two 21-inch TTs

This highly prolific class was a great improvement on the preceding P4s, with a hull large enough to carry a reasonable gun armament and two full-sized TTs. It is surprising that so high a proportion of armament weight has been devoted to gun mountings when the surrender of the after guns would possibly have allowed for a second pair of tubes. As it is, the guns are not apparently remotely directed, though the boats do carry either a Pot Head (as shown) or Skin

Head surface search radar and a High Pole/Dead Duck IFF combination. The search radar is carried on a separate mast which, apparently, folds backward.

Where the P4s were built totally of light alloys, the P6s have reverted to composite construction, though the hull is still built for planing and driven easily in calm weather to well beyond 40kts by the four diesel-four shaft machinery.

Probably, over 200 hulls were completed as torpedo-armed P6s and about a further 100 provided the basis for the Komar programme (qv). Some 50 hulls were finished without TTs, carrying in their place depth charge racks and projectors; known as the MO-VI Patrol Craft, most have now been retired. At the latter end of the 1950s about a score were re-engined with gas turbines for evaluation purposes; termed the P8 class, they were easily distinguished by their small funnel, whose presence meant the suppression of the mainmast. To give the bows more lift, with the extra power, a pair of semi-submerged foils were added forward. Not successful

as an experiment, the group reverted to diesel propulsion some years later. Still differing in detail, they were then termed P10s.

The few remaining Soviet-flag P6s are being replaced by Shershens but many remain in Algeria, China (PR), Cuba, Egypt, East Germany, Guinea, Indonesia, Iraq, Nigeria, North Korea, Poland, Somalia, Tanzania and the Yemen, though many are probably by now in poor condition.

P4 FAC (torpedo) USSR

Units: c200 built between 1950 and 1956; none now active under Soviet flag
Displacement: 25 standard
30 full load
Length (oa): 63ft
Beam: 13ft
Draught: 5ft
Machinery: Two diesels on two shafts
2,400bhp for c45kts max
Armament: Two 12.7mm or 14.5mm guns (1×2)
Two 18-inch (450mm) TTs

Although the Soviet fleet has phased out the P4, about 120 — in various stages of efficiency — are still to be found with friendly powers, Albania, Bulgaria, Cuba, China, Cyprus, Egypt, North Korea, Romania, Syria and Tanzania. Built completely of light alloys, they had the long-forecastled look of earlier craft such as the MAS or CMB. Derived from the P2, the first postwar FAC, construction began in the early 1950s with the availability of a new and reliable 1,200bhp diesel, a unit which was used up to the introduction of the Osa. Probably responding best to good maintenance, these diesels have proved less than satisfactory to some of their new owners.

The P4 presents a low profile but its main armament of only 18 inch torpedoes lacks sufficient punch to pose much of a menace. Coupled with the light guns and a hull too small to cope with anything but the most favourable weather conditions, it is a matter of comment, perhaps, that the type has lasted as long as it has.

Sarancha Missile-Armed Hydrofoil USSR

Displacement: 200 standard
250 full load
Length (oa): 190ft
Beam: 33ft
Draught: 6ft
Machinery: Two gas turbines Two diesels CODOG
Two shafts Max speed c45kts
Armament: Four launchers for SS-N-9 SSM (2×2)
One twin launcher for SA-N-4 SAM
One sextuple 23mm gun

The basic Osa hull was used for the development of a whole range of FACs but it now seems to have been superseded at last as, in 1976, the first of a new type appeared. Known as the Sarancha it may well be a full hydrofoil as opposed to a foil-assisted FAC, but little is certain about it except that it makes a significant jump in both size and offensive capacity. It has already been noted that the Styx (SS-N-2) and its later derivatives are now not really up to meeting the challenge of modern defence systems and the

SS-N-9 carried by the Sarancha may well be the chosen successor. Only the Nanuchkas have previously carried the SS-N-9 and the newcomer is only slightly shorter but considerably less beamy, relying on foils rather than beam to produce a stable launching platform. In a hydrofoil, of course, weight is at a premium and thus only two paired missile launchers are carried in place of the earlier class's triples. This, in turn, means that the superstructure can be considerably lower, though still crowned by the large dome of the associated Band Stand acquisition and control group.

Again, in spite of the weight forward, the 'pop-up' fast reaction SA-N-4 has been retained. However, the Pop Group system, hitherto always in company with this missile, is absent, replaced by the Fish Bowl antenna on the mast's leading face. It would seem unlikely that Pop Group has been superseded by the latter so it may be that a reduced performance has been accepted, possibly an inability to intercept incoming SSMs. Should this be so, the addition of

Pchela class hydrofoil.

the Gatling-type 23mm aft, together with its distinctive Bass Tilt directors, would make sense.

Further weight is saved by the adoption of a pair of GTs as main machinery but it is not clear if these drive a pair of marine screws directly (which would suggest another semi-hydrofoil) or whether they power water jets. A pair of low power diesels are supplied for use in low-speed hull-borne movements.

This extremely fast craft would be very difficult to counter in conditions that suit it, having the answer to the FAC's greatest enemy, the helicopter. It has the weaponry and visible ECM to give an incoming SSM a bad time and the horizon range of its own SSMs would be sufficient to outrange the automatic guns fitted to the majority of escorts. The 4.5 or

5-inch gun still makes sense and it should be remembered that the US Navy has found it worthwhile to develop a new, light-weight 8-inch weapon for retro-fitting to existing ships.

About 20 smaller Pchela class hydrofoils are also active. These are true hydrofoils with a semi-submerged foil forward and a full submerged foil aft. Of only 80 tons full load they carry neither missiles nor torpedoes but are armed with two twin, fully automatic 23mm guns. They have twin shafted diesel propulsion and appear to be designed for coastal surveillance, though a small sonar and half a dozen DCs can be carried so that they could probably be used effectively with helicopters in the inshore AS mode.

Surface-Effect Vehicles   USSR

In the field of the hovercraft, the Russians are following a process of development more closely akin to that of the UK than the Americans, who are concentrating efforts toward the realisation of a high-speed AS platform of up to 3,000 tons and with rigid sidewalls. The Soviet interest seems to lie in fast assault applications and their designs, so far, parallel those of the British, fully amphibious by virtue of 'noisy' airscrew propulsion and with flexible skirts.

Largest known is the *Aist*, which bears an uncanny resemblance to the British SRN4 but with the propulsion pylons mounted well aft with each pair of airscrews facing each other in a 'push-pull' arrangement. In other respects, the boxy hull, ro-ro ramps and doors, and the control cabin, the layout is very similar, though the overall length is about 13ft greater. Being a military craft the mast is more substantial for the support of more comprehensive electronics and a twin 30mm fully automatic gun mounting, similar to that on many types of warship, is sited atop the control cabin. Useful deadweight should be in the order of 60-70 tons, making them capable of carrying in excess of 500 troops, fully equipped, or about 25 smallish wheeled vehicles, or,

if equipped with a strengthened deck, four light armoured vehicles. It can also be assumed that the Russians are fully alive to the *Aist's* potential in mine countermeasures and minelaying.

Another type is the 30-ton *Gus*, of about the same size as a BH7 but with its twin engines aft. Having been developed from a commercial design it is capable of carrying only personnel and has no ro-ro potential. In addition the Russians are believed to be the only power actively developing a practical wing-in-ground (WIG) vehicle. Best visualised as a stubby-winged aircraft, it attains initial lift by thrust vectoring and then, as its velocity increases, through its wings. By limiting its flight to an elevation of about 70-100ft, a rolling bubble of air, hovercraft style, is created beneath it. Only a small forward thrust is then necessary to give the craft velocities of several hundred knots. Still very much in the development phase its forecast payload is rather more than 100 tons, giving it potential in assault from the sea or rapid AS reaction, both roles where it would not encounter high obstacles. It would seem extremely vulnerable to small ground-to-air missiles and its inability to hover, or even reduce its speed significantly, would seem to be disadvantageous.

Delta SSBN

USSR

Units: c12-15 Delta Is built since 1972
c6-8 Delta IIs built since 1973

		Delta I	**Delta II**
Displacement:	surfaced	8,500	9,500
	submerged	10,000	11,500
Length (oa):		443ft	498ft
Beam:		39ft	39ft
Draught:		30ft	30ft
Machinery: (both)		Two nuclear reactors powering two steam turbines	
		Two shafts c50,000shp for 20/28kts	
Armament:		Twelve SS-N-8 launchers	Sixteen SS-N-8 launchers
		Six 21-inch TTs	Six 21-inch TTs

Delta I class SSBN.

As with major Western powers, Russia places great reliance on her SSBN fleet for the deployment of the larger part of her nuclear strike capability and, again like them, the various stages in the deterrent's development can be traced through the submarines built to carry it. One major difference in operation is that comparable western submarines can 'lose' themselves rapidly in deep water close their bases whereas the Soviet equivalents must often traverse shallow areas which could constitute a real hazard in war. This and their constrictive geography effectively precludes the Baltic and Black Sea as bases and, in the Far East, new facilities have had to be constructed at Petropavlorsk on the inhospitable Kamchatka peninsula, adjacent to the deeps of the Kuril Trench. The area is very remote, excellent from the security aspect but a drawback in the event of war. The greatest importance is thus attached to the northern exits on the Barents Sea, easily controlled and hard by the excellent concealment of the ice cap.

When the SS-N-8 missile was introduced in 1973, its 4,000+ mile range was superior to that of the American Trident I then being developed but its physical size meant that a simple 'stretching' of the preceding Yankee class would not suffice. Thus the Delta I emerged, not only beamier and longer, but with a pronounced hump abaft the fin, and still accommodating only 12 missiles. Nevertheless, it may be that the class was produced to plan, because although, soon afterward, the Delta II was introduced, essentially similar but with an extra

section to house the 'normal' 16 missiles, the Delta I programme continued in parallel.

In appearance the exterior is well rounded and devoid of unnecessary protuberances: lightening holes have been tidied up considerably to reduce noise. The long fin acts as a stabiliser, houses a large variety of retractable sensors and being well forwards supports the diving planes, American-style. A major difference lies in the twin shafts common to most Soviet submarines.

Six defensive TTs are carried forward but the greater part of the bows is given up to the passive sonar housing, visible externally as a lighter-coloured strip; its prime task is to give the submarine adequate warning of other vessels so that it can retire undetected.

Though the Delta IIs were the world's largest submarines, they will be eclipsed by the American Ohio class but, where the latter have had large cost and time overruns, the Delta IIs are coming forward several per year and have had the SS-N-8 at sea since 1974. The SS-N-8 has been developed further into the SS-N-18, of better than 5,000 miles range and capable of carrying MIRV warheads. It is associated with the project name Typhoon and may be carried by later Deltas (known as Delta IIIs) or in an entirely new design to rival the Ohios, which carry 24 launchers. The range of the new missile will have the bonus that they can be launched from areas of sea closer to home, which can be kept fairly secure from counter-attack.

Yankee SSBN

USSR

Units: c34 built between 1967 and 1976
Displacement: 8,200 surfaced
9,700 submerged
Length (oa): 425ft
Beam: 33ft
Draught: 28ft
Machinery: Two nuclear reactors powering two steam turbines
Two shafts c40,000shp for 25/30kts
Armament: Sixteen SS-N-6 launchers
Six 21-inch TTs

In numbers, dimensions and offensive capacity the Yankees approximate fairly closely to the American Franklin/Lafayette groups and demonstrate how one state's efforts are largely geared to the negation of another's. The two series were not concurrent; at that time the USA was well ahead in SLBM development and the availability of the A2 Polaris allowed them to lay down their first hull in 1961 and the 31-boat series was completed in 1967, with later submarines carrying A3s. Only then was the Soviet equivalent to the A2, the SS-N-6 (Sawfly) ready for service, and its vehicles, the Yankees, were

not commenced until 1966, running to a series of 34, whose construction took about nine years and overlapped the early part of the Delta programme. They were constructed in both Arctic and Pacific yards.

Twin screw propulsion has been used, reducing the power required on each shaft in spite of the available shp being higher than in western equivalents but with the penalty of smaller diameters and higher revs. Otherwise, they could almost be straight copies of the Americans, with marginally greater freeboard. Hull detail is, however, not so clean, with numerous lightening holes below the casing in place of one continuous slot. This, together with the twin screws, would generate external noise additional to that created by the machinery, an undesirable feature on craft designed to operate without detection.

It has been reported that the efficacy of the SS-N-6 has been improved by the addition of MIRV heads. This could possibly be the new SS-N-17 intermediate-ranged missile being retrofitted to the class.

Hotel SSBN

USSR

Units: Eight built between about 1958 and 1962
Displacement: 4,750 surfaced
5,500 submerged
Length (oa): 377ft
Beam: 29ft
Draught: 25ft

Machinery: One reactor powering two steam turbines
Two shafts c25,000shp for 20/22kts
Armament: Three SS-N-5 launchers in Hotel II
Six SS-N-8 launchers in Hotel III
Six 21-inch TTs forward
Four 16-inch (400mm) TTs aft

Hotel II class SSBN.

With hulls closely related to those of the contemporary Echo and November classes, the Hotels are believed to have been originally intended as nuclear-propelled, torpedo-armed attack submarines, complementing the missile-armed 'conventionals' of the Golf class. Presumably the great advantages of nuclear propulsion then became more apparent and the Hotels, too, were fitted with the elongated type of fin inseparable from the early launchers.

Three of the 300-mile SS-N-4 (Sark) missiles were first carried and, as these were over 37ft in length and the pressure hull only about 29ft diameter, the reason for the fin is clear. Even though the fin is around 100ft in length — with consequences to submerged handling that can only be guessed at — only three vertical tubes were carried and an actual launch required the submarine to partially surface, an action amounting almost to suicide. Almost as soon as the class was completed, therefore, the boats went back to the yards for a retro-fitting of the 700-mile SS-N-5 (Serb), only

marginally shorter but probably capable of being launched from below the surface. As approach to the enemy's coast to this extent at the present time would be a hazardous procedure, the continued use of the class by the Russians is a little puzzling but may be for two reasons: firstly, the missiles are no longer intended for strategic work but to 'saturate' the area in which a western SSBN would be known to operate and thus almost guaranteeing its destruction, or secondly, that all overage hulls are being kept going for the purpose of a 'legalised' one-to-one replacement by modern units under the terms of the international SALT agreements.

As a possible hangover from their 'attack' origins, the Hotels carry four AS TTs aft in addition to their normal battery of six 21-inch tubes forward. Their overall appearance is rather messy and looks the compromise that it is; twin-screwed, they were the last missile armed class to mount their diving planes forward. One of the type, known as a Hotel III, was converted to a trials ship for the SS-N-8 system later to be fitted to the Deltas.

Charlie SSGN

USSR

Units: c12 built since 1968
Displacement: 4,500 surfaced
5,100 submerged
Length (oa): 287ft
Beam: 33ft
Draught: 25ft
Machinery: One reactor powering steam turbines c25,000shp for 20/30kts
Armament: Eight SS-N-7 launchers
Six 21-inch TTs

With the introduction of the 22ft long SS-N-7, the Russians had a cruise missile small enough to house within a submarine hull, in contrast to the various unlovely elevating arrangements used previously on the SS-N-3 (Shaddock) boats. In the Charlies, the already portly body swells toward the bows to provide space between pressure hull and casing for the near-vertical stowage of eight launch tubes, in two rows of four, whose flush-fitting covers are just discernible in the picture. Abaft these covers can be seen another, narrow and diagonally disposed and probably the torpedo hatch serving the forward battery of torpedoes. With all this weaponry stowed

forward, the optimum siting for a large passive sonar array has been sacrificed and that fitted has probably been built into an inferior position in the fin, a long and rounded affair that is typically Russian in appearance. The class has extremely high freeboard and resembles the Victor type and the L/B ratio of about 9:1 contrasts with that of the 13:1 or so of the preceding Echo II.

As the SS-N-7 is probably capable of a 50-mile range in an anti-ship mode, the Russians have a lead in this field as the west's encapsulated Harpoon and SM39 Exocet are hardly operational. The missile would need to rely on initial targeting from the submarine itself but then work on a 'fire-and-forget' basis, homing on its final target approach. The Charlies are believed to be triple-screwed, running normally on the wing shafts but using the centre propeller for silent manoeuvring.

Several 'stretched' Charlies are known to exist, known as Charlie IIs. Some 30ft longer, they still show only eight launcher covers and the extra hull space is possibly for improved passive electronics to enable them to launch also the SS-N-15; a smallish AS missile, capable of being nuclear-tipped and

Charlie I class SSGN.

corresponding to the American Subroc. This class would seem to be designed as a direct counter to western SSBNs and may well have the task of dogging their movements on a 'one-to-one' basis. Another pair of variants are the Papas. These are probably prototype boats, of the same general dimensions as the Charlie II but of even greater freeboard, a long low fin angular by Russian standards and, apparently, much-modified control surfaces aft.

Golf SSB   USSR

Detail of fin of Golf II class SSB.

Units: 29 believed built between 1958 and 1962
Displacement: 2,550 surfaced
3,000 submerged
Length (oa): 321ft
Beam: 30ft
Draught: 20ft
Machinery: Three diesels generators Three motors
Three shafts 6,000shp for 17/13kts
Armament: Three SS-N-4 launchers (Golf I)
Three SS-N-5 launchers (Golf II)
Five SS-N-5 launchers (Golf III)
Ten 21-inch TTs

Unique in being the only extant conventionally-propelled ballistic missile submarines, the Golfs were originally designed as large patrol boats. Probably stimulated by the American Regulus programme, the Russians quickly converted six Zulus to carry a brace

of SS-N-4 (Sark) missiles and, having proved the system's feasibility, the Golfs were recast to carry it. Nearly 30 of the class were built, introducing the long fin as a means of accommodating the large missile on a hull of lesser diameter. Like the Regulus, the Sark required a submarine to surface for actual launching but, having done so, achieved it in a much shorter time than that required for the American weapon which, being a cruise missile, needed running out on to a trainable launcher, like a small aircraft. Nonetheless, once aloft, the Regulus had a near 600-mile range compared with the Sark's 300 and this necessarily placed a Russian submarine in close proximity to an enemy coast for useful deployment, a hazard which proved the spur to the production of the 700-mile SS-N-5 (Serb).

Around 20 of the Golfs were converted to the new weapon and termed Golf IIs. They differ little

Golf I class SSB: note hatch of centre launcher open.

externally as a result, though the top of the fin is flatter in the later boats in contrast to the 'run-down' in the Golf I type. A few Golf IIIs are reported, having a fin even more monstrous for the housing of five SS-N-5s.

The class's patrol submarine ancestry is evident in the battery of 10 full-sized TTs carried, six forward and four aft. Unusually, but not unique in Soviet designs, the Golfs are triple-screwed. Any arguments for the continued retention of such out-of-date vessels have been discussed already for the Hotel class (qv) but it is worthy of note, that, since more modern SSBNs have come forward in increasing numbers, the Golf has made its appearance in the Baltic. Though extremely vulnerable in these waters, such a submarine still exercises a useful first-strike threat over the whole of West Germany and the eastern half of Great Britain. A shift to the north also places it in a position to attack any western SSBN in transit to or from Scottish bases.

Echo SSGN   USSR

Units: c34 boats completed between 1962 and 1967; only five are Echo I, remainder Echo II
Displacement: 4,900 surfaced
5,800 submerged
Length (oa): 391ft
Beam: 32ft
Draught: 25.5ft
Machinery: One reactor powering two steam turbines
Two shafts 22,000shp for 20/22kts
Armament: Eight SS-N-3 launchers
Six 21-inch TTs (forward)
Four 400mm (16-inch) TTs (aft)

With the Echo class, the Russians reached the ultimate stage in their various attempts to marry the cumbersome SS-N-3 (Shaddock) SSM to a submarine. Having proved the system with the Twin Cylinder and Long Bin variants of the Whiskey class, they began to produce two classes in parallel in about 1962, the conventionally-propelled Julietts with four Shaddocks and the nuclear Echo type with six. Firm believers in maximum armament per hull, the Soviets built only about five Echos before discovering that they could insert an extra section and thus house a further pair of launchers. About 29 of this type, termed the Echo II, were built.

The illustration clearly shows the layout with the distinctive apertures, abaft each launcher, which act as blast deflectors. Considering the unwieldy 36ft length of the SS-N-3, its elevating launchers fold down very neatly, being mounted external to the pressure hull, each in a separate watertight cylinder. Due to the Echo's slender lines, a slight increase in beam is evident in way of the second pair of launchers and the fin.

Designed for use against surface targets out to some 200 miles range, the Shaddock's performance would seem to be inhibited by the control possible from the Snoop Tray radar, whose antenna is shown extended but, as the submarine has to surface before launching, a larger installation, known as Front Piece, has its antenna mounted into a folding fairing on the forward side of the fin. As the function of this is mid-course correction, it can only be assumed that it is meant for use in the guidance of missiles fired from another vessel, remembering that the SS-N-3 and its derivative, the SS-N-12, are carried by numerous surface ships as well as submarines.

Evident also in the picture is the mast bearing the communications antenna, which folds back into the deep slot in the casing. These masts are usually sited to one side of the fin but, in the Echo, the adjacent launcher precluded it. Extremely fine-lined, the class is twin-screwed in the usual Russian fashion.

During the early 1970s the original five, termed Echo I, had their missiles removed and are now

Echo II class SSGN.

Echo I class SSN.

armed only with the rather large mixed battery of TTs common to both groups. As attack submarines, however, the Echo Is would best be restricted to 'soft' targets, being too large and too slow to stand much chance against an alert escort.

Juliett SSG

USSR

Units: c16 boats completed between 1963 and 1967
Displacement: 2,900 surfaced
3,500 submerged
Length (oa): 285.5ft
Beam: 32.5ft
Draught: 20ft
Machinery: Three diesels and three electric motors
Two shafts 6,000bhp for c18/14kts
Armament: Four SS-N-3 launchers
Six 21-inch TTs (forward)
Four 400mm (16-inch) TTs (aft) Removed from some

From any direction, the Juliett is unmistakable with its very high freeboard, long and relatively low fin and unusually wide beam. Construction began in 1961, after the SS-N-3 (Shaddock) system had been evaluated in the Whiskey conversions (qv) proceeding in parallel with that of the nuclear-propelled Echos. The SSM launchers, of which there are only four, in two pairs, are mounted similarly to those in the Echo and, though early units had the distinctive blast-deflecting scallops fitted with flush covers, this practice has been discontinued.

As with the Echo the Juliett has to surface to fire her missiles; guidance is reported to be restricted to retractable antennas, but the great length of the fin would then leave a large unutilised volume in its forward end and it is more than possible that a mid-course correction antenna is sited within. This view is given weight by the known affinity of the Soviet Fleet for mutual cooperation between submarine and surface ship. Whether the later SS-N-12 can be deployed is not known.

A full battery of TTs is carried and the attack function is underlined by the active sonar in its dome forward; both this and the passive set below have 'windows' of a distinctive hue.

The triple-diesel, triple-motor machinery fit is unusual and could explain the extreme beaminess of the class, though this feature would result also in a steadier launch platform. Though credited with but two shafts, three would seem more likely with quiet running on the centre shaft only. 'Quiet' is a relative word for the overall appearance would suggest radiated underwater noise on a par with that of a freight train. As all the SS-N-3 boats are extremely vulnerable to attack when having to surface within 200-odd miles of their target, some suspicion must linger that they have a role also in the anti-SSBN area, possibly in the 'sanitisation' of a whole sector of sea by means of a nuclear warhead should the presence of an enemy SSBN be suspected.

Whiskey SSG

USSR

Units: Up to six Twin Cylinders converted 1958-61
Six Long Bins converted 1961-64

	Twin Cylinder	Long Bin
Displacement: surfaced	1,200	1,300
submerged	1,450	1,650
Length (oa):	243ft	275ft
Beam:	21ft	24ft
Draught:	16ft	16ft
Machinery: (both)	Two diesels 4,000bhp	Two motors 2,500shp
	Two shafts 17/15kts	16/14kts
Armament:	Two SS-N-3 launchers	Four SS-N-3 launchers
	Four 21-inch TTs	Four 21-inch TTs

Whiskey Long Bin class SSG.

Whiskey Twin Cylinder class SSG.

In about 1960 the SS-N-1 (Scrubber) missile, deployed only in the Kildin and Krupnyi class destroyers, was superseded by the larger SS-N-3 (Shaddock) capable of carrying either conventional or nuclear warhead out to 200 miles. The main vehicle for the system was the Kynda class cruiser with its two quadruple launchers, and designed to counter other surface ships. To utilise the full 200-mile range, however, involved the agency of a third party for mid-course correction and, as the ship herself carried no helicopter, it was obviously planned that she should cooperate with, probably, either an aircraft or submarine. With its stealth the latter obviously appealed and its ability to stalk more closely to its target may well have stimulated early experiments in putting a single launcher on to a standard Whiskey class boat. Once these were satisfactorily completed, a further five Whiskeys were converted to the so-called Whiskey Twin Cylinder, with a pair of missiles mounted within two pressure-tight canisters, facing aft and hinged for elevation at the forward end. These did nothing for the submarine's performance as the only concession to streamlining was a fairing at the forward end, which acted also as a blast deflector. The submarine

needs to surface to launch her missiles and guidance would seem basic as the fin was not enlarged to accommodate any further retractable antennas. Whatever boats of the type still remain possess little value except perhaps for training.

In about 1961, the Twin Cylinder conversions were curtailed in favour of the improved Whiskey Long Bin. As the Juliett programme was in its early stages, the Long Bins, too, probably represent no more than a stopgap for conversions ceased as the Julietts entered service. About half-a-dozen Long Bins were produced, with four SS-N-3 launchers firing forward at fixed angles and built into a large fin of uniquely repellent appearance, bringing to mind the carapace of a large beetle. Vents can be opened in the after end of the fin to carry the missile efflux clear during launch. The two pairs of launchers are staggered in a vertical plane, the after ones firing above the forward and the arrangement required an extra 32ft section to be inserted into the hull. Guidance again is probably good only for horizon range. Four TTs are mounted forward although the boat's performances have been so degraded by their rebuilds that their use in conventional attack capacity would be highly questionable.

Victor Fleet Submarine USSR

Units: c16 Victor Is built between 1968 and 1976
c6 Victor IIs built since 1973

	Victor I	Victor II
Displacement: surfaced	4,150	4,700
submerged	5,150	6,000
Length (oa):	295ft	318ft
Beam:	33ft	33ft
Draught:	26ft	26ft
Machinery: (both)	One nuclear reactor powering two sets steam turbines	
	Probably three shafts 25,000shp for 26/30kts	
	3,000shp for 26/33kts	
Armament:	Eight 21-inch TTs	Eight 21-inch TTs

The design of the Victors appears to be one where every effort has been made to minimise hull resistance; the resulting flowing curves are, aesthetically, something of an acquired taste but have influenced opinions that the class ranks as one of the fastest in existence. Appearing in 1968, they would seem to succeed the Novembers, from which they were also developed. The earlier Type Is were rather shorter than the Novembers but as beamy,

with a free-flooding casing draining through a multitude of ports and a fin looking lower than it actually is. Unusually in Russian practice, the upper rudder protrudes from the water when the submarine is surfaced and is hinged on a skeg. Like the similarly sized Charlie class SSGNs, the Victors would seem to have three shafts, using the centre shaft only for silent propulsion.

Eight TTs are carried forward but it is very likely

136

Victor I class SSN.

loading hatches and the fin itself almost certainly contains sonars. The overall impression is of a submarine purpose-designed to stalk other submarines, probably the west's SSBNs.

About 1973 a lengthened type, first known as Uniform, then Victor II, commenced production in parallel with the Type Is. The reason for the extra length is not clear — it has been suggested that SS-N-7 anti-ship launchers have been added but this mixing of functions is unlikely. It is possible that an up-rating of machinery power has permitted a longer and more efficient hull with space for, particularly improved electronics.

A further type, code-named Alfa, appeared about 1970 but, though a couple of prototypes exist, the class does not seem to have gone into production. The design is of a displacement and size close akin to those of the American Skipjack, and the low-freeboard hull with its humped profile is also similar, though topped by a typical Russian fin in the style of that on the Victor. It would appear to be an experiment at the production of a small nuclear reactor. Its single screw propulsion is not usual in Soviet practice and the Alfa may well be an equivalent to the American *Albacore*, for research into improved hull forms.

that these can be used also for launching the mysterious SS-N-15 missile, a weapon probably similar in concept to the American Subroc and capable of planting a nuclear warhead out to a range of 15-20 miles. On either side of the casing, flanking the forward end of the fin, are generously-sized

November Fleet Submarine USSR

Units: c13 boats completed between about 1960 and 1964
Displacement: 4,300 surfaced
5,100 submerged
Length (oa): 358ft
Beam: 32ft
Draught: 25ft
Machinery: Nuclear reactor powering two sets of steam turbines
Two shafts c22,000shp for 20/25kts
Armament: Six 21-inch TTs (forward)
Four 16-inch (400mm) TTs (aft)

The Americans initially established a considerable lead over the Russians in the application of nuclear power to submarine propulsion. As a result, their earlier classes, up to the Skates, had a conventional 'Guppy' configuration and only with the Skipjacks was the high-speed single screw-form adopted. At this juncture, the Russians laid down their first nuclear attack boats, the Novembers, and adopted a tear-drop section from the outset. For a lead class

they were very large, thus suggesting that they incorporated two nuclear reactors for propulsion and are very much less handy than their western equivalents. In addition the twin-screw arrangement was retained, giving a greater degree of survivability at the expense of a poorer form and greater noise. Indeed, the class has a reputation for both machinery and hull-induced noise. The upper rudder, so much a feature of the profile of surfaced western boats, is absent, though a low, fixed stabiliser fin has been added. Though the November's fins are sited well forward, the designers did not follow American practice in the transfer of the driving planes to the fin, leaving them forward, British-style. The fin itself, however, introduced the rather exaggerated curves that have since become a feature on Soviet boats.

The class has the ability to fire torpedoes but not missiles and are regarded as second-line boats in comparison with the Victors, now emerging in useful numbers. They are, nevertheless, reckoned to be very strong submarines, capable of operation at greater than normal depths.

Tango Patrol Submarine

USSR

Units: One or two per year commissioned since
1973
Displacement: 2,700 surfaced
3,100 submerged
Length (oa): 297ft
Beam: 29ft
Draught: 20ft
Machinery: Three diesel-generator sets driving
three shafts
6,000shp for 20/20kts
Armament: Six 21-inch TTs

Neither the UK nor the USA has constructed
conventional patrol submarines for some years and
the USSR had so many from the vast expansion of
the 1960s that it was far from certain whether they
were still actively developing the type. Thus, great
interest was aroused by a new class, christened the
Tango, which appeared in 1973. Its introduction
shows that the Soviets are intent on replacing at
least some of their rapidly aging fleet of
conventionals. They are very much of a size with the
prolific Foxtrots and would seem to have inherited a
similar machinery layout. Attention has been paid to
keeping the shape clean and the fin is quite orthodox
in profile compared with the extremes of those on
the high-speed nuclear classes.

Forward of the fin, the freeboard rises smoothly to
an extra three feet or so. Besides improving
seakeeping for a boat that has to spend part of its

time on the surface, this would also increase
capacity and surface area forward. As the Russians
place their torpedo tubes in the bows, as well as
hydroplanes, passive sonar has to compete for space
and, for a boat designed primarily to act as a quiet
platform to detect incoming enemy submarines over
the continental shelf zone, electronics are vital. It has
been suggested that space has been devoted also to
the stowage of the SS-N-15 Subroc-type missile,
which can be ejected from the TTs; this would be
perfectly feasible and, indeed, likely for a
comparatively slow submarine which would have
little chance in pursuing a fast quarry, be it surface or
nuclear submarine. The earlier obsolescent classes
were constructed largely to wage a classic-type
attritional sea war but as the new Soviet navy is
geared to a short, decisive conflict, it is doubtful
whether the Tango will be produced in the vast
numbers of the former types.

Mention should be made of the quartet of Bravo
class submarines. With a length of about 225ft and a
submerged displacement of 2,900 tons they have
the look of a nuclear propelled class, having a high
speed form with a distinctive 'hump' abaft the fin.
They are, however, conventional and capable of
around 16kts submerged. As one is attached to each
of the major Russian fleets, the evidence is strong
that they are full-sized targets, profiled to give a
similar sonar response to a nuclear fleet submarine.
They are armed with a battery of six TTs forward.

Foxtrot Patrol Submarine

USSR

Units: c60 completed 1960-68
Displacement: 2,200 surfaced
2,500 submerged
Length (oa): 297ft
Beam: 27ft
Draught: 18ft
Machinery: Three diesel-generator sets driving
three shafts
6,000shp for 18/16kts
Armament: Six 21-inch torpedo tubes (forward)
Four 16-inch (400mm) TTs (aft)

Though only some 60 were completed out of a
planned 160, the Foxtrots compose about one-third
of the Soviet conventionally-propelled submarine
fleet, the increasing age of which indicates
diminishing interest in attritional ocean warfare of
the classic kind. That the only later class, the Tango
(qv) bears a close resemblance to the Foxtrot and the
long constructional programme, spanning almost the
decade both attest to the soundness of the design.

The illustration shows the appearance to be
typically Russian with the usual touch of edging

various features neatly in white. Various fittings mar the smoothness of the boat's topsides; the fin is large, rounded forward but tapering to a sharp and sloping trailing edge. Exhausts occupy the after third of the top, which is raised and faired to accommodate them. In the example shown there are two rows of 'windows', the upper are transparent, the fore covered conning position, and the lower are transmissive panels for the fin-mounted electronics. Both the Snoop Plate surface search radar and the snort induction mast are shown partially extended, and the tall communications mast, shown erected, folds flat on the after deck for submerged running. Though not readily obvious from the picture the casing around the bows is rounded (unlike that in the preceding Zulus) to house a large passive sonar array. On top is a dome for the active sonar, sometimes surrounded by a protective frame when there is a likelihood of navigation in ice.

Inherited from the Zulus was the proven triple-shaft machinery layout and the powerful torpedo battery, though the after TTs are for small-calibre AS torpedoes. Production of the class has probably ceased on commencement of the slower Tango programme but, of the six reportedly to be acquired by Libya, it is possible that some will be of new construction. A further eight had been transferred to India, a country now reported to be interested in the acquisition of an established submarine design for licensed construction in home yards.

Zulu Patrol Submarine   USSR

Zulu III class submarine.

Units: c30 completed between 1952 and 1957, some 20 still exist
Displacement: 2,200 surfaced
2,600 submerged
Length (oa): 295ft
Beam: 24ft
Draught: 17ft
Machinery: Three diesels or three electric motors on three shafts
8,000shp/3,500hp for 18/15kts
Armament: Ten 21-inch TTs

It will be noted that there exists a close similarity in dimensions between the Zulu and the later Foxtrot, which would appear to be a derivative. Similarly the Zulu dates from the years following World War II, when the influence of the newly-discovered details of the German Typ XXI was still strong. The high-speed advantages of the closed-cycle hydrogen peroxide Walther turbine were not successfully applied by either the Americans or the British because of its inherent instability, but the Russians, less experienced, embarked on a class of triple-screwed submarines designed as a high-performance class complementary to the more orthodox Whiskeys, then being built in large numbers. This new type, the Zulu, resembled the XXI in appearance also and was supposed to cruise on its centre shaft, using its Walther-powered wing shafts to boost the speed for attack purposes. Apparently, about a dozen were constructed before the Russians, too, had to acknowledge the limitations of the new technology. Conventional diesel/electric drive was substituted, about 30 boats being completed. Several variants existed. The Zulu Is had a gun armament and the IIs, IIIs and IVs had differing fin configurations. A heavy, 10-tube armament is carried by all types.

With the non-realisation of the early staff requirements, the Zulu programme petered out, leaving several incomplete hulls. Six were completed (as Zulu Vs) with a modified fin containing two vertical launch tubes for the SS-N-4 (Sark) missile, becoming the world's first ballistic missile submarines. Only stopgaps, they were never updated, and were subsequently demilitarised for research purposes.

Romeo Patrol Submarine   USSR

Units: c20 built between about 1958 and 1961
Displacement: 1,450 surfaced
1,700 submerged
Length (oa): 249ft
Beam: 23ft
Draught: 16.5ft
Machinery: Two diesels on two electric motors Two shafts
4,000/3,500shp for 18/15kts
Armament: Six 21-inch TTs

Only about 10 of the short series of Romeos still serve under Russian colours the remainder having been transferred abroad. Evidence suggests that it was planned to build them in large numbers as successors to the equally numerous Whiskeys, which they resemble closely in hull dimensions but the introduction of nuclear power and missiles caused a complete rethink on long-term plans and only the larger Foxtrots were still produced.

The bows resemble those of the Foxtrot, rounded and with a sonar dome but the fin is distinctive in the 10ft fairing on top which shrouds the snort mast, which is either of great length or incapable of full retraction. On earlier boats, such as that shown, the enclosed conning position protruded forward from the fin but, on later examples, the fin has the more orthodox type of step, possibly to increase the volume available for fin-mounted electronics. Like the Whiskey, the Romeo is a twin-screw design but with a bow-mounted battery of six TTs, for each of which two reloads are carried. Alternatively, about 36 mines can be stowed.

Six Romeos, less some of their electronics, were given to Egypt in exchange for some earlier Whiskeys. Several also went to the PRC but, subsequent to the deterioration in relationships, the Chinese have undertaken series production of Romeos, apparently as exact copies. Some of these have been transferred to North Korea.

Whiskey Patrol Submarine   USSR

Whiskey V class submarine.

Units: Over 200 built between 1951 and 1957
Displacement: 1,200 surfaced
1,500 submerged
Length (oa): 243ft
Beam: 22ft
Draught: 16ft
Machinery: Two diesels and two electric motors
Two shafts
4,000/2,500shp for 17/15kts
Armament: Six 21-inch TTs

Whiskey Canvas Bag class SSR.

Like the contemporary Zulu class boats, the Whiskeys showed the influence of German technology and the two groups of boats formed the backbone of Russian submarine strengths in the 1950s. Cross-fertilised with experience from the war-built K class, the Whiskeys were simple and strong, very suitable for mass production. Rapid series construction was achieved by building sections at widely dispersed factories and shipping them by rail or waterway to assembly yards from which possibly up to 240 were produced in seven years, half of which are still extant.

The cross-section adopted was chosen to give a minimum surface wetted area (and, thus, resistance) for a given volume. Otherwise, the design was totally uncomplicated, with a twin-screw propulsion arrangement and a four-forward, two-aft TT battery at a time when foreign practice was six and four respectively.

As can be expected on so prolific a class, there have been several variants, involving mainly changes of fin configuration. The Type I incorporated a German-style twin 25mm gun turret in a step forward of the fin; Type II was similar but with a half height after extension to the fin and a 76mm gun on the after deck. Type III was similar to Type II but with all guns removed; Type IV shared a common fin with Types II and III but included the 25mm guns and introduced the distinctive, cranked diesel exhaust which acted also as a base for the D/F loop. The final version was the Type V, which includes all boats now

operational, with no guns and a straight forward face to the fin. Though the current fin is simpler than on earlier variants, it is still rather messy by modern standards. A further sub-group exists in the Type VA, which has a six-foot high domed fitting ahead of the fin, apparently a lock for use by divers.

Some Whiskeys were converted to guided missile boats (see Whiskey Twin Cylinder and Long Bin) and a further five to radar pickets. These were fitted with a Boat Sail radar, whose enormous antenna needs to be aligned fore and aft before it can be retracted into the specially elongated fin. In its early days, the antenna was always covered discreetly immediately any foreign ship or aircraft hailed in sight; the habit earned the class the soubriquet 'Whiskey Canvas Bag'. They are now of little real value as, similar to the US Navy, the long range aircraft can do a better job — but the Russians are slow to scrap any system, however obsolete.

Those Whiskeys still under Russian colours are most probably now relegated to training duties in an operational context but many more are to be found in the fleets of Albania, China, Egypt, Indonesia, North Korea and Poland.

Quebec Patrol Submarine   USSR

Units: c20 completed between 1954 and 1957
Displacement: 500 surfaced
600 submerged
Length (oa): 185ft
Beam: 17ft
Draught: 13ft
Machinery: Two diesels and three electric motors
Three shafts 3,000/2,500hp for 18/16kts
Armament: Four 21-inch TTs

For the most part, approaches to Russian coasts are very shallow and several classes of small, defensive submarines have been produced to protect them. The only postwar class, however, has been the

Quebec, built in the 1950s contemporary with the Zulus and, like them, designed to incorporate a closed-cycle propulsion system for high speed boost. Again a three-shaft layout was adopted, with the difference that the two wing shafts had conventional diesel-electric propulsion. With the failure of the Walther turbine, the centreline shaft, too, was given an electric motor.

It is believed that only half the planned number were, in fact, completed and now compare unfavourably in almost every important aspect with the Western boats designed for similar duties, such as those in the German and Swedish navies, which are far more capacious on a shorter length, with

greatly superior battery capacity, quietness, sensors and armament.

The Quebecs are overdue for a replacement and would probably fare badly outside a protected zone. Their snort mast is of a length that demands a distinctive 'coxcomb' on the after edge of the fin, more pronounced than in the later Tango class. Only four TTs are carried, with two reloads for each or mines as an alternative.

Vigilante FAC (missile) Uruguay

Displacement: 150 standard
190 full load
Length (oa): 135ft
Beam: 22.5ft
Draught: 5ft
Machinery: Two diesels on two shafts
7,200bhp for 33kts
Armament: One 76mm gun
Two MM38 Exocet launchers (2 × 1)

Built by CMN, Cherbourg the Vigilante is a 'utility' version of the Combattante II, carrying only two SSM launchers and lacking the 40mm gun aft. With only half the installed power (two MTU 16V-538-TB91 diesels) the speed penalty is only four knots. A Thomson CSF Vega weapon control system is incorporated. Uruguay is reported to have ordered three. A patrol version is also available which, interestingly, can have a GRP-sheathed wooden hull in place of the more usual steel construction. The suggested armament would be only one 40mm and one 20mm gun with an optical control system, associated with a general-purpose radar.

Vosper Thornycroft 121ft FAC (missile/gun) Venezuela

		Laid Down	Launched	Completed
P11	Constitucion	1973	1973	1974
P12	Federacion	1973	1974	1975
P13	Independencia	1973	1973	1974
P14	Libertad	1973	1974	1975
P15	Patria	1973	1973	1975
P16	Victoria	1974	1974	1975

Displacement: 150 tons
Length (oa): 121ft
Beam: 23.5ft
Draught: 5.5ft
Machinery: Two diesels on two shafts
7,200bhp for 27kts
Armament: Even numbers
Two Otomat SSMs
One 40mm gun
Odd numbers
One 76mm gun

Large FACs by VT standards, these 124-footers are medium-sized in the current range of available designs. They do not require an extravagantly high speed so a two-shaft layout with moderately-powered machinery is adequate. Their steel hulls are powerfully built and designed to keep the sea, with a low bulwark forward improving both freeboard and appearance.

Though the diesels were supplied by MTU, the weapons fits and electronics are largely Italian in origin. The odd-numbered hulls are armed as gunboats, with a 76mm OTO-Melara forward with a Selenia-built Orion radar and an Elsag computer. The even-numbered units are fitted with a 40mm gun and with two Otomat SSMs aft, missiles with a range superior to 100 miles, cruising under inertial guidance but homing actively. If any weakness exists in this system it lays in the positive identification of an over-the-horizon target and reliance on the missile's ECM during its approach. The search and surveillance radar, whose antenna tops the rather high mast, is an SPQ-2D built under licence.

Libertad: note supports for two Otomat SSM launchers right aft.

Though nominally interchangeable gun/missile boats, a lot of work would be required to change over and they are likely to remain armed as described, though the SSMs and their containers are likely to be left ashore, for the greater part. As Venezuela is reportedly in the market for about 10 further missile-armed FACs, it will be interesting to see which is selected.

Typ 209 Patrol Submarine   Venezuela

	Laid Down	Launched	Completed
S31 *Sabalo*	1973	1975	1976
S32 *Caribe*	1973	1975	1977

Two examples of the successful West German Typ 209 export submarine (qv) built by Howaldtswerke, Kiel. A further pair were ordered in 1977. They would seem to be a counter to two similar craft under the flag of neighbouring Colombia.

Ex-US Patrol Submarines   Venezuela

	Laid Down	Launched	Completed
S21 *Tiburon* (ex-USS *Cubera*, SS347)	1944	1945	1945
S22 *Picuda* (ex-USS *Grenadier*, SS525)	1944	1944	1951

Two ex-American Balao class boats, given Guppy II conversions. Transferred in 1972 and 1973 respectively. Will probably be retired when the second pair of Typ 209s are delivered.

Vietnam

Prior to 1975 there was a fleet from North Vietnam, of Russian and Chinese origin, and one from South Vietnam, consisting of ex-American craft. Subsequent to the states' unification the majority of the South's units escaped and the remainder are now probably unserviceable. Craft believed still active are small and are:

Possibly two Komar class FAC (missile).
Three SO-I class large patrol craft.
About four P4 class FAC (torpedo).
About four P6 class FAC (torpedo).
Six Shanghai II class FAC (gun).

Yemen

North Yemen is believed to have three or four ex-Soviet P4 class FAC (torpedo) operational while the more radical South Yemen has a brace of SO-I class large patrol craft and two P6 class FAC (Torpedo). There are reports of up to three Osa I FAC (missile) being also transferred from the Soviet Union.

143

Le Fougueux Corvette

Yugoslavia

	Laid Down	Launched	Completed
PBR581 *Udarnik* (ex-P6)	1954	1954	1955

A standard French-built Le Fougeux class PC (qv) constructed to Yugoslav account with US funds.

Mornar Corvette

Yugoslavia

		Laid Down	Launched	Completed
PBR551	*Mornar*	1957	1958	1959
PBR552	*Borac*	1964	1964	1965

Displacement: 330 standard
400 full load
Length (oa): 175ft
Beam: 23ft
Draught: 6.5ft
Machinery: Four diesels on two shafts
3,200bhp for 19kts
Armament: Two 76mm guns (2 × 1)
Two 40mm guns (2 × 1)
Four MBU-1200 AS projectors

The two Mornar class corvettes are built to the same general parameters as the *Udarnik* of the Le Fougueux type. In appearance, however, they are very different, lacking the large bridge structure and funnel, and looking more like FACs. More armament is carried, with a 76mm gun in an open mounting at either end and a pair of 40mm guns similarly mounted before the bridge. The early style of Soviet AS rocket launchers fold flat on the foredeck. Superstructure is set more amidships than on the original design and there is a marked knuckle forward.

Borac

Koncar FPB (missile)

Yugoslavia

		Completed	
401	*Rade Koncar*	1977	**Displacement:** 250 full load
402	*Vlado Cetkovic*	—	**Length (oa):** 148ft
403-4 building		—	**Beam:** 27.5ft
			Draught: 7ft

Machinery: Two Proteus gas turbines of 12,000hp
Two diesels of 7,200hp Four shafts
Max speed 40kts
Armament: Two SS-N-11 SSM launchers
Two 57mm guns (2 × 1)

There is a degree of Swedish influence in these home-built boats at present under construction and though larger, may have been derived from the successful Spica classes. In spite of the strong Western bias to the design, it carries Russian missiles, in the shape of a pair of SS-N-11s sited right aft and firing forward at an angle to the centreline. Squeezed between these and the superstructure is the after 57mm mounting which has, as a result, very restricted firing arcs. Both 57mm guns are of the Bofors 170 type, laid by a Philips director.

The steel hull has a deep chine forward and has four-shaft propulsion. Two of these are driven by Rolls-Royce Proteus GTs — another carry-over from the Spica design — and the others by MTU diesels. It is noteworthy that the diesels are quite high powered in relation to the GTs and the boats could probably manage nearly 28kts on these alone; boosted CODAG-fashion by the GTs the top speed is a now-unfashionable 40kts. With controllable-pitch propellers, the shafts not in use can have their blades feathered to reduce resistance and no reversing gear is required. A class of 10 is reported possible.

In addition, the Yugoslav navy operates 10 Osa-I FAC (missile) transferred from the Soviet Union in the 1960s and about 15 Shershen class FAC (torpedo), some acquired from the same source in 1965 and some home-built since.

Heroj Patrol Submarine

Yugoslavia

		Laid Down	Launched	Completed
821	Heroj	1964	1967	1968
822	Junak	1965	1968	1969
823	Uskok	1966	1969	1970

Displacement: 1,070 submerged
Length (oa): 210ft
Beam: 23.5ft
Draught: 16.5ft
Machinery: Diesel/electric 2,400hp for 16/10kts
Armament: Six 21-inch TTs (forward)

This small class represent an improved Sutjeska and, built with Soviet armament, electronics and general know-how, probably follows their practice in being twin screwed. The submerged speed is poor by modern standards and will be improved to 16kts in the pair of 215ft follow-ons now under construction.

Sutjeska Patrol Submarine

Yugoslavia

		Laid Down	Launched	Completed
811	Sutjeska	1957	1958	1960
812	Neretva	1957	1959	1962

Displacement: 820 surfaced
950 submerged
Length (oa): 197ft
Beam: 22ft
Draught: 16ft
Machinery: Diesel/electric
1,800hp for 14/9kts
Armament: Six 21-inch TTs (forward)

These were the first Yugoslav submarines designed and built in home yards. Though a laudable attempt at independence from Soviet supply, their performance is very limited. They incorporate Soviet armament and equipment.

Detail of *Sutjeska.*

Pennant Numbers

Note: Characters in parentheses do not appear on the ship. Numbers of Russian ships are not included owing to their frequent changes.

	1	Prabparapak
	B1	Bushra
(ELPR)	1	Intrepida
(PHM)	1	Pegasus
(PC)	1	Sarasin
	PO1	Andres Quintana Roo
	PO1	Lazaga
	(PO1)	Susa
	SO1	Porpoise
	2	Hanhak Sattru
	B2	Mansor
(ELPR)	2	Indomita
(PHM)	2	Hercules
(PC)	2	Thayanchon
	PO2	Alsedo
	PO2	Matias de Cordova
	(PO2)	Sitre
	3	Ruissalo
	3	Suphairin
	B3	Nejah
	PO3	Cadarso
	PO3	Miguel Ramos Arizpe
	(PO3)	Sebha
	4	Raisio
	B4	Wafi
(PC)	4	Phali
	PO4	Jose Maria Izazgu
	PO4	Villamil
	5	Raitta
	5	Tapi
(PC)	5	Sukrip
	PO5	Bonifaz
	PO5	Juan Bautista Morales
	6	Khirirat
(PC)	6	Tongplin
	PO6	Ignacio Lopez Rayon
	PO6	Recalde
(PC)	7	Liulom
	PO7	Manuel Crecencio Rejon
	SO7	Sealion
(PC)	8	Longlom
	PO8	Antonio de la Fuente
	SO8	Walrus
	PO9	Leon Guzman
	SO9	Oberon
	P10	President el Hadj Omar Bongo
	PO10	Ignacio Ramirez
	S10	Guanabara
	S10	Odin
	P11	Barcelo
	P11	Constitucion
	PO11	Ignacio Mariscal
	S11	Orpheus
	S11	Rio Grande do Sul
	S11	Shyri
	M12	Armatolos
	P12	Federacion
	P12	Laya
	PO12	Heriberto Jara Corona
	S12	Bahia
	S12	Huancavilca

	S12	Olympus
	13	Pattani
	P13	Independencia
	P13	Elmina
	P13	Javier Quiroga
	PO13	Jose Maria Maja
	S13	Osiris
	S13	Riode Janeiro
	P14	Komenda
	P14	Libertad
	P14	Ordonez
	PO14	Felix Romero
	S14	Ceara
	S14	Onslaught
	P15	Acenedo
	P15	Patria
	PO15	Fernando Lizardi
	S15	Goiaz
	S15	Otter
	P16	Candido Perez
	P16	Victoria
	PO16	Francisco J. Mujica
	S16	Amazonas
	S16	Oracle
	F17	Kromantse
	P17	Pastor Ronaix
	S17	Ocelot
	F18	Keta
	P18	Jose Maria del Castillo Velasco
	S18	Otus
	P19	Aiolos
	P19	Luis Manuel Rojas
	S19	Opossum
	P20	Astrapi
	P20	Jose Natividad Macias
	P20	Murature
	S20	Humaita
	S20	Kursura
	S20	Opportune
	21	Simpson
	21	Surasdra
	P21	Andromeda
	P21	Esteban Baca Calderon
	P21	King
	S21	Karanj
	S21	Onyx
	S21	Tiburon
	S21	Tonelero
(S)	21	Santa Fe
	22	Chandhaburi
	22	O'Brien
	P22	Esmeraldas
	P22	Ignacio Zaragosa
	S22	Kanderi
	S22	Picuda
	S22	Resolution
	S22	Riachuelo
(S)	22	Santiago del Estero
	23	Hyatt
	23	Rayong
	P23	Kastor
	P23	Manabi
	S23	Kalvari
	S23	Repulse
	P24	Kyknos
	P25	Pigasos

	P26	Toxotis
	S26	Renown
	S27	Revenge
	P28	Kelefstis Stamou
	(SS28)	Pijao
	P29	Diopos Antoniou
	(SS29)	Tayrona
	LM31	Quito
	S31	Almirante Garcia de los Reyes
(S)	31	Salta
	LM32	Guayaquil
	S32	Isaac Peral
(S)	32	San Luis
	LM33	Cuenca
	S34	Cosme Garcia
	S40	Vela
	LT41	Manta
	S41	Vagir
(S)	41	Dos de Mayo
	LT42	Tulcan
	S42	Vagli
(S)	42	Abtao
	LT43	Neuco Racafuerte
	S43	Vagsheer
(S)	43	Angamos
	S46	Churchill
	S48	Conqueror
(S)	49	La Pedrera
	S50	Courageous
(S)	50	Pacocha
	P54	Ipoploiarhos Batsis
	P55	Ipoploiarhos Arliotis
	P56	Antiploiarhos Anninos
	P57	Ipoploiarhos Konidis
	M58	Machitis
	59	Otway
	60	Onslow
	F61	Atrevida
	61	Orion
	S61	Delfin
	62	Otama
	F62	Princesa
	S62	Tonina
	S63	Marsopa
	F64	Nautilus
	M64	Navmachos
	S64	Narval
	F65	Villa de Bilbao
	P68	Arnala
	P69	Androth
	P69	Independence
	70	Ovens
	P70	Freedom
	K71	Vijay Durg
	P71	Sovereignty
	72	Ojibwa
	K72	Sinhu Durg
	P72	Justice
	73	Onondaga
	P73	Anjadip
	P73	Daring
	74	Okanagan
	M74	Polemistis
	P74	Andaman
	P74	Dauntless
	P75	Amini

	M76	Pyropolitis
	P76	Sea Wolf
	P77	Kamorta
	P77	Sea Lion
	P78	Sea Dragon
	P79	Sea Tiger
	80	Guacalda
	P80	Sea Hawk
	81	Bayandor
	81	Fresia
	F81	Dorina
	P81	Sea Scorpion
	82	Naghdi
	82	Quidora
	F82	Otobo
	K82	Veer
	83	Milanian
	83	Tegualda
	F83	Erin'mi
	K83	Vidyut
	84	Kahnamuie
	K84	Vijeta
	F84	Enyimiri
	K85	Vinash
	K86	Nipat
	S86	Triaina
	K87	Nashat
	K88	Nirbhik
	K89	Nirghat
	K90	Prachand
	K91	Pralaya
	SS91	Hai Chih
	K92	Pratap
(PG)	92	Tacoma
	SS92	Hai Po
	K93	Prabal
(PG)	93	Welch
	K94	Chapal
	K95	Chamak
	S97	Maria van Riebeeck
	S98	Emily Hobhouse
	S99	Johanna van der Merwe
	101	Kusseh
	S101	Dreadnought
	102	Nahang
	S102	Valiant
	103	Dolfin
	S103	Warspite
	S104	Sceptre
	T107	Aldebaran
	S108	Sovereign
	S109	Superb
	S110	Glavkos
	T110	Arcturus
	P111	Sultanhisar
	S111	Nereus
	S111	Spartan
	P112	Demirhisar
	S112	Astraea
	S112	Triton
	S112	Splendid
	P113	Yarhisar
	S113	Perseus
	S113	Trafalgar
	P114	Akhisar
	S114	Papanikolis

S115	Sivrihisar	
S115	Katsonis	
P116	Kockisar	
T121	Spica	
T122	Sirius	
T123	Capella	
T124	Castor	
T125	Vega	
S126	Swiftsure	
T126	Virgo	
S131	Hangor	
T131	Norrköping	
S132	Shushuk	
T132	Nynashamn	
S133	Mangro	
T133	Norrtalje	
S134	Ghazi	
T134	Varbera	
T135	Vasteras	
T136	Vastervik	
T137	Umea	
T138	Pitea	
T139	Lulea	
T140	Halmstad	
T141	Stromstad	
T142	Ystad	
P150	Jagaren	
P151	Hugin	
P152	Munin	
P153	Magne	
P154	Mode	
P155	Vale	
P156	Vidar	
P157	Mjolner	
P158	Nysing	
P159	Kaparen	
P160	Vakoaren	
P161	Snapphanan	
P162	Spejaren	
P163	Styrbjorn	
S163	Albacora	
P164	Starkodder	
S164	Barracuda	
P165	Tordon	
P166	Tirfing	
S166	Delfin	
S170	U 21	
S171	U 22	
S172	U 23	
S173	U 24	
S174	U 25	
S175	U 26	
S176	U 27	
S177	U 28	
S178	U 29	
S179	U30	
S180	U 1	
S181	U 2	
S188	U 9	
S189	U 10	
S190	U 11	
S191	U 12	
S192	U 13	
S193	U 14	
S194	U 15	
S195	U 16	
P196	Hesperos	
S196	U 17	
P197	Kataigis	
S197	U18	
P198	Kentauros	
S198	U19	
P199	Kyklon	
S199	U 20	
203	Fremantle	
P221	Kaman	
P222	Zoubin	
P223	Khadang	
P224	Peykan	
P225	Joshan	
P226	Falkhon	
P227	Shamshir	
P228	Gorz	
P228	Lelaps	
P229	Skorpios	
P229	Gardonneh	
P230	Khanjah	
P230	Tyfon	
P231	Neyzeh	
P232	Tabarzin	
P271	Scimitar	
P274	Cutlass	
P275	Sabre	
P276	Tenacity	
P285	Jersey	
P297	Guernsey	
P298	Shetland	
P299	Orkney	
P300	Lindisfarne	
S300	Ula	
(P)	301	Bizerte
S301	Utsira	
(P)	302	Horriya
S302	Utstein	
P303	Sakiet Sidi Youssef	
S303	Utvaer	
(P)	304	Monastir
S304	Uthaug	
S305	Sklinna	
S306	Skolpen	
S307	Stadt	
S308	Stord	
309	Umitaka	
S309	Svenner	
S310	Otaka	
F310	Sleipner	
311	Mizutori	
F311	Aeger	
311	Mivatch	
312	Miznach	
312	Yamadori	
313	Otori	
313	Mizgav	
314	Kasasagi	
315	Hatsukari	
S315	Kaura	
316	Umidori	
S316	Kinn	
317	Wakataka	
S317	Kya	
318	Kumataka	
S318	Kobben	
319	Shiratori	
S319	Kunna	

320	*Hiyodori*	
S320	*Narvhalen*	
321	*Eilath*	
P321	*Denizkusu*	
S321	*Nordkaparen*	
322	*Haifa*	
P322	*Almaca*	
323	*Akko*	
P323	*Sahin*	
P324	*Kartal*	
P325	*Melten*	
P326	*Pelikan*	
S326	*Delfinen*	
P327	*Albatros*	
S327	*Spaekhuggeren*	
P328	*Simsek*	
S328	*Tumleren*	
P329	*Kasirga*	
S329	*Springeren*	
P330	*Firtina*	
331	*Saar*	
P331	*Tufan*	
332	*Soufa*	
P332	*Kilic*	
333	*Gaasch*	
P333	*Mizrak*	
S333	*Ikinci Inonu*	
P334	*Yildiz*	
P335	*Kalkan*	
S335	*Burak Reis*	
P336	*Karayel*	
S336	*Murat Reis*	
P337	*Girne*	
S337	*Oruc Reis*	
P338	*Yildirim*	
S338	*Uluc Ali Reis*	
P339	*Bora*	
P340	*Dogan*	
S340	*Cerbe*	
341	*Herv*	
P341	*Marti*	
S341	*Canakkale*	
342	*Hnit*	
P342	*Tayfun*	
343	*Hetz*	
P343	*Volkan*	
P343	*Tjeld*	
F344	*Bellona*	
P344	*Skarv*	
P345	*Teist*	
S345	*Prevese*	
F346	*Flora*	
P346	*Jo*	
S346	*Birinci Inonu*	
F347	*Triton*	
P347	*Lom*	
S347	*Atilay*	
P348	*Stegg*	
S348	*Salidiray*	
P349	*Hauk*	
S349	*Batiray*	
P350	*Falk*	
S350	*Yildiray*	
P357	*Ravn*	
P380	*Skrei*	
P381	*Hai*	
P382	*Sel*	

	P383	*Hval*
	P384	*Laks*
	P385	*Knurr*
	P386	*Delfin*
	P387	*Lyr*
	P388	*Gribb*
	P389	*Geir*
	P390	*Erle*
	401	*Rade Koncar*
	402	*Vlado Cetkovic*
	403	*Naggabanda*
	410	*Pasopati*
	412	*Bramastra*
	420	*Sparviero*
(P)	491	*Lampo*
(P)	492	*Baleno*
(P)	493	*Freccia*
(P)	494	*Salta*
(S)	501	*Primo Longobardo*
(S)	502	*Gianfranco Gazzana Priaroggia*
(S)	505	*Attilio Bagnolini*
(S)	506	*Enrico Toti*
	P510	*Soloven*
	511	*Al Saddiq*
	P511	*Soridderen*
	P512	*Sobjornen*
	513	*Al Farouq*
	P513	*Sohesten*
(S)	513	*Enrico Dandalo*
	P514	*Sohunden*
(S)	514	*Lazzaro Meconigo*
	515	*Abdul Aziz*
	P515	*Soulven*
(S)	515	*Livio Piomarta*
(S)	516	*Romeo Romei*
	517	*Faisal*
(S)	518	*Nazario Sauro*
	519	*Khalid*
(S)	519	*Fecia di Cossato*
(S)	520	*Leonardo da Vinci*
	521	*Amyr*
(S)	521	*Guglielmo Marconi*
(SS)	521	*Hayashio*
(SS)	522	*Wakashio*
	523	*Tariq*
(SS)	523	*Natsushio*
(SS)	524	*Fuyushio*
	525	*Oqbah*
	527	*Abu Obadiah*
	F540	*Pietro de Cristofaro*
	P540	*Bille*
	F541	*Umberto Grosso*
	P541	*Bredal*
	F542	*Aquila*
	P542	*Hammer*
	F543	*Albatros*
	P543	*Huitfelde*
	F544	*Alcione*
	P544	*Krieger*
	F545	*Airone*
	P545	*Norby*
	F546	*Licio Visintini*
	P546	*Rodsteen*
	P547	*Sehested*
	P548	*Suenson*
	P549	*Willemoes*
	F550	*Salvatore Todaro*

Type	Number	Name
(PBR)	551	Mornar
(PBR)	552	Borac
(SS)	561	Oshio
(SS)	562	Asashio
(SS)	563	Harushio
(AGSS)	563	Tang
(SS)	564	Michishio
(AGSS)	565	Wahoo
(SS)	565	Arashio
(SS)	566	Uzushio
(AGSS)	567	Gudgeon
(SS)	567	Makishio
(SS)	568	Isoshio
(SS)	569	Narushio
(SS)	570	Kuroshio
(SS)	571	Takashio
(SS)	572	Yaeshio
(SS)	574	Grayback
(SS)	576	Darter
(SS)	577	Growler
(SSN)	578	Skate
(SSN)	579	Swordfish
(SS)	580	Barbel
(PBR)	581	Udarnik
(SS)	581	Blueback
(SS)	582	Bonefish
(SSN)	583	Sargo ›
(SSN)	584	Seadragon
(SSN)	585	Skipjack
(SSN)	585	Seawolf
(SSN)	586	Triton
(SSN)	587	Halibut
(SSN)	588	Scamp
(SSN)	590	Sculpin
(SSN)	591	Shark
(SSN)	592	Snook
(SSN)	594	Permit
(SSN)	595	Plunger
(SSN)	596	Barb
(SSBN)	598	George Washington
(SSBN)	599	Patrick Henry
(SSBN)	600	Theodore Roosevelt
	601	Kelaplintah
(SSBN)	601	Robert E. Lee
	602	Kelamisani
(SSBN)	602	Abraham Lincoln
	603	Sarpawesesa
(SSN)	603	Pollack
	604	Pulanggeni
(SSN)	604	Haddo
	605	Kalanada
(SSN)	605	Jack
(SSN)	606	Tinosa
(SSN)	607	Dace
	608	Surotama
(SSBN)	608	Ethan Allen
	609	Sarpamina
(SSBN)	609	Sam Houston
	(S610)	Le Foudroyant
(SSBN)	610	Thomas A. Edison
	611	Nagapasa
	(S611)	Le Redoutable
(SSBN)	611	John Marshall
	612	Badr
	(S612)	Le Terrible
(SSN)	612	Guardfish
	(S613)	L'Indomptable
(SSN)	613	Flasher
	614	Al Yarmook
	(S614)	Le Tonnant
(SSN)	614	Greenling
	(S615)	L'Inflexible
(SSN)	615	Gato
	616	Hitteen
(SSBN)	616	Lafayette
(SSBN)	617	Alexander Hamilton
	618	Tabuk
(SSBN)	618	Thomas Jefferson
(SSBN)	619	Andrew Jackson
	S620	Agosta
(SSBN)	620	John Adams
	S621	Beveziers
(SSN)	621	Haddock
	S622	La Praya
(SSBN)	622	James Monroe
	S623	Ouessant
(SSBN)	623	Nathan Hale
(SSBN)	624	Woodrow Wilson
(SSBN)	625	Henry Clay
(SSBN)	626	Daniel Webster
(SSBN)	627	James Madison
(SSBN)	628	Tecumseh
(SSBN)	629	Daniel Boone
(SSBN)	630	John C. Calhoun
	S631	Narval
(SSBN)	631	Ulysses S. Grant
	S632	Marsouin
(SSBN)	632	von Steuben
	S633	Dauphin
(SSBN)	633	Casimir Pulaski
	S634	Requin
(SSBN)	634	Stonewall Jackson
	P635	L'Ardent
	S635	Arethuse
(SSBN)	635	Sam Rayburn
	S636	Argonaute
(SSBN)	636	Nathaniel Greene
	S637	Espadon
(SSN)	637	Sturgeon
	S638	Morse
(SSN)	638	Whale
	S639	Amazone
(SSN)	639	Tautog
	P640	Le'Fringent
	S640	Ariane
(SSBN)	640	Benjamin Franklin
	S641	Daphné
(SSBN)	641	Simon Bolivar
	S642	Diane
(SSBN)	642	Kamehameha
	S643	Doris
(SBBN)	643	George Bancroft
	P644	L'Adroit
(SSBN)	644	Lewis and Clark
	S645	Flore
(SSBN)	645	James K. Polk
	S646	Galatée
(SSN)	646	Grayling
(SSN)	647	Pogy
	S648	Junon
(SSN)	648	Aspro
	S649	Venus
(SSN)	649	Sunfish
	S650	Pysche

(SSN)	650	Pargo		801	Pattimura
	S651	Sirene		802	Sultan Hasanudin
(SSN)	651	Queenfish		S804	Potvis
	652	Beruang		805	Hui
(SSN)	652	Puffer		S805	Tonijn
	653	Matjan Kumbang		806	Torani
(SSN)	653	Ray		S806	Zwaardvis
	654	Aspro		807	Tjakalang
(SSBN)	654	George C. Marshall		S807	Tijgerhaai
	S655	Gymnote		S808	Dolfijn
	655	Hariman		S809	Zeehond
(SSBN)	655	Henry L. Stimson		810	Tjutjut
(SSBN)	656	George Washington Carver		811	PT 11
(SSBN)	657	Francis Scott Key		811	Katala
(SSBN)	658	Mariano G. Vallejo		811	Sutjeska
(SSBN)	659	Will Rogers		812	PT 12
(SSN)	660	Sand Lance		812	Tohok
(SSN)	661	Lapon		812	Nerevta
(SSN)	662	Gurnard		813	Palu
(SSN)	663	Hammerhead		813	PT 13
(SSN)	664	Sea Devil		814	Pandrong
(SSN)	665	Guitarro		814	PT 14
(SSN)	666	Hawkbill		815	PT 15
(SSN)	667	Bergall		815	Sura
(SSN)	668	Spadefish		816	Kakap
(SSN)	669	Seahorse		817	Barakuda
(SSBN)	670	Finback		F817	Wolf
	P670	Trident		818	Sembilang
	P671	Glaive		F818	Fret
	P672	Epée		F819	Hermelijn
(SSN)	672	Pintado		F820	Vos
	P673	Pertuisane		821	Heroj
(SSN)	673	Flying Fish		F821	Panther
(SSN)	674	Trepang		F822	Jaguar
(SSN)	675	Bluefish		822	Junak
(SSN)	676	Billfish		823	Uskok
(SSN)	677	Drum		P960	Storm
(SSN)	678	Archerfish		P961	Blink
(SSN)	679	Silversides		P962	Glimt
(SSN)	680	William H. Bates		P963	Skjold
(SSN)	681	Batfish		P964	Trygg
(SSN)	682	Tunny		P965	Kjekk
(SSN)	683	Parche		P966	Djerv
(SSN)	684	Cavalla		P967	Skudd
(SSN)	686	L. Mendel Rivers		P968	Arg
(SSN)	687	Richard B. Russell		P969	Steil
(SSN)	688	Los Angeles		P970	Brann
(SSN)	689	Baton Rouge		P971	Tross
(SSN)	690	Philadelphia		P972	Hvass
(SSN)	691	Memphis		P973	Traust
(SSN)	692	Omaha		P974	Brott
(SSN)	693	Cincinnati		P975	Odd
(SSN)	694	Groton		P976	Pil
(SSN)	695	Birmingham		P977	Brask
(SSN)	696	New York City		P978	Rokk
(SSN)	697	Indianapolis		P979	Gnist
(SSN)	698	Bremerton		P980	Snogg
(SSN)	699	Jacksonville		P981	Rapp
(SSN)	700	Dallas		P982	Snar
(SSN)	701	La Jolla		P983	Rask
(SSN)	702	Phoenix		P984	Kvikk
(SSN)	703	Boston		P985	Kjapp
(SSN)	704	Baltimore		P986	Hauk
(SSN)	711	San Francisco		P3501	Perdana
(SSBN)	726	Ohio		P3502	Serang
(SSBN)	727	Michigan		P3503	Ganas
	P730	La Combattante		P3504	Ganyang

P3505	*Jerong*
P3506	*Todak*
P3507	*Pau*
P3508	*Yu*
P3509	*Baung*
P3510	*Pari*
A5328	*Ape*
P6052	*Thetis*
P6503	*Hermes*
P6504	*Najade*
P6505	*Triton*
P6506	*Theseus*
P6092	*Zobel*
P6093	*Wiesel*
P6094	*Dachs*
P6095	*Hermelin*
P6096	*Nerz*
P6097	*Puma*
P6098	*Gepard*
P6099	*Hyane*
P6100	*Frettchen*
P6101	*Ozelot*
P6111	*S61*
P6112	*S62*
P6113	*S63*
P6114	*S64*
P6115	*S65*
P6116	*S66*
P6117	*S67*
P6118	*S68*
P6119	*S69*
P6120	*S70*
P6141	*S41*
P6142	*S42*
P6143	*S43*
P6144	*S44*
P6145	*S45*
P6146	*S46*
P6147	*S47*
P6148	*S48*
P6149	*S49*
P6150	*S50*
P6151	*S51*
P6152	*S52*
P6153	*S53*
P6154	*S54*
P6155	*S55*
P6156	*S56*
P6157	*S57*
P6158	*S58*
P5169	*S59*
P6160	*S60*

Photo Credits

Index